Praise for *Sporting Blood*

"Stringing seemingly disparate boxing stories together as intimate vignettes that document the sorrow and heartache of the most decorated—and forgotten— fighters of every generation, Acevedo strikes the reader early with a quick jab and refuses to let up."

—Christian Giudice, author of *Hands of Stone: The Life and Legend of Roberto Duran* and *Macho Time: The Meteoric Rise and Tragic Fall of Hector Camacho*

"A collection of twenty brilliant essays, Carlos Acevedo's *Sporting Blood* represents the highest level of boxing writing. Poetic and evocative, Acevedo sends readers into the darkest corners of professional boxing. These are the untold stories of some of boxing's most tragic and enigmatic figures and will appeal to fight fans and historians alike."

—Todd Snyder, author of *12 Rounds in Lo's Gym: Boxing and Manhood in Appalachia* and *Bundini: Don't Believe the Hype*

"As someone who makes a living writing about the sport and business of boxing, there is no one that educates and entertains me more about its state of affairs—past and present—than Carlos Acevedo. He's insightful, witty, enlightened, and his words often cut like a knife. I find him to be the most compelling read in our sport."

—Steve Kim, ESPN.com

"It's rare to find in one writer a restless historian, a penetrating boxing observer, and a poet who never loses sight of how 'yesterday will make you cry.' Whether he's considering an iconic figure such as Mike Tyson or a forgotten warrior like Carmelo Negron, Carlos Acevedo pursues a theme that extends far beyond boxing: the desperate quests some human beings undertake and the loneliness that runs beneath it all. *Sporting Blood* shows him working at top form."

—Paul Beston, author of *The Boxing Kings: When American Heavyweights Ruled the Ring*

SPORTING BLOOD

Carlos Acevedo

SPORTING

FOREWORD BY
THOMAS HAUSER

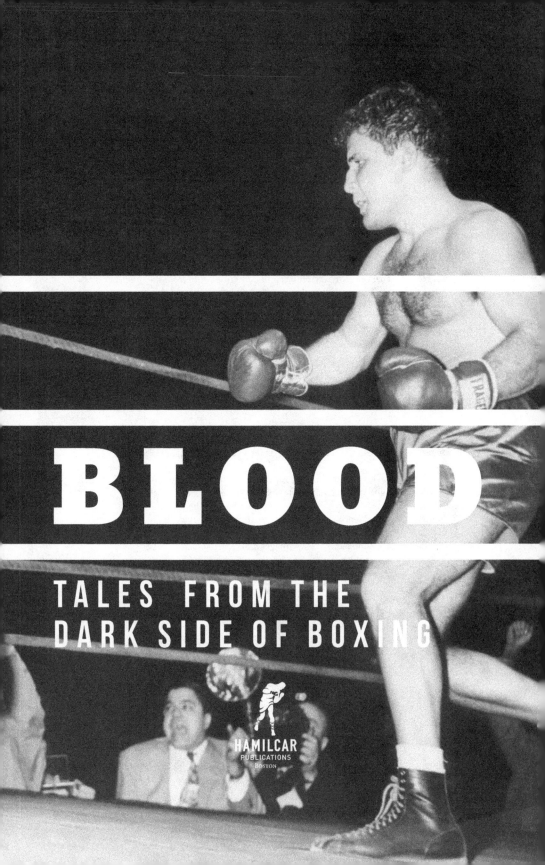

BLOOD

TALES FROM THE
DARK SIDE OF BOXING

HAMILCAR
PUBLICATIONS
Boston

ISBN: 978-1-949590-59-3

CIP data is available

www.hamilcarpubs.com

Aut viam inveniam aut faciam

On the jacket: Johnny Saxton loses to Carmen Basilio when the referee waves off their welterweight fight in the second round at the Cleveland Arena on February 22, 1957.

Frontispiece: Jake LaMotta knocks out Bob Satterfield in the seventh round of their light-heavyweight fight at Wrigley Field in Chicago on September 12, 1946.

Photo of Carmelo Negron on page 202 copyright © Geoffrey Biddle.

All other photos supplied by Getty Images and the Associated Press.

To the fallen

Contents

Foreword

The internet has changed sportswriting, particularly when it comes to writing about boxing. Very few newspapers or magazines now have a writer on staff who understands the sport and business of boxing. Meanwhile, the number of websites devoted to the sweet science keeps growing. Some of these websites are quite good. Others are awful. Reprinting a press release with a new lead is not journalism. Simply voicing an opinion without more is not journalism.

As Carlos Acevedo—the author of this book—wrote in another forum, "Boxing is immune to critical consensus because of the number of fanboys who pretend to be journalists. No other sport has such an unsophisticated mediascape covering it."

Acevedo was born in the Bronx in 1972 and now lives in Brooklyn. He was drawn to boxing as a boy, grew up reading *The Ring,* and recalls being captivated by Larry Holmes, Marvelous Marvin Hagler, and Marvin Johnson. Decades later, when the internet gave a platform to anyone with a computer and modem, he decided to write about the sweet science.

Acevedo's journey as a boxing writer began in 2007. Two years later, he founded a website called The Cruelest Sport. Since then, he has written for numerous print publications and websites, including Hannibal Boxing (his current primary outlet), MaxBoxing, Undisputed Champion Network, *Boxing Digest, Boxing World,* Remezcla, and Esquina Boxeo.

"I love the fights and the narrative that comes with them," Acevedo says. "Each fight is a story unto itself; a drama that exposes character and offers the ideal of self-determination."

I'm not sure when I first became aware of Acevedo's writing. I do remember laughing out loud years ago while reading his description of promoter Gary Shaw, who Acevedo opined "deserves credit for tenacity, like certain insects that become immune over time to Raid and Black Flag." I first quoted him in my own writing in 2011 in conjunction with less-than-stellar refereeing by Russell Mora and Joe Cortez.

"Incompetence is usually the answer for most of the riddles in boxing," Acevedo wrote of Mora's overseeing Abner Mares vs. Joseph Agbeko. "But Mora was a quantum leap removed from mere ineptitude. He was clearly biased in favor of Mares and, worse than that, seemed to enter the ring with a predetermined notion of what he was going to do. Mares had carte blanche to whack Agbeko below the belt as often as he wanted."

As for Cortez's refereeing in Floyd Mayweather Jr. vs. Victor Ortiz, Acevedo proclaimed, "Cortez, whose incompetence has been steadily growing, is now one of the perpetual black clouds of boxing. Why let Cortez, whose reverse Midas touch has marred more than one big fight recently, in the building at all on Saturday night?"

Acevedo doesn't have a big platform. He doesn't have a wealth of contacts in the boxing industry or one-on-one access to big names. In part, that's because he has never compromised his writing to curry favor or ingratiate himself to the powers that be to gain access or ensure that he receives press credentials for a fight. But Acevedo has several very important things going for him: (1) He appreciates and understands boxing history; (2) he has an intuitive feel for the sport and business of boxing; and (3) he's a provocative thinker and a good writer who puts thoughts together clearly and logically.

Look at the Contents page of this book and you'll see essays (in order) on Muhammad Ali, Jack Johnson, Roberto Durán, Esteban de Jesús, Aaron Pryor, Don Jordan, Joe Frazier, Johnny Saxton, Wilfredo Gomez, Lupe Pintor, Davey Moore, Johnny Tapia, Mike Tyson, Bert Cooper, Evander Holyfield, Sonny Liston, Jake LaMotta, Ad Wolgast, Tony Ayala Jr., Eddie Machen, Michael Dokes, Al Singer, and Mike Quarry. That's an eclectic mix. But each essay goes beyond the name of the fighter attached to it to underscore a fundamental truth about, and capture the essence of, boxing.

Acevedo calls boxing "a dark art." Phrases like "the hard logic of the ring" characterize the gritty realism of his writing. Some of the thoughts in *Sporting Blood* that captured my attention include:

- "Sadism, whether one admits it or not, is an essential part of boxing. So is masochism."
- "Nothing can take away from the terrible symmetry boxing gives its practitioners: a hardscrabble life, followed by a hardscrabble profession, followed by a hardscrabble retirement."
- "Disillusion is as much a part of boxing as the jab is."
- "In boxing, the enemies of promise are numerous: entourages, managers, promoters, injuries, other fighters. But self-destruction ranks up there with the best of the worst."
- "There is very little afterlife for a fighter who has failed to succeed."

Acevedo has an economical writing style that leads readers to the intended destination without unnecessary verbiage or digressions. Consider his description of Aaron Pryor's origins, a fighter who Acevedo describes as "one of the most exciting fighters during an era when action was a prerequisite for fame." After noting that Pryor "matched his unbridled style in the ring with an apocalyptic personal life that kept him in boldface for over a decade," Acevedo explains, "Aaron Pryor was an at-risk youth before the term came into vogue. Dysfunction was in his DNA. He was born out of wedlock in 1955 to an alcoholic mother whose moodiness could lead to impromptu gunplay. Sarah Pryor, who gave birth to seven children from five different fathers, occasionally whipped out the nickel-plated hardware when some of her brood became unruly. Years later, she wound up shooting her husband five times in the kind of supercharged domestic dispute in which the Pryor clan excelled."

"Pryor," Acevedo continues, "had a family tree whose branches were gnarled by tragedy. Its roots were blood-soaked. One of his brothers, Lorenzo, was a career criminal who once escaped from Cincinnati County Jail. Lorenzo eventually wound up doing hard time for an armed robbery conviction in Ohio. Another brother, David, became a transsexual hooker. His half-brother was shot and paralyzed by his father. His sister, Catherine, stabbed her lover to death. As if to solidify the epigenetics involved in the Pryor family—and to concretize the symbolism of the phrase 'vicious cycle'—Sarah Pryor had seen her own mother shot and murdered by a boyfriend when Sarah was a child."

In a little more than two hundred words, Acevedo has painted a portrait. Do you still wonder why Aaron Pryor had trouble conforming to the norms that society expected of him?

In a chilling profile of Tony Ayala Jr., Acevedo writes, "In the ring, he was hemmed in by the ropes. For more than half his life, he was trapped behind bars. The rest of the time? He was locked inside himself." Ayala spent two decades in prison in conjunction with multiple convictions for brutal sexual assaults against women. Acevedo sets up the parallel between Ayala's misogynist conduct and his ring savagery with a quote from the fighter himself about boxing. "It's the closest thing to being like God—to control somebody else," Ayala declared. "I hit a guy and it's like, I can do anything I want to you. I own you. Your life is mine, and I will do with it what I please. It's a really sadistic mentality, but that's what goes on in my mind. It's really evil. There's no other way to put it. I step into that dark, most evil part of me and I physically destroy somebody else, and I will do with them what I want."

Acevedo also has a gift for dramatically re-creating the action in classic ring battles. After recounting the carnage that Ad Wolgast and Battling Nelson visited upon each other on February 22, 1910, he observes, "What Wolgast and Nelson produced was not, in retrospect, a sporting event, but a gruesome reminder of how often the line between a blood sport and bloodlust was crossed during an era when mercy was an underdeveloped concept in boxing."

A vivid description of the December 3, 1982, title bout between Wilfredo Gomez and Lupe Pintor is followed by the observation, "At the core of these apocalyptic fights, where two men take turns punishing each other from round to round, lies the question of motivation. Not in the sporting sense; that is, not in the careerist sense or anything so mundane as competition, but in an existential sense. And while boxing lends itself far too often to an intellectual clam chowder (common ingredients: social Darwinism, atavism, gladiatorial analogies, talk of warriors), the fact remains that what Gomez and Pintor did to each other, under the socially sanctioned auspices of entertainment, bordered on madness."

This is powerful writing. Enjoy it.

Thomas Hauser
New York City
January 2020

A Ghost Orbiting Forever

MUHAMMAD ALI, 1942–2016

We were between TV sets for a while back then, touch and go during the "Running on Empty" era, living just off Bathgate Avenue in the midst of an asphalt hell. When was that? Was it '76 or '78? Who can tell? The Mets were awful; Gerald Ford told us all to drop dead, seething Travis Bickle had already painted the East Village red and Howard Cosell, using his best nasal twang, intoned, "Ladies and gentlemen, the Bronx is burning." By then, they had even torn down the El, leaving us marooned among the arson ruins, the Latin Crowns and the Golden Guineas, "Son of Sam" in gaudy newsprint, the blackout of '77 and the anarchy steaming in its wake. We had little in those days—less than that, maybe. But my dour old man bought me an Ali-Superman DC Special from a corner newsstand on Fordham Road. Then: long nights by the windowsill, streetlamp and moonlight igniting the stillness. There he is, again, back to haunt: A real-life superhero—a black man, no less! Goddamn!— in the middle of what looked like Zero Hour. Call that a revolution, if you want.

◆ ◆ ◆

"Know that the life of this world is merely a sport and a pastime."
　—The Koran

◆ ◆ ◆

During his exile years, from 1967 to 1970, Muhammad Ali barnstormed the college lecture circuit and performed ministerial duties for the Nation of Islam. He starred in an off-Broadway play. He filmed a bizarre fantasy sequence against a toupee-wearing Rocky Marciano in a computer-generated matchup whose algorithm, like something HAL might have calculated with sinister intent, determined that Marciano would score a late-round TKO. Ali reinforced his fame, as well as his ideas, on national television so often, he probably logged more screen time than Ed Sullivan or Michael Landon. There he was, dissent with pizzazz, razzing Jack Paar, Jerry Lewis, William F. Buckley, Joey Bishop, Merv Griffin, and David Frost. He appeared on *Face the Nation* and on PBS, where, more than once, he expressed admiration for notorious desegregationist George Wallace during an interview.

◆ ◆ ◆

Although Ali was part of the roiling zeitgeist, his stance on the Vietnam War was slightly ahead of its time. There were teach-ins across the country in 1965 but "The Ballad of the Green Berets" was at the top of the pop charts a year later and "Operation Rolling Thunder" had not yet galvanized the general public. By the end of 1965, there were 184,000 US soldiers in Vietnam. Four years later, that number reached 542,000. Privately, President Lyndon B. Johnson referred to Vietnam as "a raggedy-ass, fourth-rate country."

◆ ◆ ◆

"I ain't no Christian. I can't be, when I see all of the colored people fighting for forced integration getting blowed up. They get hit by stones and chewed up by dogs and they blow up a Negro church and don't find the killers. I get telephone calls every day. They want me to carry signs. They want me to picket. They told me it would be a wonderful thing if I married a white woman because this would be good for brotherhood. I don't want to be blown up. I don't want to be washed down sewers. I just want to be happy with my own kind. I'm the heavyweight champion but, right

now, there are some neighborhoods I can't move into. I know how to dodge booby traps and dogs. I dodge them by staying in my own neighborhood. I'm no troublemaker. I don't believe in forced integration."
—Muhammad Ali, 1964

◆ ◆ ◆

That a naive young man who fainted after getting his first kiss from a high school sweetheart would someday turn into the most prominent member of a lucifugous sect is hard to imagine. With its odd cosmology, its talk of "white devils," its militant stance and its hellfire outlook—so in tune with the times—the Nation of Islam shocked the heartland.

◆ ◆ ◆

Ali kept boxing out of the cultural dustbin in the mid-1960s when network television all but abandoned the red-light district of sports in the wake of the Kefauver hearings and the tragic live-feed battering of Benny Paret. Only a few years before Ali made his pro debut, boxing could be seen on network television five or six nights a week, not as an afterthought or as a time-buy, not as off-peak filler for multiplex channels, but as an integral part of the dawning pixel era. While Ali fought almost exclusively on closed-circuit theater bookings, he dragged his showman/shaman act everywhere he went, provoking the media into spontaneous outrage, reverence, wonder, befuddlement.

◆ ◆ ◆

Although Ali was raised in a middle-class family, his father, Cassius Clay Sr., boiled over from the dispiriting day-to-day humiliations that made being a "Negro" in mid-twentieth-century America such an existential torment. Clay Senior, who was aghast when his son joined the Nation of Islam and changed his name to "Cassius X," almost certainly drove Ali to what most of the country, at the time, referred to as the "Black Muslims." As a child, Ali heard his embittered father repudiate White America over and over again. He also heard Clay Senior extol the philosophy of Marcus Garvey, whose "Back to Africa" movement may have given Ali the urge for separatism. Not for Ali, the risks of the Freedom Riders, voter-registration drives, boycotts, picket lines. Once, Ali—then Cassius Clay and still in high school—attended a demonstration in Louisville. A white woman dumped a bucketful of water from an apartment window over him. Soaked, Ali disavowed protests instantaneously. But to chastise Ali for his noninvolvement at a time when thousands risked their lives on behalf of the civil rights movement is to miss the point altogether: Segregation was official Nation of Islam ideology. And Elijah Muhammad and Malcolm X were not the only black men to rail against integration. When Stokely Carmichael took over the Student Nonviolent Coordinating Committee, one of his first acts was to oust its white members.

◆ ◆ ◆

What little most Americans knew about the Nation of Islam, they had learned from *The Hate That Hate Produced*, a documentary that aired in five parts in 1959. Even for a sect that mixed Islam with Marcus Garvey, Father Divine, the Protocol of the Elders of Zion, and Philip K. Dick, the Nation of Islam, during the 1960s, was, for whites and some blacks as well, beyond the pale. This was, mind you, a Black Nationalist movement that tried to work out some sort of pact with the Ku Klux Klan and with George Lincoln Rockwell and the American Nazi Party. And some of its enforcers, usually responsible for meting out beatings to keep the rank and file in line, graduated to assassination when they gunned down Malcolm X at the Audubon Ballroom in Harlem on February 21, 1965.

Despite its militant stance, the Nation of Islam turned its gunsels mostly on its own. A few days before his assassination, Malcolm X held a press conference in New York City, where he essentially apologized for the Nation of Islam. "I feel responsible for having played a major role in a criminal organization," he said. "It was not a criminal organization at the outset; it was an organization that had the power—the spiritual power—to reform the criminal." In the end, what matters most, perhaps, is the grassroots effect of the Nation of Islam: thousands of young (African) Americans rehabilitated after prison terms, or taken off street corners, eschewing drugs and liquor, well-spoken, given a sense of self-worth, no longer future zeros, their bow ties exclamation points on new lives.

◆ ◆ ◆

October 1, 1975—Muhammad Ali TKO 14 Joe Frazier, Araneta Coliseum, Quezon City, Philippines

"We went to Manila as champions, Joe and me, and came back old men."
  —Muhammad Ali

◆ ◆ ◆

More than any other boxer, Ali openly acknowledged the physical toll his vocation took on him. This introspection, rare among fighters, who, more than any other athletes, must maintain a self-regard that borders on megalomania, underscored his belief that boxing, in some ways, was beneath him. He conceded his physical limitations as early as 1971, while being pestered by insects during an interview with Ira Berkow. "These flies keep flying around me," he said. "They must know I'm not all that I used to be. They must see the little gray hairs that been growing in my head lately." His worst years as a fighter, post–"Thrilla in Manila," saw him descend into the earthbound world of the average professional boxer. These were his years of decay. Ali began, like any other run-of-the-mill pug, to get the close decisions—against Ken Norton and Jimmy Young. He clowned his way through several dreary mismatches. He lost his title to a virtual amateur, Leon Spinks, retired after winning the rematch, and, with the promise of millions for a comeback, challenged Larry Holmes in a virtual suicide mission. Already he was beginning to show signs of the damage common to fighters who do not acknowledge the hazards of their trade. While magazines urged him to retire, his celebrity status, paradoxically, grew, particularly among litterateurs, ideologues, and the same people he once terrified as a cohort of Malcolm X: Middle America. By the mid-1970s, Ali was co-opted by the mainstream and his new ubiquity was based on the very same capitalist dream machine the rebellious 1960s looked to undermine. Ali was in the movies. Ali had his own Saturday morning cartoon. Ali starred on television. Ali earned sponsorships from D-Con, batteries, and Bulova. With the radical chic sheen now gone (Revolution Road in America hit a Dead End in 1981 with the final explosive dissolution of the Weather Underground and the Black Liberation Army), Ali was safe enough, sanitized enough for Madison Avenue and Mego.

◆ ◆ ◆

In 2003, Bill Ayers showed up at the Film Forum in New York City for a Q&A after a screening of *The Weather Underground*. He was a harmless-looking man, soft spoken, wearing glasses and two earrings. Someone in the audience asked him about the sexual habits of revolutionaries on the run.

◆ ◆ ◆

What separated Ali from the contemporary fighter, an unusual species of blowhard, was his willingness to concretize his boasts where it mattered most: inside the ring. Yes, Ali was an unstoppable braggart, a man whose self-aggrandizement (which preceded his social consciousness by several years) was too often conflated with racial pride, but there was little disconnect between his proclamations and his achievements. Not only did Ali face the very best heavyweights of two eras, but he also faced a slew of tough contenders whose own legacies were stonewalled by the fierce competition of the 1970s: Ken Norton, Ron Lyle, and Earnie Shavers. When Ali returned from his exile, which lasted three and a half years, he faced the number-one-ranked heavyweight in the world: Jerry Quarry.

◆ ◆ ◆

What Ali did in the ring was not revolutionary for the simple fact that not a single distinguished heavyweight in his wake could reproduce his style. In a way, Ali was like Dizzy Gillespie, whose virtuosity—one step beyond—could not be duplicated or surpassed for nearly thirty years, or until Jon Faddis began hitting notes not even Gillespie could reach in his prime. Of course, there were variations on the Ali style among the heavyweights—think of flashy Greg Page and flamboyant Michael Dokes—but, for the most part, smaller fighters adopted its main ingredients. The closest a heavyweight came to successfully incorporating the Ali method may have been jab-and-dance master Larry Holmes, who sparred with Ali in the early-1970s and went on to butcher "The Greatest" in one of the saddest spectacles ever seen in a boxing ring.

But the flashpoint reflexes, the improvisatory moves, the stamina needed to dance gracefully for fifteen rounds, the explosive hand speed, the decking, dodging, and darting (all done seemingly in double-time)—these had never been seen before among the bigger divisions. After all, his aspiration as a fighter was madness: to resurrect Sugar Ray Robinson as a heavyweight. More influential, of course, was his personality, part vaudeville, part rassling routine, part mad preacher, part the Dozens. Egotism, insult, exhibitionism, incivility—Ali changed boxing in more ways than one. Even during the most primitive era of prizefighting in America, when fights to the finish were common, a certain amount of gentility was expected. When John Morrissey defeated John C. Heenan to retain his heavyweight title in a gruesome slugfest in 1858, the occasion, blood-soaked or not, called for a strange ritual etiquette: "All the courtesies of war followed with the utmost grace at the end of the close of the fight. Morrissey was carried over to his fallen foe and, in the French style, kissed his hand in token of his valor."

◆ ◆ ◆

Because Ali was a "common man" symbol for a revolutionary movement primarily sparked by middle-class baby boomers, he was adopted with almost comic blind faith by activist liberals, despite the fact he was often intrinsically opposed to their ideals. Ali did not drink. He did not smoke. Drugs were strictly verboten. He was well-dressed and clean-shaven. *The Feminine Mystique* by Betty Friedan was the last book he would thumb through. His disavowal of involvement during the struggles of the civil rights era was in stark contrast to the philosophy of disobedience practiced by progressives throughout the 1960s. Worst of all, perhaps, his segregationist stance was distinctly at cross-purposes with the Utopian vision of his newfound champions. Later, when Ali was accepted by moderates and liberals alike, his hobnobbing with brutal—even insane—despots such as Idi Amin, Mobutu Sese Seko, Ferdinand Marcos, Muammar Gaddafi, and "Papa Doc" Duvalier was something his leftist backers could only cringe over.

To make matters even more perplexing for some liberals, Ali was a Republican in the 1980s, supporting Ronald Reagan, Orrin Hatch, and George H. Bush, among others. But Ali, more than anyone, understood the complexities and contradictions of his own myth. This was made clear by the publication of *Muhammad Ali: His Life and Times* by Thomas Hauser in 1991. Oral biographies had been in the air at the time—Jackson Pollack by Jeffrey Potterton, Truman Capote by George Plimpton, and Edie Sedgwick by Jean Stein, for example—but these were all written after their subjects had died. *Muhammad Ali: His Life and Times* was unique in that it was an authorized work and, in that, its subject had few qualms, if any, with negative testimony about his life and actions. What were his personal sins, whatever they were, compared to a life lived at public white heat for over twenty years?

◆ ◆ ◆

"I've made my share of mistakes along the way but if I have changed even one life for the better, I haven't lived in vain."
　—Muhammad Ali

Fugitive Days

pril 5, 1915—Down, at last, in the twenty-sixth round of a bout fought under a blistering sun before thousands of hecklers, even there, in Havana, more than three hundred miles away from American bedrock. Down, and at the feet of "The Pottawatomie Giant," Jess Willard, a cowpuncher who lumbered out of the Great Plains, shucking spurs, lassos, chaps, all the way to the heavyweight championship of the world.

From the moment he lost his title to a primitive "White Hope" in an equally primitive ring set up in Cuba, Jack Johnson—renegade, dandy, scourge of America (where, to his everlasting misfortune, interracial marriage was banned in several states)—was a burnt-out case. Even before losing to Willard and relinquishing his status as "The Black Avenger," Johnson had sent a telegram to his mother in Chicago that read in part: "I AM TIRED OF KNOCKING AROUND."

Oh, yes, Johnson has been wandering, through fugitive days, for years, ever since fleeing Chicago in 1913 after being convicted of violating the Mann Act, a federal law meant to curb prostitution but that was occasionally used to enforce Bible Belt virtue by prosecuting celebrities with libertine tastes. (Indeed, Johnson was not even the most famous celebrity tripped up by the Mann Act; that distinction goes to Charlie Chaplin, acquitted in 1944, or perhaps rock 'n' roll pioneer Chuck Berry, who spent nearly two years in prison after being convicted of transporting a fourteen-year-old across state lines for immoral purposes.) And Johnson was a staunch devotee of lowlife: Although he ran a lavish club in Chicago, his preferred milieu was brothels. And his preferred company? Prostitutes, usually more than one at a time, and, to the dread of most Americans, white prostitutes.

When Johnson took up with a pale-as-alabaster nineteen-year-old courtesan within weeks of his first wife committing suicide, public fury prompted legal action. After his future mother-in-law charged Johnson with kidnapping her daughter, Lucille (who would eventually marry Johnson in a bid to avoid testifying against him in court), authorities closed in. But it was an earlier tryst with another working girl, Belle Schreiber, that ultimately led to his Mann Act conviction on May 13, 1913.

A larger-than-life embodiment of what sociologist Thorstein Veblen had recently called "conspicuous consumption," Johnson swaggered through the early twentieth century at odds with the established racial mores of the United States. Like other hell-raisers of his era—Abe Attell, Stanley Ketchel, and Ad Wolgast—whose days and nights were perpetual scandals, Johnson lived life without a speedometer. Unlike his fellow rowdies, however, Johnson was black. That fact, combined with his audacious attitude—his defiance, his drinking, his omnivorous sexual appetite—in an age when black men were still targets for lynch mobs, made Johnson the object of near-hysterical outrage. Whereas his title-winning knockout of Tommy Burns had merely caused shock, his thrashing of Jim Jeffries in 1910 spurred race riots across the country. Not only did Johnson pummel Jeffries, but he also humiliated "The Boilermaker," boldly taunting and grinning, gold-capped teeth glittering in the sun, as he dealt out nearly fifteen rounds of punishment.

In the wake of the Civil War, institutionalized slavery morphed into "Jim Crow" laws, a series of municipal rulings whose sole purpose was to disenfranchise blacks throughout the South. But Johnson was born in Galveston, Texas, in 1878, an active seaport that naturally functioned, for commercial purposes, as an international zone. Under these utilitarian circumstances, Galveston found itself both racially mixed and relatively tolerant. Compared to growing up in Mississippi or South Carolina, childhood in Galveston seemed almost idyllic. "No one," Johnson said, "ever told me that white men were superior to me."

Whether Johnson consciously took on the role of racial revolutionary or not, his actions required extraordinary courage. He stood out, virtually alone, on the bleak horizon of pre–civil rights America, a symbol of resistance to many black Americans. "I always take a chance on my pleasures," he once said.

Sentenced to 366 days in prison for his reckless disregard of all that Jim Crow prohibited, Johnson fled America on June 24, 1913, an outlaw on the run certainly, but with his overriding sense of *joie de vivre* still intact. He toured England, Argentina, France, Germany, Barbados, Spain—all without a Baedeker at hand.

Two years later, however, he was an exile to himself. As champion, Johnson earned more than the racist cartoons and rotogravures his notoriety generated. No matter how loathed he was by a public that viewed his personal excesses as a blatant disregard for the retrograde moral order of the ironically named Progressive Era, Johnson was an exemplar of sporting supremacy in an age when the heavyweight championship could still be viewed in near-mythical terms. That status, left behind in Havana, could no longer help him in exile. A few days after being stopped by Willard, a dejected Johnson boarded a steamship bound both for Europe and for several unsettled years of a life that had long since spiraled out of control.

When Johnson arrived in London in May 1915, he was not met with the fanfare that had greeted him on previous trips. Without the distinction of being heavyweight champion, Jackson was already on his way to has-been status. His revue, *Seconds Out*, played to waning box-office receipts, and his personal life, which is what ultimately led to his prosecution in America, prompted mass revulsion. In addition, his quicksilver moods—he was sued for assault at one point—soured everyone around him. In January 1916, Johnson was ordered to leave England under the Aliens Restriction Act. With World War I raging across the Continent, he ultimately decided that neutral Spain would be his safest option.

In Barcelona, Johnson was still enough of a curiosity to attract his share of attention. He opened a short-lived advertising agency called "The Information," performed in parody bullfights, revived his vaudeville act, and played the carefree boulevardier for a retinue of hangers-on. Even without the 24/7 digital age paparazzi of today, Johnson remained part of the international glitterati. In fact, he might even have been the generator of the worldwide press he received while in exile. Wire stories about

Johnson could be read from Australia to England to Toronto to all the major cities in the United States. If "The Information" could be said to be a functioning enterprise, then it was on behalf of Johnson himself. Here is Johnson single-handedly destroying a submarine; there is Johnson ready to run for mayor of Barcelona; and now a report or two on how Johnson has acquired King Alfonso as a patron.

Ultimately, however, Johnson knew that making enough pesetas to continue living high style under straitened Old-World circumstances would involve his fists. Nearly a year after losing his title to Willard, an out-of-shape Johnson returned to boxing by scoring a dubious seventh-round stoppage over Frank Crozier on a theater stage that doubled as a ring in Madrid.

As a pro in America during the last lawless era in boxing, Johnson understood the lucrative kinship between prizefighting and carny sideshows. With that in mind, he hooked up with one of the unlikeliest figures ever to step into a boxing ring. Born in Switzerland in 1887 to British parents, Arthur Cravan, whose real name was Fabian Lloyd, was one of the first personalities to kick-start the Dada movement in art. Cravan was a one-man modernist-wrecking crew who published an irreverent literary journal called *Maintenant* filled with pre-surrealist verse and diatribes against his contemporaries. For years, Cravan had idolized Johnson, and he included "Lil' Arthur" on his list of cultural heroes alongside Rimbaud and Wilde. "After Poe, Whitman, Emerson, he is the most glorious American," Cravan rhapsodized. "If there is a revolution here, I shall fight to have him enthroned king of the United States."

Inspired by seeing Johnson perform his vaudeville routine in France a few years earlier, Cravan transformed poetry readings and lectures— where he often held forth wearing only a jockstrap—into free-for-alls, sometimes firing a pistol into the air and, more often than not, hurling objects as well as insults at the startled crowd.

Despite their apparently unbridgeable backgrounds, Cravan and Johnson were remarkably similar. Both men were nomads who had crisscrossed the world; both men were provocateurs who had been thrown in jail more than once. And, of course, both men were boxers, although Cravan gloved up mostly in salons and ateliers when boxing was a fad among artists such as Picasso, Braque, and Miro. In fact, his only distinction as a fighter was winning the amateur light-heavyweight championship of France in a walkover.

One last similarity brought them together in Barcelona: both men were on the run. Despite his riotous approach to life and art, Cravan was obsessed with avoiding conscription and thereby the killing fields of Europe. As the carnage spread across Europe, Cravan wound up in Spain, where he and Johnson hatched a plan to meet in the ring. They made arrangements not as opponents but as co-conspirators: Johnson, low on cash, looking for a quick fix, and Cravan, a rootless draft dodger trying to amass ship fare to New York City, where even the bohemian crowd of Greenwich Village would be startled by his sociopathic antics when he got there.

On April 23, 1916, Johnson and Cravan squared off at the Plaza de Toros Monumental in Barcelona. Over the years, the events surrounding the Johnson–Cravan fight have been embellished to the point of being fictionalized. This, in part, is because so many chroniclers have relied on the memoirs of Blaise Cendrars, a poet and eccentric who elevated the imagination above all else. His recollections of the Barcelona affair are as reliable as the war reminiscences of Baron Munchausen.

In his whimsical account of the fight, Cendrars claimed that Johnson kayoed Cravan in the first round and that the crowd erupted into a riot, rushed the ring, and set the arena on fire, forcing officials to throw Johnson into jail overnight for his own protection. None of this was true. With pioneering Spanish film director Ricardo de Baños on site to record the events, Johnson and Cravan were prepared to extend their travesty for as long as possible in hopes of cashing in on theater replays. There would be no first-round knockout. But what was meant as a profitable lark turned into a full-fledged hoax when D. Felix Suarez Inclan, the local magistrate, informed the participants that prizefighting in Barcelona, while tolerated, was unauthorized. As such, Johnson and Cravan were advised to go easy, and the police were ordered to intervene at first blood.

Trying to convince a crowd that the inept Cravan could last a few rounds against even an aging and flabby Johnson was no easy task, and the bout dragged on, marred by clinching and posing until Johnson mercifully put an end to the hoax with a single blow that legitimately dropped Cravan on his face in the sixth round. It was such a dreadful fight that

Johnson was unable to profit from it as he had hoped. The film footage was useless, and word-of-mouth forced Johnson to enter the ring under similar but less remunerative circumstances across Spain. In an interview with *El Nuevo Mundo* dated March 15, 1918, Johnson was asked how much of his money he had saved during his storied career. He replied, with aplomb, "Not a cent. With the same ease that it came, it went, and the same hands that won it lost it."

Once a clotheshorse who changed lavish outfits twice a day, Johnson was now night-crawling through the winding streets of Madrid looking especially threadbare for a dandy who had, years earlier, been compared to Beau Brummell. For Johnson, keeping solvent meant hustling from day to day. Because Spain had little interest in boxing—its national idols were superstar toreros Juan Belmonte and Joselito—Johnson saw his money-making prospects dwindle.

In March 1919, Johnson returned to Havana—site of his diminishment four years earlier—and upon disembarking, immediately announced that his loss to Willard in 1915 had been a fix. Unfortunately, this startling claim distressed the Cuban government, which promptly issued a warrant for his arrest. Again Johnson sailed on, this time to Mexico, where some brave entrepreneurs assured Johnson that there was a fortune waiting for him in setups. In keeping with his knack for chaos, Johnson arrived during turbulent times in the wake of the Mexican Revolution. There, he publicly called for black Americans to abandon the United States for the more racially tolerant Mexico, a move that verged on sedition.

At odds with the United States over oil rights, President Venustiano Carranza saw Johnson as a public-relations opportunity he could not pass up, and so he welcomed Johnson to Mexico City. Under the patronage of Carranza, Johnson waltzed through exhibitions, put on his strongman act, and eventually ran a bar in Tijuana. But Carranza would not live long enough for Johnson to truly prosper. Ousted by a coup after appointing a figurehead to the presidency, Carranza was assassinated before he could flee Mexico. With Carranza dead, Johnson found himself the enemy of yet another state. Ordered to pack his bags by the Mexican government, Johnson contacted the Bureau of Investigation and offered to negotiate terms of surrender. For seven years, Johnson had wandered across the world, often under duress, and now, with nowhere else to go, he was ready to trade one form of exile for another.

On July 20, 1920, Johnson met US agents at the Los Angeles border, where crowds had gathered on both sides to see the former heavyweight champion of the world relinquish the last thing he had of value: his freedom. Always ready for a publicity op, Johnson, in a ratty suit, paused dramatically before crossing so that photographers could capture the moment. And then, Jack Johnson, for years a Janus-like symbol of both hatred and pride, stepped over the border and, once again, into the unknown.

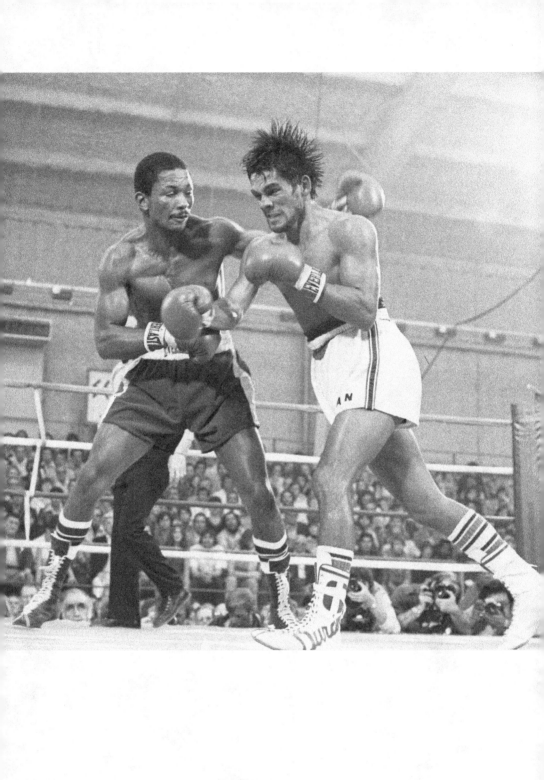

The Last Goodbye

THE RIVALRY BETWEEN ROBERTO DURÁN AND ESTEBAN DEJESÚS

He came a long way to see his nemesis, Esteban de Jesús, in his dying days, out to Río Piedras and to a converted milk factory where the malarial sunlight filtered in through grimy windows overlooking sickbed after sickbed. Now wraithlike, 90 pounds, and seeking solace from a future afterlife, de Jesús had been an addict, a killer, a convict, one of the top lightweights in the world, and, for a little while at least, a national hero, the first man ever to beat Roberto Durán.

◆ ◆ ◆

With José Torres retired and Carlos Ortiz, the gifted ex-champion whose prime began during the *West Side Story*–era, nearing the end of a creaky comeback, New York City was ready for another Puerto Rican star. In 1972, Esteban de Jesús, born in hardscrabble Carolina, Puerto Rico, debuted at the Felt Forum in Madison Square Garden, stopping George Foster in eight rounds. A stablemate of Wilfred Benitez and trained by Gregorio Benitez, de Jesús was a precise counterpuncher with a ruinous left hook and enough dark secrets to last a lifetime. After building a record of 33-1, de Jesús, already dabbling in the nightlife, set his sights on bigger targets—and the temptations that often accompany such ambition. In New York City he had impressed the *afición* with his sharpshooting skills, but not many believed he would be a threat to young Roberto Durán, the recently crowned lightweight champion stalking greatness.

If New York City was impressed by de Jesús, it was wonderstruck by Durán, who coldcocked Benny Huertas in his Madison Square Garden debut in September 1971 and less than a year later trampled stylish Ken Buchanan for the lightweight championship of the world. Even after building up an insurmountable lead on the scorecards, Durán could not resist his own malicious nature. A split-second after the bell ending the thirteenth round, "Hands of Stone" buried a shot below the belt that left Buchanan writhing on the canvas in agony. Poor Buchanan was ruled unable to continue, and Durán was declared the TKO winner, beginning a reign of terror that would last for the rest of the decade. Brash, bold, and brutish, Durán reveled in his reputation for savagery.

Durán, born in 1951, was too old to have benefited from the social programs of Omar Torrijos, the Panamanian strongman who seized power in 1968. As a child, he hustled around on the dusty streets of El Chorrillo, a Panama City slum that could have doubled as the setting for a Graham Greene novel. For the rest of his life, Durán would be hungry— for money, for women, for celebrity, for combat. In the years to come, he would kayo a woman who charged him after a fight, brawl with opposing trainers during gym sessions, turn press conferences into impromptu melees, and publicly greet Juanita Leonard—married to Sugar Ray, boxing royalty in his heyday—with a middle finger. Most infamously, perhaps, Durán chilled a national audience when he spoke disdainfully about Ray Lampkin, still in distress and soon to be carried out of the ring on a stretcher after Durán had nearly decapitated him with a wrecking ball hook. "I was not in my best condition," he told a live television audience. "Today I sent him to the hospital. Next time I will send him to the morgue." But winning the title had given Durán a chance to satiate some of his pangs, and his gluttony would cost him the next time he fought in Manhattan.

Because Durán and de Jesús both had reputations in New York City, where boxing-mad Latinos supported their countrymen as a matter of national pride, a matchup between them was inevitable. They met in a nontitle scrap on November 17, 1972, before a partisan crowd of 9,144. Less than three weeks earlier, de Jesús had scored a ten-round decision over journeyman Don McClendon in San Juan. Now, for $10,000, de Jesús was about to headline Madison Square Garden—still the fight capital of the world—against a rampaging lightweight with unlimited potential.

What was supposed to be a mere distraction from carousing turned into a nightmare for Durán within thirty seconds of the opening bell, when de Jesús landed a snapping right hand that stung him and followed up with a sweeping left hook that nailed Durán flush on the jaw. Stunned, Durán crashed to the mat for the first time in his career. When referee Arthur Mercante completed the mandatory eight-count, Durán dove into the fray again, but he could never claw his way back into the fight.

By feinting and making himself a moving target, de Jesús kept Durán off-balance from round to round, peppering the future legend with jabs, hooks, and the occasional cross. At the sound of the final bell, a disgusted Durán turned away from de Jesús with a defiant gesture of his glove. The unanimous decision went to Esteban de Jesús.

Over-the-weight fights against top contenders were holdovers from the 1920s, '30s, and '40s, and Durán manager Carlos Eleta continued the tradition by denying de Jesús an immediate rematch for the title. "After that fight, we went with [trainer] Ray Arcel to a restaurant and Durán was crying," Eleta told Christian Giudice, author of *Hands of Stone*. "I told him you don't win the fight in the ring but in training. . . . He wanted the rematch immediately, but I postponed that fight so that he could get out of this feeling. I waited until he was ready and then I told him that he would fight de Jesús again." Years later, Freddie Brown, who co-trained Durán alongside Ray Arcel, broke down the upset succinctly to *Sports Illustrated*. "He had just won the title and he was having a lot of fun celebrating. He didn't take de Jesús seriously. It didn't mean anything to him. He came to New York to play."

After scoring the biggest win of his career, de Jesús went on to post a pair of decisions over contender Ray Lampkin and a knockout over former super-lightweight champion Alfonso "Peppermint" Frazer. Durán, meanwhile, released his raw fury in successful title defenses against Jimmy Robertson, Hector Thompson, and Guts Ishimatsu. It took a career-high payday of $125,000 to lure him into a rematch against de Jesús—this time in Panama.

On March 16, 1974, de Jesús and Durán squared off before nearly sixteen thousand spectators at the Gimnasio Nuevo Panama in Panama City, where the dry season guaranteed temperatures of over one hundred degrees at ringside. After a grueling struggle to make weight, de Jesús was so drained that Gregorio Benitez tried to postpone the fight under the pretext of a cut de Jesús suffered in sparring. A $40,000 purse convinced de Jesús to enter the ring under unfavorable circumstances. For his part, Durán was training harder than ever before. Not only was he scheduled to face the only man who had ever beaten him, he was also worried about supernatural forces. Even for boxing, with its near-surrealist air, such a concern seemed beyond the pale. According to Christian Giudice, de Jesús had gathered warlocks in his camp in order to hex Durán.

If de Jesús was worried about the inferno-like conditions, he seemed oblivious to them when the opening bell rang. Both men forced a torrid pace in the dizzying heat. Durán, well prepared for his only conqueror, fought with the trademark frenetic style he had been unable to muster in the first bout. Still, de Jesús seemed ready for the onslaught, and for the second time in as many fights, he toppled Durán with a lashing hook barely a minute into the first round. For Durán, who jumped to his feet quickly, the possibility of having been the victim of bad juju must have seemed all too real as he took the mandatory eight-count.

From that point on, Durán and de Jesús—the best lightweights in the world—warred toe-to-toe until one of them began to wilt. It was de Jesús who succumbed. With less than a minute remaining in the seventh round, a clubbing right hand dropped de Jesús to his knees. He beat the count but took more punishment over the next few rounds, and at the end of the tenth, he told Benitez that he could go no further. Unmoved, Benitez pushed de Jesús out of the corner for one last stand, which lasted less than thirty seconds. Sensing the kill, Durán moved in on a wobbly de Jesús with both hands churning. A looping right sent an exhausted de Jesús crashing to the canvas, where he took the full count on his knees.

Although de Jesús had absorbed a beating from Durán (as well as one from Antonio Cervantes in losing a decision for the WBA super-lightweight title in May 1975), he rebounded by outpointing Guts Ishimatsu for the WBC lightweight title in Bayamon in May 1976. In winning the WBC championship, de Jesús became part of a unique geographic renaissance. From 1975 to 1978, Puerto Rico, an island with the population of Wales at the time, produced a slew of world champions, including Angel Espada, Sammy Serrano, Wilfred Benitez, Alfredo Escalera, and Wilfredo Gomez. Before Gomez skyrocketed to the kind of fame that bordered on religious mania in the late 1970s, it was de Jesús who captured the imagination of Puerto Rico. During that era, Wilfred Benitez was recognized for his eccentricity as much as he was for his precocious ability, and Alfredo Escalera, although popular, was admired chiefly for a crowd-pleasing style emphasized by his habit of carrying a snake into the ring with him. De Jesús, on the other hand, exuded class. His neat counterpunching style, mixed with nimble footwork and an accurate jab, was the blueprint from which Gomez and future champions such as Edwin Rosario and Victor Callejas plotted their own nifty moves.

De Jesús defended his WBC title three times in Bayamon, turning back Hector Julio Medina, Buzzsaw Yamabe, and Vincent Mijares—all by stoppage. Finally, nearly four years after their last meeting, the scene was set for de Jesús and Durán to renew their hostilities, this time for the undisputed lightweight championship. A few months after beating de Jesús in Panama City, Durán spoke to the *Miami Herald* about his toughest foe: "I would not like to step into the ring again with Esteban," Durán said, "but if it comes to it, I will knock him out again." According to promoter Don King, staging the rubber match was just short of hard labor. "It was a job just to get the two managers of the fighters to even think about a match," King told *Sports Illustrated*. "They had fought twice and neither wanted to fight a third time. First I convinced de Jesús. But the hard part was convincing Eleta. Then, when we did agree, trying to find a site that pleased him was almost impossible. One place was too cold; the next too hot. A third place, somewhere in Africa, was OK, but then Eleta didn't think he could get Durán's money out. He finally said yes to Las Vegas."

Except for a few heated insults exchanged before their previous fights, Durán and de Jesús were fierce but not enraged competitors. In the days before their unification match, however, Durán made his feelings about de Jesús clear. "I don't like him for a lot of reasons," Durán said, "mostly because he is the only man ever to beat me. And he is the only man to ever knock me down. I don't like him for a lot of reasons, but I have to respect him for them." Their rivalry reached critical mass at the weigh-in when both camps took part in a scuffle that made the usually unflappable Don King jittery about the possibility of having to postpone the fight.

On January 21, 1978, Durán and de Jesús met at Caesars Palace in a bout broadcast nationally by CBS. Already hollowed out by a drug habit that predated his championship reign, de Jesús looked slack during the prefight instructions. He entered the ring a 5-7 underdog that afternoon, but the truth was that de Jesús, at twenty-six, was only the latest nostalgia act to hit the Vegas strip.

To make matters worse for de Jesús, he was now facing a Durán at his absolute peak. Durán, a juggernaut when he flattened de Jesús two years earlier, answered the opening bell by jabbing and circling. By adding guile to his attack, Durán ensured that de Jesús never had a chance at victory. Although he boxed well in spots, de Jesús was forced into the uncomfortable role of aggressor for most of the fight. In the twelfth round, he closed in on Durán, who connected with a trip-wire right hand—half cross, half uppercut—that dropped de Jesús in a heap. Showing remarkable courage, de Jesús crawled across the ring and hauled himself upright with the aid of the ropes. When the action resumed, Durán battered his bruised adversary with both hands until the fight was finally halted.

A year after unifying the lightweight title, Durán would abandon his title to focus on the welterweight division, where in less than two years he would notch his greatest achievement: a stirring win over Sugar Ray Leonard in the first superfight of the 1980s.

For de Jesús, losing to Durán in their rubber match accelerated his downward spiral. Manny Siaca, who trained de Jesús in the last stages of his career, told the *New York Times* that de Jesús no longer believed his career could be salvaged. "He felt depressed, that it was the end for him, that he didn't have it anymore."

In his last fight, de Jesús challenged Saoul Mamby for the WBC super-lightweight title in Bloomington, Minnesota, far away from the bright lights of Las Vegas and New York City, and as chief support to the main event featuring Larry Holmes–Scott LeDoux. On July 7, 1980, Mamby stopped de Jesús in the thirteenth round.

In retirement, de Jesús began making headlines for all the wrong reasons. Long considered a tropical Arcadia after years of travel brochures, celebrity cruises, and sun-washed tourism commercials, Puerto Rico has always had a dark heart at its center. As a hub between South America and the United States, Puerto Rico has been a drug-running stopover for trafficking, with the inevitable tragic consequences. Even now, on the verge of being a failed state, Puerto Rico is suffering from a heroin scourge that has left thousands of lives in tatters. Now adrift among the junkie subculture in Puerto Rico, de Jesús saw his drug habit grow worse. He was arrested during a raid in San Juan and charged with possession of heroin.

Then, on November 27, 1980, fueled by a potent combination of heroin and cocaine, de Jesús turned a road-rage incident into a tragedy when he shot and killed an eighteen-year-old after a high-speed chase on an expressway. He was convicted of first-degree murder and sentenced to life in prison. At Rio Piedras State Penitentiary, de Jesús became a preacher, and daily prayer meetings became part of his routine. In 1985, when de Jesús found out that his brother (with whom he shared needles to inject heroin) had died of AIDS, he had himself tested by prison officials. The result was a death sentence: de Jesús tested positive for HIV.

Within a few years, de Jesús was so ill that his sentence was commuted on the condition that he remain in an AIDS clinic for treatment. "The doctors tell me that I have anywhere from one to four years to live," de Jesús said in a television interview in February 1989, "but I hope God will support me longer." There would be no reprieve for the magnificent lightweight whose troubles—combined with his losses to Durán —would permanently overshadow his career. Three months later, he was dead.

A few weeks before he died, however, an ailing de Jesús received a visit from Roberto Durán, whose empathy brought him to Puerto Rico from hundreds of miles away. Durán met his ex–rival for the fourth and final time in a weathered milk factory converted into a makeshift sickbay.

During the late-1980s the growing AIDS epidemic sparked a national panic. Before that, however, before the number of AIDS deaths spiked from hundreds in 1982 to more than fourteen thousand in 1989, AIDS was virtually a taboo subject. It took the death of Rock Hudson, ex-Hollywood leading man, to bring sharper national focus to the AIDS crisis. Best known for his roles in Douglas Sirk melodramas and Doris Day comedies in the 1950s and '60s, Hudson was the first recognizable face of a mystifying disease too often thought of as the bane of the underclass. Hudson, rich, famous, and preserved forever on celluloid as a hand-some young man, died in 1985. By the late 1980s ACT UP, playwright Larry Kramer, Elizabeth Taylor, and the Aids Memorial Quilt (unfurled in front of the White House in 1988) raised awareness of an illness that had a near-apocalyptic air about it. Even then, however, AIDS victims suffered discrimination and the process by which the disease spread was still shrouded in ignorance. Under any circumstances, it seemed, AIDS was something to fear with almost pathological intensity. But Durán immediately moved in to embrace de Jesús. "When I see him there so thin," Durán told Christian Giudice, "my tears run out because he used to be . . . a muscular guy. I start crying and I hug him, and I kiss him and I tell my daughter to kiss him."

This act of compassion was captured in a photograph that was distributed worldwide by the Associated Press. In stark black and white, it reveals two warring selves, now achieving another kind of glory, an acknowledgment of human frailty and the bonds between us all, a haunting *memento mori*.

Right on for the Darkness

ON AARON PRYOR, 1955–2016

ne must still have chaos in oneself to be able to give birth to a dancing star."
—Friedrich Nietzsche

◆ ◆ ◆

From the beginning, Aaron Pryor, who died on October 9, 2016, was at odds with the world. Or, perhaps, the world was at odds with him. One of the most exciting fighters during an era when action was a prerequisite for fame, Pryor matched his unbridled style in the ring with an apocalyptic personal life that kept him in boldface for over a decade.

Pryor was an at-risk youth before the term came into vogue. Dysfunction was in his DNA. He was born—out of wedlock—in 1955 in Cincinnati to an alcoholic mother whose moodiness could lead to impromptu gunplay. Sarah Pryor, née Shellery, who gave birth to seven children by five different fathers, occasionally whipped out the nickel-plated hardware when some of her brood became unruly. Years later, she wound up shooting her husband five times in the kind of supercharged domestic dispute in which the Pryor clan excelled.

◆ ◆ ◆

Pryor had a family tree whose branches were gnarled by tragedy and whose roots were blood-soaked. One of his brothers, Lorenzo, was a career criminal who escaped from Cincinnati County Jail and eventually wound up doing hard time for an armed robbery conviction in Ohio. Another brother, David, became a transsexual hooker, while his half-brother was shot and paralyzed by his father. His sister, Catherine, stabbed her lover to death. As if to solidify the epigenetics involved in the Pryor family—and to concretize the symbolism of the phrase "vicious cycle"—Sarah Pryor had seen her own mother shot and murdered by a boyfriend when Sarah was a child.

◆ ◆ ◆

As an eight-year-old already at sea in chaotic surroundings, Pryor was molested by a minister. Shame was never far beneath the surface of a man who would eventually earn millions of dollars and worldwide fame as one of the most exciting fighters of his era. On the streets of Mount Auburn and Avalon—where race riots in 1967 and 1968 left bloodstains caked on the sidewalks—Pryor was left to his own devices in a time and place where social services barely existed. As a young boy, he was virtually homeless for years, couch surfing when he could, sleeping in doorways or under awnings whenever his mother locked him out of the house. He was an Over-the-Rhine dead-end kid before finding refuge in a boxing gym as a teenager.

◆ ◆ ◆

After losing a decision to Howard Davis Jr., in an Olympic trials box-off in 1976, Pryor returned to Cincinnati at loose ends. That same year, he made his debut, as a late substitute, and earned a payday of $400 against an ex-kickboxer. By contrast, Davis Jr., had a contract from CBS in hand worth nearly $300,000 before he had ever stepped into a pro ring. The TV gold rush had begun, and Pryor had no chance to stake a claim. Soon Pryor became the hired help—as a sparring partner—for the stars who had left him behind: Davis and Sugar Ray Leonard.

◆ ◆ ◆

Not long after signing Pryor to an exclusive deal, Madison Square Garden—in those days one of the top promotional firms on the East Coast—called a press conference to announce that "The Hawk," then a lightweight, could not get a meaningful fight. So in 1980 Pryor turned to the Robin Hood of prizefighting, Harold Smith, for help. Smith, with money embezzled from Wells Fargo, managed to lure WBA super-welterweight champion Antonio Cervantes to Cincinnati, where Pryor rebounded from an early knockdown to overwhelm and eventually stop the defending champion, who had as many successful title defenses under his belt as Pryor had fights.

◆ ◆ ◆

Like Leon Spinks, the ditzy man-child sent careening through short-lived fame, Pryor often received press coverage that bordered on mockery. It was Spinks who became the target of talk-show hosts and a Richard Pryor skit, but Pryor was no less susceptible to lampooning than "Neon" Leon. His pre–hip-hop Kangols, Cazals, and Day-Glo tracksuits were ready-made for ridicule. Malapropisms popped out of his mouth like Mentos. The bad press he received, he said, was due to "misrepresentation of my personality." Later, he removed the gold cap from one of his front teeth, began wearing suits in public, and even toted a briefcase from one press junket to another.

◆ ◆ ◆

What made Pryor appealing was a fierce ring style seemingly at one with a personal outlook that bordered on madness. Pryor scored five consecutive stoppages in defense of his junior welterweight title and in the process astonished viewers with his frenzied performances. For Pryor, being knocked down often meant popping right back up to charge at his opponent before the referee could issue the mandatory eight-count. Gaetan Hart, Lennox Blackmoore, Dujuan Johnson, Miguel Montilla, Akio Kameda—all were worn down by Pryor and his cyclone attack.

◆ ◆ ◆

As much chaos as Pryor surrounded himself with between fights—he made headlines in 1980 for being shot by his then-girlfriend Theresa

Adams—in the ring, everything was a strange kind of zen. "Controversy is still going to come, because that is my style and some people still don't like me," Pryor once told *KO Magazine*. "I don't care, they just want to see me get beat. I still got something to prove to those people. I still want them to say, 'That nigger's crazy,' about me."

◆ ◆ ◆

Three world titles into his career, Alexis Arguello finally broke into the mainstream after stopping heartland teen idol Ray Mancini in a 1981 lightweight title defense. After scoring a brutal thirteenth-round TKO, Arguello captured the imagination of a national television audience by consoling Mancini with a tenderness antithetical to the general mores of a blood sport. You could not ask for a saintlier contrast to Aaron Pryor.

◆ ◆ ◆

November 12, 1982—The Orange Bowl, Miami, Florida: Aaron Pryor TKO 14 Alexis Arguello

Before the bell rang, Pryor shadowboxed, paced, flurried with intensity. As he was being announced, he pointed his gloved fist at Arguello and held his pose, glowering, for nearly a minute. "I intended to make Alexis believe that I was going to . . . kill him," Pryor later recalled. Soon the men met at ring center and nearly twenty-four thousand spectators watched, spellbound, as Pryor and Arguello abandoned themselves to bloodlust.

◆ ◆ ◆

"After the fight was stopped, Arguello was stretched out on the floor with an oxygen mask held to his face. For the moment, he was not an athlete, not an admirable public figure, but the victim of an accident, as if he had been hit by a drunken driver, or a coal mine roof had fallen on him."
—George Vecsey

◆ ◆ ◆

There would be no salvaging either man. For both Pryor and Arguello, the future would be an illusion. "After I beat Arguello is when I started to lose myself," Pryor once recalled. "I didn't know quite who I was for a long time."

◆ ◆ ◆

At last, Pryor had earned the respect and distinction he had craved his entire life. Or had he? Within hours, his greatest accomplishment was eclipsed by the actions of his trainer, Carlos "Panama" Lewis. Twice—after the first round and after the thirteenth—Panama Lewis instructed Pryor to drink from a mysterious black bottle—"The one I mixed." "The Black Bottle" was not black at all, in fact, but a strange Robert Ryman off-white. Grainy video reveals that it seemed to be wrapped in athletic tape as if to hide its contents.

Panama Lewis would go on to serve a prison sentence for removing the padding from the gloves of Luis Resto in a 1983 fight against Billy Collins Jr. "I had seen Panama Lewis getting to do this with Aaron one time," recalls Frankie Sims, former co-trainer of Pryor. "He was getting ready to cut the inside of the gloves and take the pads out. I looked right at him and shook my head. 'Don't do that man.' He knew I was dead serious, and so he didn't cut out the pads, but he was very crooked in my opinion. He didn't help Aaron's reputation at all."

◆ ◆ ◆

Pryor essentially trained himself for the rematch with Arguello in 1983. Sparring numberless rounds sans headgear, Pryor was hospitalized for a thunderous migraine. Under-conditioned, surrounded by chaos, and already battling a drug addiction that would leave him on the brink of death more than once, Pryor battered Arguello in Las Vegas, scoring a tenth-round TKO and leaving the limelight for a life on the margins.

◆ ◆ ◆

After being introduced to crack by his wife, Pryor spent the next ten years in a perpetual haze. A *Sports Illustrated* profile in 1985 revealed Pryor, death-in-life, gray and skeletal, his surroundings as dreary as those of a drifter wandering the streets from day to dire day. For Pryor, nothing mattered now except the rush. He placed his life and his career on a funeral pyre. "Miami is the drug capital of the U.S. There are drugs at every other door. Living in that environment, I reached out for some help," Pryor recalled. "My wife had divorced me. I was so hurt by rumors of the black bottle that I had no energy. I reached out and certain people did not give me their right hand. They gave me drugs."

◆ ◆ ◆

Pryor rallied in 1984, against limited Nicky Furlano in Toronto, where he labored to a fifteen-round decision and revealed in the process a fighter—a man—who was beginning to fray. A year later, in 1985, Pryor struggled to a narrow points win over Gary Hinton in Atlantic City and disappeared, undefeated, into a permanent midnight.

◆ ◆ ◆

"I ain't The Hawk now. The Hawk is dead. I'm a ghost."
  —Aaron Pryor, 1985

◆ ◆ ◆

The mid-1980s, neon and glitz for some, were some of the bleakest years for Pryor. He was divorced for a second time. In October 1986, he was arrested for assaulting his mother. In 1987 he was shot in the wrist and held hostage by a pair of baseheads and his mother tried to have him committed. In 1989, he was arrested for possession of drug paraphernalia. There were more lawsuits and canceled fights than can be remembered. He went through trainers, managers, and promoters the way a hanging judge went through outlaws in the West.

Finally, after the lost years passed him in a blur, Pryor was sentenced to six months in prison for drug possession. For more than one court appearance, Pryor, who appeared indefatigable in the ring, overslept and arrived late. Recalled Pryor: "I immediately became a night person. There's no such thing as a crackhead being a 'day person.' The crackhead is up all night and sleeps all day. I also became very undependable. Whenever anyone asks a crackhead to do something, they'd better not hold their breath waiting for it to happen. The person using the crack only thinks of themselves, how something will benefit them, and the next time they are going to get high. They're not thinking about picking up the kids from school, meeting the in-laws for dinner, or having a family get-together on Sunday. It's all about getting high."

◆ ◆ ◆

This was not the kind of habit that led to a few weeks in the Betty Ford clinic or could be overcome by an intervention. It was *Do the Right Thing, J Is for Junkie, Night of the Living Baseheads* deterioration. For loose change, a shambolic Pryor shadowboxed on street corners. Occasionally, he even sparred against neighborhood toughs in alleys and backyards. He shuffled from one crack house to another, took beatings from conscienceless thugs, suffered sexual degradation, and slept on curbsides under harsh lamppost light. Every urban wasteland was a mirror image of another during that era. Crack vials shattered beneath feet, abandoned buildings were repurposed for shooting galleries and smoking dens, crosswalks were ruled by vicious sentinels wearing Timberlands and waving Glocks. All blue hours were splintered by the pop-pop-pop of gunshots, the nonstop wail of sirens, and the falling, booming bass beat of Jeeps cruising the risky streets. Then the sun would rise again on chalk outlines, spent shells, sidewalks caked in flaking blood. But you would never think to find someone as accomplished as Aaron Pryor in that netherworld.

◆ ◆ ◆

"One time, a dope dealer thought I was so high that he could manipulate me into believing that I owed him $5,000. I argued with him and he pulled a gun on me and started firing at me point blank. I pulled out my own gun and started firing back. In a flash, there were two other guys by his side firing automatic weapons at me. It was a good old Wild West show. The bullets were whizzing by me and putting holes in my car. We must have been only twenty feet from each other. When I emptied my gun, I got in the car and drove off. That was the kind of madness I was living in."
—Aaron Pryor

◆ ◆ ◆

In 1987, more than two years after his last fight, Pryor faced hard-hitting ex-prospect Bobby Joe Young at the Sunrise Musical Theater in Fort Lauderdale, Florida. It was too much for a disintegrating Pryor. Years of squalor had left him with a gray pallor. His vision, suspect for years, may have deteriorated to the point where he should not have been allowed in the ring. Before the fight began, Pryor had his mouth bloodied in a scuffle with Young's trainer, Tommy Parks. Young scored a knockdown in the first round, staggered Pryor repeatedly, and dropped the ex-champion hard in the seventh with an overhand right. As the referee tolled the mandatory eight-count, a wobbly Pryor dropped to one knee and made the sign of the cross. The referee reached ten.

◆ ◆ ◆

His umpteenth comeback, in 1990, was a travesty. A fly-by-night promoter named Diana Lewis decided that Pryor would be enough of a sideshow attraction to make the harsh phrase "blood money" a remunerative reality. Nearly blind in one eye, Pryor was granted a license to fight in Wisconsin, whose Department of Licensing and Regulation ruled that denying the tattered Hawk the right to fight was tantamount to discrimination. Pryor stopped Daryl Jones, his pal of many years, in three farcical rounds and returned to the streets.

◆ ◆ ◆

"I got so depressed, I contemplated suicide. Plenty of times. Not because the money was gone or even that I had wrecked my life. I wanted to die because I couldn't find a way to live. I didn't know how to start a new life."
—Aaron Pryor

◆ ◆ ◆

"All of it had to do with drugs. With crack. He has been assaulted—mentally, physically, sexually. He's been beaten, not just with fists, but

with guns, sticks, bats. Some of these leeches have taunted him to shadowbox for them. They have mocked him, humiliated him, threatened him. All for what? A little rock of cocaine? For that trash, they've made him beg. Made him do unimaginable . . ."
    —Cincinnati trainer Mike Brown, 1993

◆ ◆ ◆

Lying in a crack house, seemingly on the verge of death, Pryor had an epiphany. He was rushed to a hospital with bleeding ulcers and underwent surgery. When he was released after two weeks—now sporting a long scar across his stomach, the last of several life marks—he headed straight for a church and to a new beginning, one that lasted for more than twenty years. Pryor became a deacon and a motivational speaker. He trained amateur fighters in Cincinnati. Aside from a few national television appearances alongside his son, Aaron Pryor Jr., a journeyman super-middleweight, "The Hawk" no longer had the spotlight on him. This new anonymity was a sign of serenity—something Pryor had earned with blood and sweat. The same way he had earned his Hall of Fame status in the ring.

◆ ◆ ◆

"I've had a phenomical . . . just a phenomical life."
    —Aaron Pryor

The Catastrophist

THE TROUBLED WORLD OF DON JORDAN

"Chaos" is the only suitable word to describe the career of Don Jordan. Nearly sixty years after he first won his welterweight title, Jordan remains a mystery without a solution. Not only did he bewilder spectators with his desultory performances, he also mystified trainers, sportswriters, police officers, mobsters, and historians, few of whom bothered to trace a career that read more like a case study than the narrative of a boxer. Welterweight champion only long enough to make two defenses and accidentally TKO nefarious Frankie Carbo, Jordan left behind a legacy as befuddling as that of Iron Eyes Cody or D. B. Cooper. Like many fighters in the 1950s, Jordan was dogged by ties to mobsters, but it was his own instability that ultimately led to his spectacular crash.

Donald Lee Jordan was born on June 22, 1934, in Los Angeles to a sprawling family estimated to have had anywhere from between eighteen to twenty-two children. Son of a former amateur boxer, Jordan revealed his wild side early, running with street gangs as a teenager and spending time in various reformatories. "I wasn't a tough kid," Jordan once told Lee Greene. "I was real quiet. I just had one big fault. I liked to fight." His nickname, "Geronimo," was earned during his stint gangbanging in the Russian Flats section of Boyle Heights in East L.A. Jordan dropped out of high school, married at age sixteen, and decided to put his fists to better use.

After a short stint in the amateurs, Jordan turned pro as a lightweight in California in 1953. A converted southpaw with a snappy jab and a busy left hook, Jordan won the state lightweight title less than two years after his debut, defeating Joe Miceli, Art Ramponi, and former champion Lauro Salas on his way to a 20-2 record.

In 1955 Jordan lost two decisions to buzz-saw Art Aragon, and subsequently fell into a slump, dropping six of his next twelve fights. Although he managed to beat another ex-champion in faded Paddy DeMarco, Jordan lost decisions to Jimmy Carter, Orlando Zulueta, Joey Lopes, L. C. Morgan, and, for the California State welterweight title, Charley "Tombstone" Smith. A slew of knock-over fights in Mexico, where his fluent Spanish and ring finesse made him a popular draw, put Jordan back on track, and when he returned to Los Angeles he hooked up with a used car salesman named Don Nesseth, who turned Jordan over to trainer Eddie Futch and Jackie McCoy for development. An improved Jordan soon ran off a hot streak that included decisions over Isaac Logart and Gaspar Ortega.

Even with his career gathering momentum, Jordan was unable to curb his reckless nature. Bad habits, the kind that sabotage athletic pursuits, were *modus vivendi* for Jordan. "Not only did Jordan drink but he was a chain cigarette smoker," recalled Jackie McCoy. "Not many fighters do that. This guy never stopped smoking. But somehow he won the welterweight title." Jordan, however, did not draw the line at martinis and Marlboros. In one of the strangest stories to ever come across police blotters involving a boxer, Jordan was arrested on November 8, 1958, for firing arrows from a sixty-inch target bow at two women after a dispute. Jordan was booked for assault with a deadly weapon. A belligerent and obviously blotto Jordan could easily have been charged with resisting arrest as well. "While being questioned by detectives," reported the *Los Angeles Times*, "Jordan tried to grab the bow and arrow after threatening to shoot the officers and a newspaper reporter–photographer team." Charges were later dropped, but in time other problems, the kind endemic to boxing in the 1950s, would arise.

When Nesseth asked Jackie Leonard, matchmaker at the Hollywood Legion, to approach IBC viceroy Truman Gibson for big fight exposure for Jordan, he unknowingly set off a chain of events that would eventually change the course of boxing history. No sooner was Gibson in the mix than Jordan was matched up with rugged Virgil Akins for a shot at the welterweight championship. Akins, who won the vacant title by annihilating Vince Martinez in 1958, would be making his first defense against Jordan. Hard-punching "Honeybear" was considered "inconsistent," one of several euphemisms tossed around boxing in the 1950s, but as a fighter with friends in low places, it is nearly impossible to say how much of his hit-and-miss career was legitimate and how much was not. On December 5, 1958, Jordan plastered the 3-1 favorite over fifteen dirty rounds before 7,344 fans at the Olympic Auditorium to win the welterweight championship. His unexpected victory would have dramatic repercussions.

It is hard to imagine someone as erratic as Jordan—who was arrested for possession of marijuana only three weeks after winning the world title—causing the downfall of Frankie Carbo, but truth, as they say, is stranger than fiction. When Nesseth refused to give Carbo a "cut" of Jordan after the Akins match, "Mr. Gray," along with malignant sidekick Blinky Palermo, resorted to threats. Threats gave way to action, and Jackie Leonard, mistakenly thought by Carbo to be a willing go-between for his underworld shenanigans with Jordan, was beaten senseless by unknown assailants for taking his jitters to authorities. Several arrests, indictments, and trials later, Carbo and Palermo were convicted of conspiracy and extortion for their schemes involving Jordan and were each sentenced to long bids in prison. The mob stranglehold on boxing had been loosened, courtesy of a prizefighter for whom collateral damage was merely second nature. Even as Carbo and Palermo stewed on the witness stand, Jordan was partying with Mickey Cohen, poster boy of L.A. gangster chic, and drawing the enraged scrutiny of the California State Athletic Commission.

In 1959 Jordan defeated Akins in a rematch at the Kiel Auditorium in St. Louis and then made his second—and last—title defense a few months later against former sparring partner Denny Moyer in a dull and sparsely attended bout in Portland. For the Moyer fight, Jordan, who often trained like a man with hypersomnia, weighed in at 148.5 pounds and had to sweat down to the limit. "We never knew what kind of shape he would be for a fight," Jackie McCoy told Dave Anderson. "Eddie Futch used to train him. When he was getting ready for a fight with Gaspar Ortega he came down with a terrible cold. I thought we should call off the fight, but Futch said, 'No, he might show up in worse shape.' Jordan, amazingly, finished strong and won."

For the next few months, Jordan alternated between night crawling through Los Angeles, battling his ex-wife in court, and testifying to grand juries about racketeers. Finally, the impulsive Jordan decided to make his own career moves. Against the advice of his managers—and with McCoy seeing his cut reduced to training fees only—Jordan went on a short winter tour of South America, where unknown Luis Federico Thompson promptly knocked him out in Argentina. Jordan blamed his first stoppage loss on a mysterious "virus" that might actually have been a combination of mononucleosis and jake leg.

Humiliated, Jordan returned to Los Angeles to recover over the holidays. Before long, however, he found himself in one rumpus after another. First, he was suspended by the California State Athletic Commission after refusing to appear for a physical without explanation; then he was arrested on a DWI charge after crashing into two parked cars. Next Jack Urch of the Athletic Commission pointed the finger of suspicion directly at "The Geronimo Kid" by bluntly stating, "We want to know why Jordan persists on palling around with Mickey Cohen." Lastly, Jordan incurred the wrath of the NBA when he preposterously agreed to a "tune-up" bout with journeyman Candy McFarland less than two weeks before a scheduled defense against Benny Paret. At odds with his brain trust and full of near-surrealist irrationality, Jordan turned down a $12,500 television date with Don Fullmer to face McFarland at Baltimore Stadium for less than $1,400.

On May 16, 1960, after a rain delay of two days, McFarland, undistinguished but earnest, cuffed Jordan into a stupor over ten rounds and copped an easy decision. "It was the best kind of workout I could have got," Jordan blithely told the press. Oddsmakers immediately installed him as a 3-1 underdog against Paret.

By this time Jordan was considered not only a "cheese champ," but serious trouble as well. Nevada state boxing commissioner Jim Deskin, vexed by the loose cannon about to step into the Las Vegas Convention Center, assigned a security detail of police detectives to stake out the Jordan training camp. On May 27, 1960, in the first nationally televised bout from Las Vegas, Paret pounded Jordan over fifteen monotonous rounds. "As early as the fifth round," reported *Sports Illustrated*, ". . . it was clear that Don Jordan had lost everything but courage." And courage was not nearly enough for the 4,805 spectators who booed intermittently as Paret churned away at a champion who could have doubled as a Penitente that night.

Never one for damage control, Jordan compounded his troubles by signing over his entire $85,000 purse for the Paret bout to co-managers McCoy and Nesseth in order to hook up with Las Vegas–based hotel impresario Kirk Kerkorian. "I'd fight ten times for nothing to get rid of Nesseth," Jordan snarled. Kerkorian, a former amateur boxer, knew little about the labyrinthine world of prizefighting, and, it could be said, his signing of Jordan proved it. With lawyers hounding him for alimony payments, Jordan decided that he would need a little incentive to step into the ring and held promoters ransom for $2,000 in the dressing room. He got the payoff, but that was the last time Don Jordan had things his own way in the topsy-turvy world of boxing.

Over the next two years, Jordan would hit the skids running and would win only two of his last eleven fights. The boxer with graceful footwork, snappy combinations, and a precision jab seemed to vanish overnight. Other than Carmen Basilio, Tony DeMarco, and Ludwig Lightburn, Jordan suffered his humiliating free fall at the hands of one middling pug after another. On October 5, 1962, Jordan hit bedrock after being "stopped" in the first round by "Battling" Torres at the Olympic Auditorium, where Jordan had won the welterweight title less than four years earlier. The California State Athletic Commission immediately suspected a fix and suspended him for life. Jordan, only twenty-eight at the time of the Torres fiasco, never fought again. His final record stands at 51-23-1-1.

Today Don Jordan is all but forgotten. If he is remembered at all it is for the sudden tailspin that sent him crashing from welterweight champion to complete washout in less than two years. Why did such a talented boxer unravel so suddenly? Was it the drinking, the carousing, the smoking? Certainly other fighters—from Abe Attell to Harry Greb—burned candles at both ends without sputtering out so quickly. Did the strange virus he claimed was responsible for his loss to Luis Federico Thompson linger on and affect his performances? Or was it merely hard luck? The kind of luck a rough-and-tumble man like Jordan might believe was the only kind he could expect?

In 1973, over a decade removed from his short-lived and tumultuous heyday, Jordan earned more notoriety after a bizarre interview with Peter

Heller. Akin to some of the jailhouse ramblings of Charles Manson, the former welterweight champion of the world claimed, among other things, to have been a paid assassin as a child in the Dominican Republic and to have been a factotum for the underworld throughout his career. One outlandish claim followed another until, finally, the question of veracity became moot. His answers were "true" insofar as they functioned as dark correlatives to his fractured psyche. "Winning the championship was the most awful experience of my life," Jordan told Heller. "Believe me, it was awful. It was not a thrill to me. I was involved in certain situations, activities not to my advantage, shall we say. I was involved in certain things; to win was not as thrilling as I thought it would be as a fighter. When I lost it I was happy. I was more happy losing it than winning it."

Boxers, like recently paroled felons, often have difficulty adjusting to the "outside" when their careers are over, and in this respect, Jordan was no different. He struggled with alcoholism, divorced for a second time, and found it difficult to make a living. "I went from job to job," he told the *Los Angeles Times* in 1970, "I was a swamper in a produce market, a machinist in the shipyards, and a carpet layer. I found there were more people in public against me than there were when I was fighting."

A few steady years working for Douglas Aircraft in Santa Monica were followed by a stint as a longshoreman in Wilmington. It was there, in the rugged waterfront district of Southern California, that Jordan was savagely beaten during a robbery on September 30, 1996. Two thugs attacked Jordan in broad daylight and left him for dead in a parking lot. He lingered in a coma for nearly five months before dying on February 13, 1997. He was sixty-two years old. Two men suspected of the murder were later released due to insufficient evidence. His senseless and tragic death was a fitting exclamation point to the unruly life of a boxer who once muttered the bleakest of aphorisms: "But all man knows when he fights he must lose."

Dark Sun

REMEMBERING JOE FRAZIER

Joe Frazier, whose first fight with Muhammad Ali—an event that attracted worldwide attention—sealed his legacy as one of the defining American sports figures of the last fifty years, died of liver cancer on November 7, 2011. He was sixty-seven years old. Although Frazier was heavyweight champion from 1968 to 1973, he will certainly be remembered most for his vicious trilogy with Ali, one marked by malice, anguish, and regret.

Frazier and Ali first swapped punches on March 8, 1971, in a fight that transcended sports and became a social and political happening. Among the luminaries seated at ringside in New York City that night were Hubert Humphrey, Joe Louis, Woody Allen, Diana Ross, the Kennedys, J. Edgar Hoover, David Frost, Alan Shepard, and Joe DiMaggio. Even famed matador El Cordobés was there. Burt Lancaster did commentary for the closed-circuit audience, and Frank Sinatra, on assignment for *Life* magazine, took photos from the ring apron. "This is the biggest event in the history of the planet Earth," Ali said, only half-joking about "The Fight of the Century."

In retirement, Frazier seemed like a man chased by ghosts. Overshadowed by the legend surrounding the charismatic Ali, Frazier felt that his own legacy was diminished, and he bristled at having his accomplishments undermined. His seething rivalry with Ali went far beyond boxing, and over the years developed into a sports tragedy with a *dramatis personae* of two. "Joe Frazier truly despised Ali," wrote Ali's personal physician and cornerman Ferdie Pacheco.

In the ring, Frazier embodied the hard-earned dignity unique to prize-fighters who cannot—or will not—separate boxing from such concepts as honor, pride, and respect. "I guess you could say I was just about always the underdog," Frazier told the *Philadelphia Daily News*. "But all that just makes me work harder. It makes me love harder."

◆ ◆ ◆

Born on January 12, 1944, and raised in a shack in Beaufort, South Carolina, among palmettos and the long shadow of Jim Crow, Joseph William Frazier began toiling on the barren family farm by the time he was five years old. One of twelve children, Frazier picked vegetables at fifteen cents a crate and helped his father, a sharecropper, run white lightning. Even then his life was hard labor, prefiguring the grueling career ahead of him, and Frazier seemed to be on a fast track to callused middle age. "I quit school after the ninth grade," he told Dave Anderson in 1971. "I wasn't learning anything. I was just there taking space. I had the mind of a man early. You name it—outlook, girls, bread. I was chasing girls when I was thirteen. I was married at sixteen. When I was in school, I'd go into the class and look at the teacher's legs."

Not long after dropping out of school, Frazier hopped on a Greyhound and headed east to live with relatives in Brooklyn. Already married and a father, Frazier soon moved to Philadelphia, where he worked long hours in a slaughterhouse, sharpening his left hook on hanging sides of beef, an idiosyncrasy Sylvester Stallone would appropriate for his film character Rocky Balboa. A few short years later, Frazier, who took up boxing at a local Police Athletic League to lose weight, was in Japan competing in the 1964 Olympics. Incredibly, as a replacement for an injured Buster Mathis, Frazier won a gold medal, defeating Hans Huber by decision in the finals despite fighting with a broken thumb.

Frazier returned from Tokyo with his medal, empty pockets, and vague dreams of becoming the heavyweight champion of the world. With the help of Philadelphia businessman Bruce Baldwin, a syndicate of sporting shareholders formed a group called Cloverlay to back Frazier as he pursued his career.

Under the tutelage of Yank Durham and, later, Eddie Futch, Frazier became the most destructive heavyweight force to emerge since the grisly heyday of Sonny Liston and a throwback to the freight-train style of Jack Dempsey. Pure aggression in the ring, "Smokin' Joe" tore after opponents at the sound of the opening bell, wielding one of the deadliest weapons in boxing: a left hook whose cruel torque had been partially perfected by a broken arm suffered in his youth. His arm had been poorly set and when it healed, it remained slightly crooked.

From 1967 to 1971, Frazier cut a swath of terror through the heavyweight ranks. Among the notable fighters he defeated were George Chuvalo, Manuel Ramos, Bob Foster, Buster Mathis, Oscar Bonavena, Doug Jones, Jerry Quarry, Eddie Machen, and Jimmy Ellis. Frazier did not only beat these fighters but, for the most part, demolished them. Jones retired. Quarry was pummeled before losing via cuts. Chuvalo suffered a broken orbital bone. Machen never won another fight. Neither Foster nor Ellis knew they had each been decked more than once. Ramos, who had never been stopped until he had the misfortune of answering the bell against Frazier, hit the skids running and never looked back, winning only four of his next twenty-seven bouts and suffering nine knockouts along the way to nowhere fast. Out of all the contenders Frazier met, only Bonavena, tough as whalebone, managed to last the distance.

Even then, however, Muhammad Ali, who had lost his title in the grimy backrooms of boxing commissions, was beginning to dog Frazier. A crowd of protesters gathered outside Madison Square Garden the night Frazier knocked out Buster Mathis for the New York State version of the heavyweight title. They gathered on behalf of Ali, whom they considered the true world champion. Unifying the division in 1970 by beating Ellis, who had won an elimination tournament to determine the WBA champion, did little to earn Frazier the respect he felt he deserved. Although he was undefeated and a gate attraction in New York City, Frazier knew that he would have to face Muhammad Ali to silence his detractors.

If Ali was boxing's transcendent countercultural icon, the darling of the jet set and the burgeoning radical chic movement, then Frazier was its John Henry, steel-driving his way through the hardest sport of all with strength, determination, will, and an almost pathological zeal for training.

But it was Ali who drew headlines and caused a commotion wherever he went. Stripped of his livelihood in 1967 for refusing induction into the Vietnam War, Ali lost three and a half years of his athletic prime before returning to the ring—and to a different world—in 1970. "Politics had banned him from the ring and politics brought him back," wrote sports journalist Robert Lipsyte. "As more Americans caught up with Ali's anti-war sentiments, his refusal to be drafted seemed less like dodging than standing up for principle." After being granted a license to fight in Atlanta while his conviction for draft evasion was under appeal, Ali returned to the ring on October 26, 1970, and stopped Quarry in three rounds. When a court order allowed Ali to fight again in New York City, he scored a fifteenth-round TKO over Bonavena and immediately targeted Joe Frazier as his next opponent.

Frazier and Ali agreed to meet in Madison Square Garden. Both men were guaranteed $2.5 million each, an outlandish sum of money in 1971. No sooner was the fight announced than Ali began to hurl insults at Frazier. "Joe Frazier is too ugly to be champ," he said. "Joe Frazier is too dumb to be champ. The heavyweight champion should be smart and pretty like me. Ask Joe Frazier, 'How do you feel, Champ?' He'll say, 'Duh, duh, duh.'" He called Frazier "The Great White Hope" and an "Uncle Tom."

Frazier had no chance against Ali outside of the ring. With his jive esoterica, impish doggerel, and outlandish persona, Ali was simply too glib for the quiet, hardworking man who had grown up dirt poor on a subsistence farm. In addition, Frazier was going up against the zeitgeist. Vilified during the mid-1960s, Ali returned to the spotlight in the wake of My Lai, Helter Skelter, Altamont, and the first draft lottery since World War II. Against the chaos of National Guard deployments, the civil rights revolution, political assassinations, the catch-22 quagmire of the Vietnam War, and one raging riot after another, Ali rose out of the ashes to become a symbol of courage and righteous rebellion. "After a while, how you stood on Ali became a political and generational litmus test," sportscaster Bryant Gumbel explained to Thomas Hauser. "He was somebody we could hold on to, somebody who was ours. And fairly or unfairly, because he was opposing Ali, Joe Frazier became the symbol of our oppressors."

Later, Ali would say he was only trying to promote the fight to ensure its box-office success, but the cruelty of his taunts could not be shrugged off—at least not by Frazier. No longer was his bout with Ali simply a sporting event; to Frazier, it was about revenge. "He had me stunned," Frazier told journalist William Nack in 1996. "This guy was a buddy. I remember looking at him and thinkin', What's wrong with this guy? Has he gone crazy? He called me an 'Uncle Tom.' For a guy who did as much for him as I did, that was cruel. I grew up like the black man—he didn't. I cooked the liquor. I cut the wood. I worked the farm. I lived in the ghetto. Yes, I 'tommed.' When he wanted me to help him get a license, I 'tommed' for him. For him! He betrayed my friendship. He called me stupid. He said I was so ugly that my mother ran and hid when she gave birth to me. I was shocked. I sat down and I said to myself, I'm gonna kill him. OK? Simple as that. I'm gonna kill him!"

But the heated political and racial overtones soon began to take on a dangerous cast as well. Frazier received death threats, and when he arrived in New York he was assigned a security detail led by NYPD detective Joe Coffey, who refused to let Frazier do his roadwork. "I couldn't allow it," Coffey told *The Ring* in 1992. "He would have been too vulnerable. So he'd put on his rubber suit and he'd run in place and shadowbox in the room. We turned the Pierre Hotel into a gym." Frazier's children were also threatened and remained in Philadelphia with bodyguards. For his part, Ali arrived at the weigh-in at Madison Square Garden with a police escort to help him navigate the chaotic streets, overrun by fans, protesters, and assorted midtown loonies. His team was so worried about the mob that Ali was not allowed to leave Madison Square Garden. He spent the next ten hours in the press room, resting on a cot.

Although Frazier could not compete against Ali's wit, between the ropes and under the hot lights, he was more than enough to handle the self-proclaimed "King of the World." After fifteen pitiless rounds, forty-five minutes of mayhem couched in sporting terms, Frazier earned a unanimous decision over Ali in Madison Square Garden before 20,455 fans and an estimated worldwide audience of more than three hundred million. Joe Frazier had won "The Fight of the Century," but he had to be helped back to his corner after the final bell. When he hobbled out of the ring that night, Frazier, like Ali, left behind pieces of himself that could not be recovered. He was in and out of the hospital for weeks after the fight and would never be the same fighter again.

On January 22, 1973, Frazier was brutalized by George Foreman in a little over five minutes in Kingston, Jamaica. It was a fight that no one associated with Frazier wanted to see take place, and one that Frazier did not train particularly hard for. "There was too much partying going on," Eddie Futch told Ronald K. Fried. "It was the wintertime and he was down there in the balmy Jamaica atmosphere and the jet-setters from New York and from Philadelphia had come down to the hotel . . . and there was just a big party going on." Against the implacable Foreman, who entered the bout with thirty-four knockouts in thirty-seven fights and no defeats, Frazier hit the canvas six times before referee Arthur Mercante stopped the carnage.

After a points win over Joe Bugner in London, Frazier and Ali met again in a rematch that fell far short of the original. Before the bout, however, Frazier and Ali continued their hostilities, brawling on the set during a televised interview with Howard Cosell. They hit the floor in a heap after Ali had called Frazier ignorant and, during the scrum, Frazier tried to twist off Ali's foot. The fight itself was not nearly as interesting. On January 28, 1974, Ali and Frazier met in Madison Square Garden for a second time in a dull waltz marred by referee Tony Perez and by the spoiling tactics of Ali, who won an uneventful decision over twelve rounds.

When Frazier and Ali met for the final chapter of their blood feud, this time in Quezon City on October 1, 1975, they saw their vendetta played out with less skill but, incredibly, more ferocity than ever before. Again, Ali brought his special brand of wordy malice to the promotion, calling Frazier a "gorilla" and referring to Frazier as "the only nigger in the world ain't got no rhythm." Ali also carried around a small rubber gorilla, a prop he quickly named "Joe" and abused with a flourish. While Ali mocked, Frazier fumed. "It's real hatred," he said. "I want to hurt him."

They were hollow men in the ring that October morning, no less so for the fury with which they battled. Despite their diminished physical resources, they revealed, once again, the terrible beauty of prizefighting. The "Thrilla in Manila" was a CliffsNotes for sadism. For twelve grisly rounds, both men took turns hammering at each other until it seemed as if only one outcome was possible. Fittingly for a fight that resembled an inferno, there was no air conditioning in the Araneta Coliseum. "Never before in my forty years of boxing involvement had I experienced heat like this," wrote Ferdie Pacheco. "I survived the corner work by wearing a towel that was soaked in cold water and filled with ice cubes on the top of my head."

Finally, when Frazier began having difficulty seeing out of his swollen left eye, Ali rallied in the thirteenth, and in the fourteenth, he landed combinations that staggered Frazier all over the ring until, mercifully, the bell rang to end the round. On his stool, battered and weary, Frazier remonstrated with a concerned Futch, who was ready to intervene. Across the ring in the opposite corner, Ali sat slumped, arms outstretched and draped over the ropes, being tended to by his trainer, Angelo Dundee, ready to yield. Years later, cornerman Wali Muhammad recalled the moment for Thomas Hauser: "After the fourteenth round, Ali came back to the corner and told us, 'Cut 'em off.' That's how tired he was. He wanted us to cut his gloves off. And Angelo ignored him." Futch, however, could not ignore how badly hurt Frazier was. He signaled to referee Carlos Padilla and the fight was over. So, too, was one of the fiercest rivalries in sports history. Frazier would never forgive Futch and, in the years to come, he would disparage his former trainer at every turn. "Don't talk to me about Eddie Futch," Frazier said. "He became a big hero with the press. Such a caring man. Don't talk to me about him."

Even after the pain and disappointment of Manila, Frazier continued fighting. To make matters worse, Frazier, whose poor eyesight was not yet common knowledge, entered the ring for some of his last fights wearing contact lenses. Eight months after losing to Ali, Frazier squared off against George Foreman once again. In the prizefight netherworld of Uniondale, New York, Frazier was again mauled by Foreman, who dropped him twice in the fifth round, sending him staggering into retirement. A restless Frazier returned in 1981 and fought to an ugly draw against an ex-felon named Floyd "Jumbo" Cummings in a fiasco staged in Chicago. Finally, Frazier, then thirty-seven, retired from the ring for good.

There are few happy endings in boxing. Most fighters struggle in their post-fight years, and Frazier was no exception. He drank excessively. His marriage crumbled. He was arrested for DWI—a charge he later beat—and suffered from a variety of illnesses—hepatitis, high blood pressure, diabetes—and a car accident in 1989 left him with chronic back pain for the rest of his life.

Frazier tried his luck as a trainer, but even boxing was no longer good to him. In 1984, his son, Marvis, was knocked out in the first round by Larry Holmes in a suicidal title shot, and Joe Frazier Jr., a talented welterweight, saw his potential undercut by drug abuse and prison time.

Eventually, Frazier also lost his fortune, and by the late 1990s he was living above his gym on North Broad Street in Philadelphia.

Oh, there were good times too, of course, because Frazier was a lively man, one who enjoyed a party and being recognized in public. He worked the trade shows, hammed it up for the WWF, toured with his R&B band, starred in television commercials, made cameo appearances in a few films, and gave his time to several charitable organizations. He was also a tireless signer of autographs and always had a moment for his admirers.

At times, however, there was a melancholy air around him, a darkness. Burt Watson, once Frazier's business manager, told of Frazier's bitterness toward Ali in an interview with Mark Kram Sr. more than twenty years after Manila. "For a long time, I didn't understand what was eating at him, then I did. Ali doesn't know how deep he cut into Joe. You don't do to a man what he did to Joe where we come from . . . to Joe, it was total betrayal by Ali. The acclaim Ali gets eats at him. Joe is the only legend still disrespected. Ali robbed him of who he is. To a lot of people in this city, Joe's still ignorant, slow-speaking, dumb, and ugly. The tag never leaves him. Ali can't even talk and he's still the prize."

For nearly thirty years, Frazier brooded over Ali. Affable in public and at memorabilia signings, Frazier found it difficult to be gracious about the man who had caused him so much anguish. Taking credit for Ali being a trembling hulk of a man afflicted by Parkinsonism is Richter scale–level hatred, yes, and Frazier could not withhold his rage. At one point, years ago, a drunken Frazier had to be kept away from Ali by George Foreman and Larry Holmes at a function. "Truth is," he once said, "I'd like to rumble with that sucker again—beat him up piece by piece and mail him back to Jesus." He also wanted, he said, to push Ali into the Olympic flame when "The Greatest" lit it during the opening ceremonies in 1996. In a similar grim vein, Frazier told Kram, "If we were twins in the belly of our mama, I'd reach over and strangle him."

Joe Frazier had a career record of 32-4-1, with twenty-seven knockouts. When he revealed that he had been nearly blind in his left eye throughout his fighting days—the result of a cataract—he instantly turned a distinguished career into some sort of sporting miracle.

From 1968 to 1971, with Ali in exile, Frazier was the dominant heavyweight force in boxing, and when Ali returned to settle matters once and for all, it was Frazier who won. *The Ring* rated Frazier the top-ranked heavyweight in the world for six consecutive years—from 1967 to 1972—a distinction few fighters can claim. Frazier was also voted *The*

Ring "Fighter of the Year" three times. He was elected to the International Boxing Hall of Fame in 1990 as part of the inaugural class of inductees.

Although Frazier often seemed bitter about his legacy, he was well aware of what he had accomplished—even if others were not. In an article published to commemorate the twentieth anniversary of "The Fight of the Century," Frazier told *The Ring*, "I just love knowing I did what I did."

So do we, Joe. So do we.

Strange Days

THE JOHNNY SAXTON STORY

Johnny Saxton was one of the most controversial champions of the postwar era. Gifted, but ultimately baffling, Saxton trailed skulduggery—and worse—wherever he went. If Primo Carnera can be considered a dreadful symbol of gangland regulation of boxing in the 1930s, then Saxton may very well be the poster boy of the Mafioso-controlled 1950s. Although he won the welterweight championship twice, no one can be certain about his accomplishments in boxing. His connections to mob figures Frankie Carbo and Blinky Palermo resulted in several peculiar situations, and his career was later overshadowed by tragic circumstances beyond the ring.

Born in Newark, New Jersey, on Independence Day, 1930, Johnny Saxton lived a life of nearly impossible symbolic significance. As a child, the luckless Saxton was bounced from relative to relative before being sent to the Colored Orphan Asylum in the Bronx. Founded in 1836 in Manhattan, the Colored Orphan Asylum was eventually torched to the ground during the Draft Riots of 1863; it then reappeared in Riverdale in the early 1900s.

Saxton, as can be expected under the circumstances, was a troubled child. "From the very beginning he had the tendency toward mischief," wrote John C. Ross, "and required constant counseling. Later, when he was placed in a foster home, he had to be returned to the orphanage occasionally because of his inability to make the proper adjustment." Saxton took up boxing in the local Police Athletic League and eventually disciplined himself enough to remain permanently with his foster mother, Hortense Pierson, in the Bedford–Stuyvesant section of Brooklyn.

After winning thirty-one of thirty-three amateur bouts, two national AAU championships, and a Golden Gloves title, Saxton turned pro in 1949 under the guidance of Bill "Pop" Miller. Early in his career, Saxton trained at the Uptown Gym in Harlem and sparred with the likes of Sugar Ray Robinson, Ike Williams, and Sandy Saddler. Miller, perhaps in deference to the dark power structure of the day, introduced Saxton to Blinky Palermo who, in turn, bought Miller out for a reported $10,000.

A cautious stylist with a busy jab and good footwork, Saxton was never a hit with the crowd. Like former lightweight champion Sammy Angott, Saxton, although a sound technical boxer who showed occasional flashes of brilliance, was prone to clinching and mauling.

Saxton went unbeaten in his first forty contests. Among the fighters he defeated on the way to a 39-0-1 record were Ralph Jones, Charlie Salas, Joe Miceli, Tony Pellone, Luther Rawlings, Freddie Dawson, and future welterweight champion Virgil Akins. Blinky Palermo had once manufactured a similar record for one of his earlier prospects: "Blackjack" Billy Fox. Unlike Fox, however, Saxton had natural talent to burn. Bob Richelson summed up his early promise in a 1953 article for *Boxing*: Saxton was, he wrote, "generally regarded, with the possible exception of Floyd Patterson, as the greatest prospect to come out of the Golden Gloves since Ray Robinson."

But even then, there were troubling signs. A curious lethargy, for example, often afflicted many of his opponents: Ramon Fuentes, Lester Felton, Johnny Bratton, and Livio Minelli all slipped into inexplicable hypnotic states when facing Saxton. Felton was disqualified; Minelli, who could not even manage to muster up family honor as motivation (since Saxton, after all, had whipped his brother Aldo in 1950), was tossed by referee Ruby Goldstein for sheer ineptitude; Fuentes was so passive that the crowd hurled trash into the ring; and Bratton nearly had his purse withheld for his somnambulism act. Saxton was acutely aware of his unpopularity. "I've always been knocked," he told the press in 1957. "Let's face it. Saxton's always been a bad guy. I haven't been on the good side of nobody."

In 1953 Saxton had his undefeated run snapped by whirlwind contender Gil Turner, and six months later he dropped a decision to veteran

Del Flanagan. Despite these two losses and a subsequent draw against Johnny Lombardo, Blinky Palermo used his connections to obtain a title shot for his fighter.

Saxton won his first championship at the expense of Kid Gavilan in a fight widely considered to be fixed. On October 20, 1954, Saxton slipped away with a fifteen-round decision in Philadelphia, but there would be no ticker-tape parade thrown in his honor. "I congratulate you—on your luck," Frank Weiner, chairman of the Pennsylvania Athletic Commission, told the new champion after the match. Arthur Daley called the fight "the equivalent of a double no-hitter" and "undoubtedly the worst prizefight ever held." Little of note occurred during the bout. Saxton refused to lead, backpedaled meticulously, counterpunched sparingly, and, when the ineffectual Gavilan so much as hinted at a move, held brazenly. "That was just not his night," Saxton told *SPORT* magazine in 1963. "You have those off nights. Anybody has them. He had one."

Gavilan wept openly after the fight and complained bitterly about getting "the business." His accusations were bolstered by thunderclouds of rumors that had swirled prior to the match. Like the infamous Billy Fox–Jake LaMotta hoax (also a Carbo–Palermo co-production), the Saxton–Gavilan outcome appeared to be widely known in advance. Bookmakers in New York reportedly refused to accept wagers on Saxton. "It was an open secret," Budd Schulberg told *The Observer* years later. "All the press knew that one—and other fights—were fixed. Gavilan was a mob-controlled fighter, too, and when he fought Billy Graham it was clear Graham had been robbed of the title. The decision would be bought. If it was close, the judges would shade it the way they had been told."

Some of the curious decisions Gavilan received in his own fights raised the possibility that "The Cuban Hawk" followed story lines that were handed to him. When the script called for him to lose, however, Gavilan got testy. "A possible explanation of the putrid affair," wrote Dan Parker in *Sports Illustrated*, "is that . . . Carbo . . . saw that the Keed not only was getting balky but also was slipping rapidly, and, to keep control of the title, arranged with Blinky to pass it along to Saxton. Gavilan apparently was suspicious from the start, as he pulled out of the match twice." And his outburst to the media probably sealed his fate as far as title fights were concerned. In an era where rematches were the norm, it is impossible to account for the fact that Gavilan—one of the most popular fighters in America and a television staple—never received a return bout with Saxton.

After winning the welterweight crown, Saxton participated in two non-title scraps: a monotonous decision victory against Ramon Fuentes (in which the only action of the evening was provided via audience participation) and a surprise points loss to talented but obscure Ohio contender Ronnie Delaney in a non-televised match that Saxton was widely expected to win. Then, on April Fool's Day, 1955, in his first defense of the championship, Saxton was demolished by Tony DeMarco in fourteen rounds. A raucous crowd of nearly nine thousand Bostonians watched hometown favorite DeMarco, officially a 3-1 underdog, drop Saxton with his trademark left hook and batter "The Fighting Orphan" along the ropes until referee Mel Manning halted the slaughter. Although he fought courageously and with more brio than previously noted for, Saxton took a beating from the rugged DeMarco, and this fight may have been the catalyst for the downward spiral that followed.

After a string of soft comeback wins, Saxton regained the welterweight title by outpointing Carmen Basilio in Chicago on March 14, 1956, in a fight that raised as many—if not more—eyebrows as the Gavilan washout had in 1954. The *New York Times* reported that when the decision was announced, "The reading of these tallies . . . set off a derisive din that shook the stadium rafters. It was sustained for ten minutes, died down a bit, then rose again when the preliminary bouts that follow the main event entered the ring." All of Chicago, not just the crowd of 12,145 and the live television audience of millions, seemed to be in an uproar. The press hinted at sinister forces behind the scenes; Basilio spoke bluntly, but eloquently: "It was like being robbed in a dark alley"; the Illinois State Athletic Commission quickly launched an investigation that led, as most investigations do in boxing, to a dead end. In an interview with Dale Shaw several years later, Saxton scoffed: "Fight writers. What do they know? I won it." Then, in an uncanny echo of the Gavilan match, he added, "Basilio had a bad night."

Saxton cashed in on his repeat notoriety the same way he had after the Gavilan fight: with three more nontitle bouts, including a solid rematch win over contender Gil Turner. Then, on September 12, 1956, Saxton was stopped in a return with Basilio. Although Saxton had been banned from fighting in New York State due to his underworld associations, Julius

Helfand, chairman of the New York State Athletic Commission, convinced that Basilio could not get a fair shake in Chicago or Philadelphia—or anywhere else, for that matter—consented to stage the bout in Syracuse despite his animosity toward the "mobster" element. A 2-1 favorite, Saxton was feisty and competitive in the early rounds, but Basilio, relentless as always, wore his opponent down with a body attack. By the eighth round, Saxton had been pounded to a near standstill. Referee Al Berl intervened in the ninth with Saxton reeling helplessly around the ring, blood streaming from a split lip. "I cut him, I banged him, I hit him real hard, took all the fight out of him," recalled Basilio, boiling a prizefight down to its brutal essence.

Five months later, a third—and unnecessary—match with Basilio lasted only two rounds before Saxton was bludgeoned to the canvas. "When Saxton fell," reported John C. Nichols, "it was obvious that he was out. Indeed, it appeared that he would never be able to move before he was counted out, though he surprised everyone by getting to his feet again." Saxton rose, but—in what can easily be read as a symbol for the black days to come—was too wobbly to continue.

From 1956 to 1962 Saxton lived through the kind of nightmare scenario Kafka might have dreamed up. But even before he lost his title and slipped into despair, there had been signs of erratic behavior. In June 1954, for example, Saxton was arrested for threatening his wife, Vivian, with a loaded gun only three months after the couple had exchanged wedding vows. Only a few months prior to his rematch with Basilio, in June 1956, Saxton was arrested for an early, if peculiar, example of road rage when he attacked two waiters sitting in a car double-parked on a Queens street. Unable to squeeze past the offending vehicle, Saxton decided to play traffic cop with a baseball bat and a lug wrench. "BOXER IN NONTITLE BOUT" read the headline in the *New York Times*. Charges were later dropped.

If his personal life was pandemonium, the boxing ring offered no relief. In his first fight after the loss to Basilio, Saxton was knocked down twice and stopped by old foil Joe Miceli in four rounds. His adviser, Ben Stamper, summed it up concisely: "He just seemed to fall apart all at once." Saxton was next knocked out in a non-sanctioned match with a New Jersey State trooper on a roadside in Newark. Stopped for a traffic offense, Saxton claimed that the officer had insulted his wife and that he had emerged from his car to defend her honor. He was dropped by a single blow—a "sucker right" as Saxton put it—and became a running joke for newspapers along the eastern seaboard.

Saxton remained idle for a year before returning to score an unpopular decision over club fighter (and previous victim) Barry Allison on October 10, 1958. A points loss to undefeated Denny Moyer followed, and, in his last fight, Saxton was bludgeoned by Willie Green in four rounds. The strange career of Johnny Saxton was over. He was twenty-eight years old.

In retirement Saxton, a high-school dropout, found himself adrift. And broke. He got a job as a dockworker to make ends meet. Like many boxers from similarly bereft backgrounds who suddenly hit the big time, Saxton spent his tens and twenties as if they had expiration dates stamped on them. After the parties and the his-and-hers Cadillacs, it was the IRS, patron bogeyman of prizefighters, who relieved Saxton of his house in Flushing and an apartment building he co-owned in Harlem. After losing his job on the waterfront, Saxton became increasingly depressed. "I used to take these long walks," he told Dale Shaw. "Vivian told me to get some help, to do something. I didn't know what to do. I couldn't fight. I was troubled."

On March 4, 1959, Saxton proved just how troubled he was when he was arrested on a burglary charge that netted him $5.20 and an "orlan" cape. Saxton jumped from a second-story fire escape and tried to dash down an alleyway to freedom, but he was caught and subdued by three police officers in a ferocious scrum. He languished in the bullpen for a few days before his bail was anonymously posted, and, after being released, walked the streets of Harlem with sunglasses to avoid being recognized. By then Vivian, unable to endure his volatile ways any longer, had left him.

On April 4, 1959, Saxton was arrested for burglarizing a five-and-dime store in Atlantic City. Another scuffle with the police ended with Saxton being handcuffed and hauled to prison in tears. Saxton would later claim that he was hoping to be shot by the pursuing officers in a fruitless attempt at "suicide by cop." Nothing, not even the awful fulfillment of a death wish, seemed to be going right for Saxton. In prison, he attempted to hang himself with a makeshift noose made of socks in a second suicide attempt whose failure could only have been another blow to his shaky sense of self. After being cut down from his useless gallows,

Saxton became "hysterical," and when his volatile behavior continued, he was sent to Ancora State Hospital in New Jersey.

"When I came here," he told James Stewart-Gordon during his stay in Ancora, "I wanted to get out of life. I knew I couldn't fight no more. I was supposed to have got big money from fighting on TV, but I never saw it. No one ever gave me more than a couple of hundred dollars at a time. Now I'm here in the hospital. That's what boxing did for me." After two years of therapy and psychotropic drugs, Saxton was released. The former welterweight champion of the world returned to New York City, rented a furnished room in Brooklyn, and geared up for another round with the legal system.

In 1962 District Attorney Frank D. O'Connor of the Queens County Courthouse dismissed outstanding charges against Saxton after he had been declared "punch-drunk and legally insane" at the time of his arrest. By contrast, in Atlantic City, the court ruled Saxton fit for trial even though Dr. Harry Brunt, medical director of Ancora, reported that Saxton "had the mentality of a 10-year-old child" and that his brain appeared to be one-quarter damaged. Charges were eventually dropped in New Jersey as well, and Saxton shuffled into a new life. "It was hustle and bustle ever since I quit fighting," he lamented in 1964.

Over the years Saxton lived the patchwork life of many down-and-out fighters. He worked as a "floor manager" at a nightclub; he volunteered for a youth program in Harlem; occasionally he trained an aspiring fighter; he spent time as a security guard at the Brownsville Community Center in Brooklyn; here and there he gave private boxing lessons. By the 1990s he was found living in squalor in a New York City apartment sans electricity. Eventually, he wound up in a retirement home in Lake Worth, Florida, where he was diagnosed, for the second time in his life, with dementia—this time the pugilistic kind.

Although his career was marred by smoke and mirrors, there is no doubt that Johnny Saxton was a talented boxer. His achievements as an amateur are particularly impressive. At the time Saxton was dominating the amateur ranks, boxing was still the number-two sport in America, and hundreds—perhaps thousands—of tough youngsters competed every year for amateur trophies in the late 1940s. In the end, however, it seems that he was willing to cut corners in order to achieve success and, ultimately, a sense of distinction.

Not many fighters had kind words for Blinky Palermo. Johnny Saxton, on the other hand, although left nearly penniless despite earning several large paydays during his career, never showed bitterness about the man of whom Coley Wallace once said: "He ruined boxing for me." In 1955 Saxton issued a strange and ambiguous statement to the press after being singled out by New York State Athletic Commission Chairman Julius Helfand for consorting with unsavory types: "Since my first professional fight in 1949, Frank Palermo has been my manager, friend, and adviser. He has been honest and trustworthy in every dealing we have had during my career. I now hold the welterweight championship of the world. I am going along with Palermo."

Even after his career was over and his life was in shambles, Saxton was magnanimous about his former manager. By then Palermo was already serving a long prison sentence for his various crimes against boxers and boxing. "I blame myself," Saxton told Dale Shaw. "What I wanted, I wanted. What I wanted, I got, man. From the beginning. Right from the beginning." What Saxton wanted more than anything was to be like his idols Joe Louis and Sugar Ray Robinson. Perhaps he wanted to be like them too much.

W. C. Heinz once related an interesting story, one with an O. Henry twist, about Sugar Ray Robinson. "One afternoon I got to the gym early," he wrote, "and over in a big corner, in the half-light, I saw Robinson working on the big bag. I stood there and marveled at his natural grace, the speed and fluidity with which he turned on his variety of combinations. It seemed to me that at the age of thirty he looked better than ever, and then he stopped and turned around. It was Johnny Saxton."

Saxton, who died in 2008, fought professionally from 1949 to 1958 and retired with a record of 55-9-2. He was, despite the half-light, a good boxer. For a little while, as welterweight champion of the world, he managed to shuck off bleak anonymity.

The Hurting Kind

WILFREDO GOMEZ VS. LUPE PINTOR

"The tragedy of machismo is that a man is never quite man enough."
—Germaine Greer

◆ ◆ ◆

Wilfredo Gomez and Lupe Pintor, two young men who had both chosen a blood sport to pursue their dreams of distinction, shared other similarities as well. Both men rose from desperate poverty, both men battled weight scales as strenuously as they battled their opponents, and both men were world champions. Finally, both men were sporting icons in their countries. This, to a degree, is where they differed: while Pintor was a popular boxer in Mexico, Gomez was a national hero in Puerto Rico, where his larger-than-life status may have played a defining role in their fight. On December 3, 1982, they turned a boxing ring into an inferno.

José Guadalupe Pintor Guzmán was born in Cuajimalpa, Mexico City, where he grew up in almost unimaginable poverty. One day Pintor returned home from school to find his father waiting for him at the door. "Here, from now on, you study, or you eat." Pintor dropped out and began selling snow cones in the streets of Cuajimalpa, where bullies often capsized his cart and roughed him up. Naturally, this led Pintor to the nearest gym to learn the art of self-defense. From there, Pintor would become a two-time world champion and one of the few moneymakers below the lightweight division in the early 1980s.

Throughout a career that began in 1974, Lupe Pintor suffered the kind of bad luck that seemed almost paranormal in retrospect. First, Pintor saw his world-title dreams delayed because he shared the same manager, "Cuyo" Hernandez, with reigning bantamweight champion Carlos Zarate. Then his inconsistent performances cost him back-to-back decisions in 1978, just as he had solidified himself as a contender on the heels of a twenty-two-fight winning streak.

When Pintor finally met Zarate in the ring, on June 3, 1979, he instantly became the most unpopular Mexican in Southern California when he was the beneficiary of a scandalous decision, one even he seemed surprised to have received. On national television, Pintor was visibly shocked as the verdict was announced in his favor. To make matters worse, the scorecards were so scattershot as to beggar the imagination. Judges Art Lurie and Harold Buck both tabbed Pintor the winner at 143-142. But Bob Martin did not just dissent—he rebelled. Somehow, Martin scored the bout an eye-popping 145-133 in favor of Zarate. Boxing is the last surrealist outpost, and its madhouse ethos materialized in Pintor–Zarate almost as if to solidify the natural order of things in a sport where chaos is intrinsic. Martin, inexplicably, was unaware that the fight was being judged on the ten-point must system and spent half the fight scoring on the soon-to-be obsolete five-point system. When he realized his mistake, Martin went back to his scorecard and simply doubled up the tabulations for each round. His Rube Goldberg solution resulted in a mathematical fiasco.

Zarate was so hurt by the decision that he immediately retired when his appeal to the WBC was denied. Now Pintor was the man who had inadvertently forced a beloved fighter into the shadows. As if determined to bolster his lousy reputation, Pintor began his reign as a farce. He spent a couple of days in a Mexico City jail, reportedly for assaulting a police officer responding to the scene of a fender bender, and he lost a nontitle bout six months after the Zarate debacle, an embarrassing setback made doubly so by the fact that the fight took place in Sonora, Mexico, for a negligible purse. Even his timing was off. By the time Pintor won his world title, the red-hot bantamweight scene in Los Angeles had cooled off. Over the span of a decade, Ruben Olivares, Alfonso Zamora, Carlos Zarate, Frankie Duarte, Chucho Castillo, Jesus Pimentel, and Rafael Herrera lit up the Inglewood Forum and the Olympic Auditorium week after week. Unfortunately for Pintor, he arrived when nothing remained but memories. Only Alberto "Superfly" Sandoval and Alberto Davila were box-office attractions among 118-pounders as 1980 closed in. (Right up to his title challenge of Gomez, his misfortune continued: Before the fight, promoter Don King, claiming financial disaster because of poor ticket sales, reduced the purses of both headline matchups. Pintor saw his $750,000 payday cut by $150,000.)

For years Pintor had been struggling both with his weight and with critical negligence. Because of the *Outer Limits* quality of his win over Zarate, Pintor received only grudging respect during his bantamweight title reign despite defending his title on the road, often against stiff competition. From February 1980 to June 1982, Pintor fought eight times, a stretch that included wins over Sandoval, Elijiro Murata, Johnny Owen, and Alberto "Tweety" Davila. In 1980, his tragic bout against Owen, held at the Olympic Auditorium, brought Pintor a measure of bitter fame when "The Merthyr Matchstick," only twenty-four years old, died as a result of injuries suffered during the fight. His title defense against the popular Sandoval drew a sellout crowd to the Olympic Auditorium, and he earned $175,000 for his kayo of Seung Hoon Lee. At his best—which was a rare sighting, since he was often weakened by his struggles making weight—Pintor was an intelligent pressure fighter with a withering left hook and staying power. But he had worn himself out battling the scales. Pintor decided to move up to junior featherweight, where a match against Wilfredo Gomez promised him the biggest payday of his career—and the most potential danger.

Wilfredo "Bazooka" Gomez was the closest thing to Roberto Durán and, for better or worse, the personification of machismo in the ring. Like Pintor, Gomez, born in Santurce, Puerto Rico, was raised in poverty. (In another similarity between them, Gomez sold candy on the streets to help his parents.) When Gomez was fifteen, he falsified his age to qualify for the Olympics. In 1972 he represented Puerto Rico as a scrawny flyweight in the tragic Munich games where, after a first-round bye, he dropped a decision to Mohamed Selim and was eliminated from the bracket. Two years later, Gomez won gold at the 1974 Central American and Caribbean Games held in the Dominican Republic and the World Championships in Havana, where he scored a knockout in every round.

As Gomez became the hottest amateur in Puerto Rico, he attracted a slew of potential managers and promoters. Eventually, Gomez signed with Yamil Chade and Carlos Eleta, who managed Roberto Durán. Here is where Gomez went from a prospect to a phenom. In the early 1970s, Panama was a boxing hotbed. Roberto Durán, Ismael Laguna, Ernesto Marcel, Enrique Pinder, Antonio Amaya, Peppermint Frazer, Rigoberto Riasco, and Jorge Lujan were some of the champions produced by the Puente Del Mundo. "Panama is where I learned everything," Gomez told Christian Giudice. "I graduated from boxing school there. It was the best boxing school in the world. That was where I perfected my lateral movement and where I learned to move side to side. I learned to do a move where I would come in with my lead left hook and then follow with my straight right hand. The Panamanians claimed to have invented that technical style of boxing. They were technical and very polished boxers."

Like so many other fighters, Gomez had grand(iose) plans for his boxing afterlife. He was in his early twenties when he formed Bazooka Enterprises, an optimistic incorporation meant to encompass real estate, acting, and sponsorship deals. But the glittering nightlife that undercut so many of his compatriots also depleted Gomez little by little. Esteban de Jesús, Hector Camacho, Victor Callejas, Wilfred Benitez, Edwin Rosario—all Puerto Rican champions incapable of mastering the limelight. In contrast to the relative anonymity of most American pugs, prizefighters were (and still are) genuine celebrities in Puerto Rico, and, until the arrival of Felix Trinidad in the early 1990s, no one raised the collective blood pressure of Boricuas the way Gomez did. Part of this was because of his good looks and earthy demeanor; part of it was because of his fierce ring style, modeled on that of his idol, Durán, whose intensity was both fascinating and frightening. Aside from a draw in his professional debut, Gomez did not go the distance in a fight until nearly a decade into his career. He won the WBC super-bantamweight title in 1976 and had captured the imagination of the Puerto Rican *afición*, even if Sonny Werblin, who ran Madison Square Garden in the late 1970s, once asked, vis-a-vis Gomez, "What the hell is a super-bantamweight?"

Gomez was 32-0-1, with thirty-two knockouts, when he moved up to featherweight and challenged WBC titleholder Salvador Sanchez in 1981. Although Sanchez was an established champion in another division, Gomez paid little heed to the threat he presented. A smooth-boxing counterpuncher with supernatural endurance and stamina, Sanchez was the stylistic antithesis of the stereotypical Mexican slugger epitomized by his contemporaries José "Pipino" Cuevas and Bazooka Limón. At twenty-two years old and with a record of 40-1-1, Sanchez was in his prime. Why would Gomez overlook such a dangerous opponent? Recent form might have been one reason. Sanchez was coming off a fifteen-round decision over Nicky Perez, a man whom Gomez had annihilated three years earlier. In addition, Sanchez had struggled to a dubious points win over Pat Ford, a performance Gomez viewed from ringside at the Freeman Coliseum in San Antonio. After the decision was announced, Gomez entered the ring and shoved Sanchez. "I remember Wilfredo had a big talk with Sanchez in San Antonio," cornerman Don Kahn told Christian Giudice. "The promoter sent Wilfredo up into the ring after the fight . . . and Wilfredo went and pushed him as if it was a real fight. Sanchez also took it seriously, too, and the trainers got involved, and it became a big brawl in the ring. Wilfredo was always like that. He was a tough guy to deal with."

Despite being considered the best featherweight in the world—even with Eusebio Pedroza as a co-titlist—Sanchez had a record whose highlights remained a pair of stoppage defeats of weatherworn Danny Lopez and decisions over hard-punching but limited Juan Laporte and perennial contender Ruben Castillo. These facts might have given Gomez cause to underestimate Sanchez. Mostly, however, it was his outsized sense of self. Ego is as essential to a fighter as a pinpoint jab is, but the same confidence that drove Gomez to batter one title challenger after another also prompted him to cut corners in training and disregard his opponents. A little over a month before the fight, Gomez was lolling on a cruise ship when Don King reached him via phone and urged him to abandon ship and begin training. As if he had suddenly realized how reckless he had been, Gomez begged King to postpone the fight. In the early 1980s, the intricate closed-circuit television model—hundreds of theater/arena locations across the country outfitted with satellite dishes, projectors, decoders, and so on—was nearly impossible to roll back, and King refused to delay the promotion.

Only hours before the scheduled weigh-in for the Sanchez fight, Gomez was four pounds above the limit: plastic suits and a sauna were his last debilitating hopes for making the 122-pound mark. A weakened

Gomez eventually managed to make weight, but his hopes of becoming a two-division champion were all but shattered. From the outset, Sanchez, poised and calculating, was in control. He dropped Gomez within thirty seconds of the opening bell and went on to batter "Bazooka" until the fight was halted in the eighth round. In all, Gomez, who fought back valiantly throughout the bout, was knocked down twice, bled freely from his nose, and suffered a broken orbital bone.

While Puerto Rico declared a national day of mourning, Gomez was on his way to becoming a recluse. For three months the handsome playboy with a passion for mirror balls and sleek sports cars let shame paralyze him. "Losing," he once said, "is worse than dying." When he returned to the ring, it was, surprisingly, as a junior featherweight. To keep himself close to fighting weight, and perhaps to keep the demons at bay, Gomez fought five times in the first eight months of 1982 and scored kayos in title defenses over a trio of competent if not inspiring challengers: Juan Kid Meza, Roberto Rubaldino, and Juan Antonio Lopez.

On August 12, 1982, the boxing world was shocked when Salvador Sanchez, only twenty-three years old, died after a late-night car crash in Queretaro. Gomez mourned not only the death of his rival but also the possibility of vindication in a potential rematch. "Sanchez was a good athlete who trained seriously and knew his business," Gomez told *World Boxing*. "He was a professional and a gentleman outside of the ring. I was overconfident for our fight. Everyone said I was going to win and I didn't expect that kind of fight from him. He caught me with a surprise punch in the first round, and I never recovered from it. I was undertrained. I had problems making weight and was too weak. I always thought I could beat him, but I can never prove it. When I heard of his death, I could not believe it. He was a legend."

With Sanchez gone, Gomez was ready to make his seventeenth title defense, this time against another storied Mexican fighter: Lupe Pintor. Wilfredo Gomez–Lupe Pintor was the opening bout of a doubleheader headlined by Thomas Hearns and Wilfred Benitez at the Superdome in New Orleans, Louisiana. "The Big Easy" had been one of the most important boxing cities in America in the nineteenth century, but its importance had diminished year after year, until boxing became a mere afterthought. In 1978 Muhammad Ali had inaugurated boxing at the Superdome, defeating Leon Spinks to reclaim the heavyweight championship of the world, and a mini-renaissance began in New Orleans, where ABC televised cards featuring Sugar Ray Leonard, Roberto Durán, Victor Galindez, and Marvin Johnson. In Gomez–Pintor, the Superdome had its last high-profile fight of the 1980s.

Normally phlegmatic, Pintor seemed unusually irritable during the lead-up to the fight. "He is a man who thinks, because he weighs a few pounds more than me, he can beat me," Pintor told *Newsday* about Gomez. "He thinks because Sanchez weighed two more pounds than he did, he lost. Two pounds, for God's sake! He never learned that is the size of a man's heart that wins for him. Gomez has a heart that is underweight."

Pintor could not have been more wrong.

Upstaging Thomas "Hitman" Hearns, one of the most exciting fighters of the 1980s, was no easy task, but Gomez and Pintor managed it within a minute of the opening bell. Where referee Octavio Meyran had to exhort Hearns and Benitez to mix it up—"Fight, fight!" he shouted—his counterpart for the cofeature, the grandstanding Arthur Mercante, merely needed to stay out of the way.

Over the first few rounds, it seemed as if Gomez would overwhelm Pintor with his trademark aggressiveness. He darted in and out, working behind a quicksilver jab and throwing whistling overhand rights that seldom missed. From time to time, Gomez would force Pintor against the ropes, where "Bazooka" rattled off combinations that shook Pintor to his boots. But Pintor had his own image to worry about, that of the man who would uphold the legacy of Salvador Sanchez, and he began returning fire in the third round.

Except for his unexpected brawl with Carlos Mendoza and his brutal loss to Sanchez in 1981, Gomez had never been in such a firefight before. Although Pintor had moved up from bantamweight, his blows, especially his crippling left hook to the body, clearly affected Gomez.

In the sixth round, the darker lessons Gomez had learned in dusty Panama gyms began to surface. With Pintor pinned against the ropes, Gomez started mixing deliberate—and potentially debilitating—elbows into his combinations. At the end of the round, referee Arthur Mercante deducted a point from Gomez, who had already been warned several times for low blows.

As the grueling rounds went by in a violent blur, Gomez grew more and more disfigured. With his cheekbones swollen, his eyes shut into slits, and his nose splayed, he seemed on the verge of collapse. In the later rounds, his chief cornerman would rush across the ring when the bell sounded, like a firefighter or a lifeguard, and carry Gomez back to his corner for the brief respite between rounds. Because Pintor was a long-distance fighter— he had scored several late stoppages—he did not appear discouraged at any point in the fight, even when Gomez was flaying him with hooks and right crosses. Trying to outlast Gomez was a painful strategy, but Pintor seemed relatively fresh despite the punishment he had taken.

"We felt we'd get the kayo before the fifth round," Yamil Chade would later say. "But Wilfredo wasn't in the best condition. For four years he has lived the happy life, new friends, parties. God gave us many things and one thing is temptation. I don't blame him."

The twelfth round was a phantasmagoria of violence, with both men slugging from bell to bell. Gomez sent Pintor reeling across the ring early and moved in for the kill. Trapped against the ropes, Pintor countered well, but Gomez lashed him again and again with stinging blows until he finally decelerated. At the end of the round, Pintor seemed on the verge of a TKO win when he shook Gomez with a barrage punctuated by a snapping uppercut just before the bell rang. Macho to the last, both men exchanged taunts before returning to their corners.

By the thirteenth, Gomez was throwing arm punches and wobbling around the ring. Several times, he was visibly hurt by Pintor, who exhorted Gomez to slug. Through sheer will and heart—which combined to form a strategy, of sorts, based wholly on defiance—he kept attacking with a ferocity that belied his dwindling physical condition. Although Gomez was exhausted, he forced Pintor back occasionally with his cyclonic flurries. It was hard to believe that, after the trauma they had inflicted on each other, both fighters were still standing. These were, after all, supremely conditioned athletes, but they were also men who had trained a lifetime to inflict damage on their opponents. More than anything, they were the hurting kind.

At the core of these apocalyptic fights, where two men take turns punishing each other from round to round, lies the question of motivation. Not in the sporting sense—that is, not in the careerist sense, or anything so mundane as competition—but in an existential sense. And while boxing lends itself far too often to an intellectual clam chowder (common ingredients: social Darwinism, atavism, gladiatorial analogies, talk of warriors, and so on.), the fact remains that what Gomez and Pintor did to each other, under the socially sanctioned auspices of entertainment, bordered on madness.

Central to boxing is the concept of hypermasculinity, but Gomez took "the manly art" to near-parodic lengths. Whether he was partying through the night, trying to intimidate his opponents with cryptic allusions ("I kill them slowly"), physically assaulting reporters, or openly proclaiming his indestructibility, Gomez was machismo in action on a twenty-four-hour basis. His self-image was now distorted, a reflection of his feverish constituency—Puerto Ricans overcome by nationalist fervor and who had invested Gomez with a symbolic power that far exceeded sporting partisanship. After all, Puerto Rico had declared a national day of mourning when Gomez lost to Salvador Sanchez. This cognizance—of his outsize stature to an island of millions—seemingly drove Gomez beyond his physical threshold against Pintor.

For Gomez, the memory of his loss to Sanchez, along with his cultivated public image, pushed him forward. In 1981, former light-heavyweight champion Jose Torres tackled the subject of machismo for *The Ring*. "Ads, commercials, and, indeed, all the media itself, are dedicated to identifying—and hyping—male machismo," Torres wrote. "So much so that boxing crowds in Latin countries immediately boo if a defensive fighter is successful in preventing his opponent from connecting solidly while not doing much himself in return. . . . These days men who choose boxing as their occupation in Latin countries do so with the conviction that lumps, lacerations, cuts, broken bones, and blood are important distinguishing emblems—not necessarily of defeat but are, instead, honorable and dignified badges of victory. There is not much fun in winning unless you can show evidence of machismo."

It was Pintor who would succumb to the pace. Just as Gomez seemed incapable of reaching the final bell, much less rallying, he unleashed a roundhouse right that caught Pintor behind the left ear and dropped him, heavily, on the seat of his pants. With a look of surprise on his face, Pintor beat the count, but the punishment accumulated during nearly forty minutes of combat had caught up with him seemingly all at once. Gomez drove Pintor back and pinned him against the ropes, where he unleashed a whiplashing left hook that connected flush. Pintor dropped to one knee and pitched over with a thud. As Pintor tried to regain his scattered senses, referee Arthur Mercante halted the fight without issuing a count. The crowd erupted, euphoric. In a neutral corner, Gomez, battered almost beyond recognition, was too exhausted to celebrate with zeal. He raised his arms overhead, wearily, before his cornerman lifted him up in victory.

After the bout, Gomez contemplated retirement because of the damage he had suffered. And Pintor? "For my part," he once wrote, "I suffered for days from a powerful headache, and I decided to take a long break." Neither man was ever the same after their encounter at the Superdome, despite some future successes in the ring. Bad luck continued to pursue Pintor, at least for a while. Not long after losing to Gomez, he was seriously injured in a motorcycle crash that forced him into retirement. But he returned to win a featherweight title in 1985, upsetting Juan Meza via decision on a nationally televised card aired from Mexico City. Pintor lost his title in his first defense and fought haphazardly until 1995, with nothing to show for it but a string of losses and a diminution of his legacy. For years, Pintor has worked for the Mexico City Metro; now and then he reappears, relatively unscathed, to give an interview, where he invariably names Gomez as his most difficult opponent.

After blitzing two patsies over the next year, Gomez moved up a division and outpointed Juan Laporte to win a featherweight title in 1984. When Laporte snapped his streak of knockout victories, you could see that the end was near. Other fighters show symptoms of decline by struggling with inferior opposition or by losing outright, but Gomez proved he was slipping just by going the distance in a relatively easy victory. In his next outing, he was battered to defeat by a young Azumah Nelson and then won a third title via a hometown decision against Rocky Lockridge. Well past his prime, he was knocked out by a historical footnote named Alfred Layne in 1985 and, after two meaningless comeback wins, Gomez spiraled into a netherworld of drugs and liquor. Today, Gomez suffers from the effects of his grueling career, his swaggering persona now replaced by an almost childlike demeanor. To see him now is to recall, almost dreadfully, his words after he had triumphed over Pintor: "When I fight," he said, "I fight to the death."

Yesterday Will Make You Cry

THE SHORT, TRAGIC CAREER OF DAVEY MOORE

The skyscraper canyons of midtown Manhattan might as well have been a world away from the ruins of the South Bronx, where burned-out Plymouth Dusters and Chevy Bel Airs were permanently parked on crumbling sidewalks; vacant lots, overrun by knotweed and hypodermic needles, pockmarked block after shambolic block; and pyromaniacs used abandoned tenements as so much oversized tinder night after endless night.

In the 1970s, New York City, a twentieth-century Stone Age, teetered on the brink of collapse. The homicide rate had more than doubled since the mid-1960s and bankruptcy loomed over one of the most famous metropolises in the world. It was like something out of a J. G. Ballard novel: dystopia in asphalt, and the South Bronx was Ground Zero.

Davey Moore, who would rocket to near stardom after winning a world title in only his ninth pro bout, fought his way out of Morrisania, a slum that had long ago earned its notoriety as a national symbol of urban blight. Raised by a single mother who passed him along from one relative to another, Moore shared a deprived background all too common among prizefighters. "Davey was raised very poor, from the real ghetto," his mother, Lee, told the *New York Times*. "Many times I used to send him to school with an empty stomach. I had to work, and Davey just drifted around from people to people. But Davey never had a problem in his life and I never had the police knocking at my door."

Somehow, Moore avoided the numberless pitfalls of his Soundview neighborhood. "I grew up in a bad environment, and if you let the environment control you, you were in trouble," Moore told *World Boxing* in 1981. "I was always with the books, but it was rough in the streets, and I was always pretty good with my hands. My friends said go to the gym, but I kept procrastinating." Then, when he was fifteen, Moore made his way to the Morrisania Recreation Center where he met his eventual trainer/manager Leon Washington, an ex-club-fighter who saw promise in his brash new charge. And Moore was a quick study. He won four Golden Gloves titles during the days when tens of thousands would still gather across the city to watch amateur boxing. Moore also made it to the finals of the Olympic trials in 1980, losing a decision to future undisputed welterweight champion Donald Curry.

Before Moore turned pro, he had already announced accelerated career plans to the media. But not even Moore, who had signed with Top Rank and had already been featured on national television, envisioned a title shot against newly crowned Tadashi Mihara after only eight pro outings. Nor could Moore imagine that his first championship opportunity would take place in Tokyo as a pit stop en route to an even more exotic locale: Johannesburg.

Bob Arum, who had previously staged lucrative heavyweight fights in Pretoria and Sun City, was now looking for pay dirt with Charlie "The Silver Assassin" Weir, a deadly puncher with a unique patch of white streaking his hair. Weir was a box-office supernova across Cape Town and Durban. Not even the moral stain of apartheid could prevent Arum from making money in South Africa. Unfortunately for Arum, Japan was part of a global sporting boycott against South Africa, and its officials would likely have suspended Mihara for signing a contract to defend his title against Weir. What looked like a dead end for Arum soon became just another open road for "Bottom Line Bob" to do what he did best: find a way to cash in. Arum drafted Moore, then a welterweight with an 8-0 record, into service, matching him against Mihara in Tokyo for a purse of $30,000. For Arum, Moore was simply a go-between, someone who would transport the WBA title from Japan to South Africa, the curious boxing El Dorado of the early 1980s. Cool, cocky, and confident, Moore signed an unusual two-fight contract that called for him to face Weir within ninety days of annexing the title. All Moore had to do, of course, was win. On February 2, 1982, Moore became part of the first wave of neophyte champions created by new weight classes, splintered titles, and the ascendant sanctioning bodies, when he pummeled Mihara into a sixth-round stoppage.

The stage was set for Moore, as an underdog, to face Weir in Johannesburg. To the surprise of the partisan crowd at Ellis Park Stadium, Weir was no match for Moore, who used his hand speed and combination punching to batter "The Silver Assassin" from the opening bell. After scoring seven knockdowns, Moore was declared the KO winner, having upended both Weir and Arum, who soon after abandoned South Africa entirely.

Although he had a shiny title belt strapped around his waist, Moore, to most observers, was nothing but the personification of boxing decadence. In his next title defense, however, Moore stopped respected veteran Ayub Kalule in the tenth round of a back-and-forth struggle in Atlantic City, New Jersey. A grinding southpaw and an ex-WBA super-welterweight titlist himself, Kalule entered the bout against Moore having lost only to Sugar Ray Leonard. Skeptics were now ready to look at Moore as something other than a rookie fluke. "I was a big believer in Moore," says Steve Farhood, who covered Moore for *KO Magazine*. "While he had been rushed to the title, he was a young fighter who was already battle-tested. By beating the big-punching Charlie Weir on the road in South Africa, and successfully defending against an excellent and underrated fighter in Ayub Kalule, who was 40-1 at the time, Moore had won over a lot more people than just me."

An aggressive boxer-puncher who sacrificed defense for offense, Moore fought with verve, often skipping after his opponent, and ripping off eye-catching flurries. Among his drawbacks were poor balance and an upright style that invited counters. His biggest flaw, however, was his temperament. Despite his amateur pedigree, Moore loved to brawl, especially on the inside, and this trait, gold to television viewers across America, was often brutally compounded by his shoddy defense. But what he lacked in finesse he more than made up for with an exuberance that would make him one of the action stars of the early 1980s.

After flattening Indianapolis club fighter Gary Guiden in three rounds on January 29, 1983, in another successful title defense, Moore was now in a position to face his first truly recognizable opponent: Roberto Durán,

"Hands of Stone," the tarnished legend ready to atone for a past that was never far enough behind him. The match was set for June 16, 1983.

In the years since his humiliating surrender to Sugar Ray Leonard in the infamous "No Mas" debacle, Roberto Durán, formerly the most revered fighter in the world, had become little more than a pot-bellied barfly whose roadwork consisted of chasing women. Day after day he watched his greatness wither. The pastel colors of *Miami Vice*–era Florida, where Durán partied hard, clashed violently with his slow disintegration. A dreary loss to Kirkland Laing in September 1982, after Durán had already dropped a decision to Wilfred Benitez in a junior-middleweight title challenge, seemingly sealed his fate as a top attraction.

When Arum plucked Durán off the scrap heap after the Laing fiasco, it looked like nothing more than a cynical exercise in flesh peddling. By then, Durán was as unfashionable as lava lamps or mirror balls. One by one his allies fell by the wayside. He was abandoned by his manager, Carlos Eleta; by his trainers, Freddie Brown and Ray Arcel; by his cornerman, Panama Lewis; by his interpreter, Luis Henriquez. Even Don King, a man who would rush into a burning oil tanker to rescue a crumpled dollar bill, cut him loose. Now, Durán was alone with his ghosts. "A lot of people turned their backs on me," Durán said. "I was depressed. I did not care. I did not care enough to train hard."

But Durán reignited his passion by bludgeoning José "Pipino" Cuevas (on the same day Moore walloped Guiden) in a fight that hearkened back to his glory days. For Durán, a feverish sellout crowd at the L.A. Sports Arena brought back the adrenalin rush. Poor Cuevas, once a wrecking machine with a left hook that tore heavy bags off their hinges, lasted less than four rounds. "I'm not the Durán of old," Durán said after dismantling Cuevas, "but I'm better than most of the champions I see." He might have been talking about Davey Moore, who was, after all, a rookie.

It goes without saying, of course, that prizefighters are inveterate risk takers. If the occupational hazards they face in the ring are not enough, the nagging injuries that sometimes accompany them under the lights compound their exposure to danger. And Moore had enough troubles before answering the bell against Durán that they might have functioned, collectively, as dark premonitions of what was to come. First, Moore had torn a ligament in his knee a day after knocking out Gary Guiden and was forced to wear a cast for weeks, preventing him from staying fit between bouts. Even more disturbing, however, was the fact that Moore had undergone oral surgery only a few days prior to facing Durán. A freak punch during a sparring session fractured some of his teeth and, after Moore suffered through pain for most of his training camp, a dentist insisted on surgery. Finally, Moore failed to make weight and needed time in a steam room to boil down to 154 pounds. What would compel a fighter to compete under such unfavorable circumstances? For Moore, a $300,000 guarantee, plus percentages of the gate and the closed-circuit receipts, were enough to shrug off any misgivings. This heedless attitude would cost him dearly.

Under normal circumstances, Durán would have been considered merely a carpetbagger against the Bronx-born Moore, who lived roughly half an hour away from Madison Square Garden. To the *afición*, however, Durán remained what Jose Torres once called "the high priest of machismo." Along with the 20,069 spectators who shoehorned into Madison Square Garden—the first sellout there since Ali–Frazier II in 1974—thousands of New Yorkers milled, feverishly, along 8th Avenue, kickstarting an impromptu block party to celebrate the graceful savagery of "Cholo." It was, after all, his birthday. Roberto Durán had turned thirty-two on the day he would be born again.

As superstitious as ever, Durán entered the ring accompanied by a Cuban spiritualist, a woman who performed an understated *santeria* ritual before the two combatants were brought to ring center. The partisan crowd shook Madison Square Garden to its foundations, rattling Moore, who realized that any hometown advantage he might have had probably vanished the moment tickets were printed for the bout.

Not long after the opening bell rang, Moore found himself with much more serious worries. With only a few seconds left in what had been a tentative opening round, Durán thumbed Moore in the right eye. Throughout his career, Durán had been considered a dirty fighter—going all the way back to the night he won the lightweight title against Ken Buchanan via ruthless low blows—and Moore would never give him the benefit of the doubt in future interviews. "The thumb was planned, it wasn't no loose jab," Moore told *KO Magazine*. "You don't punch like that, especially in the first round, you still got your strength. He knew he couldn't beat me straight up."

Handicapped by limited vision, Moore was forced to work in close against a fighter who not only excelled at trench warfare but lusted for it. "I was going to try to surprise Durán in the first and if I couldn't, I was going to box him and try to take him out in the late rounds. But after he thumbed me in the right eye, the plan went out the window." While his eye continued to swell shut, Moore confronted another gruesome problem in the third round: a pair of plastic caps he wore on his teeth as a consequence of his surgery cracked after Durán landed a thudding uppercut. Almost immediately, Moore began to bleed from his mouth.

Of all the skills a boxer has to master, none is as mystifying as pain management. Masking hurt in the ring is essential for a world-class professional. Rarely does a fighter wear a look of agony the way Moore did against Durán from round to round that night. He shuddered, winced, staggered, grimaced, flinched—every blow Durán landed seemed to affect Moore. As brave as Moore was, as much as he returned just when he seemed on the verge of being overwhelmed, he was on borrowed time in the ring. By the fifth round, it was clear that Moore would last only as long as his body held out, and at the end of six rounds, it looked as if Moore would disintegrate. He bled from his mouth and nose. His right eye was barely a slit, nearly impossible to peer through. The body shots he had taken had sapped his energy. Although he threw and landed his share of combinations, they did little to discourage Durán. "Every time I tried to hit him, I telegraphed," Moore recalled after the fight. "My right eye was so swollen, and he was moving to my right, so every time I tried to punch him I had to turn my head. He knew the punch was coming and he would ride with it." Whenever Moore would open up, Durán would punish him with debilitating counters.

In the seventh round, Durán seemed to revel in the bloodshed. He tore into Moore with both hands, a sneer breaking across his face from time to time, and landed digging shots to the ribcage. Finally, a booming right hand sent Moore skidding on the seat of his trunks. For a moment, Moore sat on the bloodied canvas, his face knotted in pain, before he wobbled to his feet and was saved by the bell.

Between rounds, trainer Leon Washington seemed reluctant to let Moore continue. Unfortunately, he sent Moore out anyway, out into one of the most infamous beatings of postwar boxing. A nearly defenseless Moore reeled under a two-handed onslaught that must have conjured up memories of Willie Classen, Duk-Koo Kim, and Johnny Owen. Both his mother and his girlfriend fainted in their ringside seats. Near the apron, where New York State Athletic Commission appointees were gathered, hoarse cries to stop the slaughter competed against the roar of the euphoric crowd. Yet referee Ernesto Magana seemed spellbound by the butchery taking place before his eyes. Even when Washington tossed a blood-splotched towel into the ring, Magana failed to acknowledge it. To put an end to a seemingly imminent tragedy, Top Rank official Jay Edson ducked through the ropes and forced Magana to act.

When it was all over, Durán, now a three-division champion, was overcome with emotion. All of Madison Square Garden serenaded him with a rhapsodic version of "Happy Birthday." Meanwhile, a battered Moore stood off to the side, mumbling to himself. "I can't believe it," he repeated, over and over again.

It would be three long years before Moore would challenge for another world title. On August 24, 1986, Moore was stopped by journeyman IBF super-welterweight champion Buster Drayton in ten rounds. As if to underscore how much of an afterthought he had become to an American public he had once thrilled with his freewheeling style, Moore faced Drayton in Alpes-Maritimes, France. There was nothing left for Moore now except the inevitable: life as a stepping-stone. The last dreary years of Davey Moore were a jarring contrast to his days as a shooting star, when he was part of the 1980s renaissance in the United States, when his bouts were aired on NBC, when he invariably trotted around the ring, arms raised, in a victory lap most notable for his sparkling grin. Moore would now recall something boxing writer Trevor Wignall once lamented: "It is impossible to conceive of anything more hideous than the fate of the unsuccessful boxer."

Only one highlight marked his post-Durán career—a second-round TKO of triple-crown king and former wunderkind Wilfred Benitez in 1984—but even that achievement cried out for an asterisk. Benitez suffered a broken ankle after suffering a knockdown in the first round and, unable to defend himself in the second, was rescued by the referee before he was seriously hurt. Even though Moore had scored a headline win, it was clear he was no longer the same fighter. "If Moore was indeed ruined by Durán, it was more than just the physical beating he took," says Farhood. "Remember, birthday-boy Durán was the crowd-favorite that night at the Garden despite the fact that Moore was a New York kid. That had to have a negative psychological effect. And Moore was supposed to beat a faded Durán, so expectations were high. Moore fought ten more times after Durán and went only 6-4. He was still young, but no longer fresh. It is obvious he was not the same fighter."

Not only did Moore have to suffer the physical and psychological side effects of his dismantling at the hands of Durán, he also had to face his new standing in the harsh winner-take-all boxing economy. "I go from one million to $15,000?" Moore asked, incredulously. "You mean my stock dropped that low?" Later, it would drop even further. The last two fights of his career, only a few years down the road, would earn Moore a combined total of $6,500. In just five years, Moore went from headlining Madison Square Garden—the most famous arena in the world—to making a dismal appearance in front of a few hundred at a Sheraton Hotel in East Rutherford, New Jersey.

When he was a young star on the rise, Moore was one of the few who benefited from the whims of boxing, a sport as capricious as the gods of the Greek myths. Now, everything seemed against him. Inactivity, injuries, managerial squabbles, shrinking paychecks. One cancellation after another kept Moore idle, and when he did fight, it was without his typical flair. A questionable disqualification loss to Louis Acaries in Paris killed any momentum Moore, now less dedicated to conditioning, had gathered following a pair of comeback wins. After Drayton stopped him, Moore suffered beatings from Lupe Aquino and John David Jackson. His last fight took place in Staten Island, where Moore stopped a tomato can with a 14-20 record.

Misfortune followed Moore beyond the ropes as well. On June 2, 1988, Moore died in a freak accident. When his Dodge Raider began to roll down his driveway, Moore tried to stop it, only to slip and be dragged underneath the SUV. Moore, whose bank account was nearly empty, who was still accepting pickup fights, who had no life insurance, was crushed to death. He was twenty-eight years old. His final record stands at 18-5, with fourteen knockouts.

The better world Davey Moore had made for himself far from the bleak streets of Morrisania—a neat house in Holmdel, natty clothes beyond a pair of shell-toe Adidas, a nifty black Porsche to speed over to the Times Square Gym, national fame as a marquee TV attraction with a lollipop grin—lasted less than five years. What Durán did to him left him more than just shell-shocked; it left him, to an extent, bereft. "How did I feel after the fight?" he once asked. "Heartbroken."

Under Saturn

JOHNNY TAPIA, 1967–2012

"The past is inevitable."
—Delmore Schwartz

2.

Look: there he is, a faraway blur, caught for an instant in the slipstream of time. Is it ESPN or USA? Is it 1989 or 1990? There are mullets in the crowd, oversized glasses, some Zubaz, maybe. The picture is scratched and grainy, like a silent film or something viewed in a kinetoscope, but you can still see the tattoo of Christ on his chest. Years later his body will be scarred by a wickerwork pattern of ink, but for now this stark image— set against skin as pale as alabaster—is made all the more startling by its solitude over two decades ago. Fast hands, quick feet, a full head of hair, a nose not yet misshapen by the rigors of his profession. A knotted heart behind the crown of thorns. He is handsome still. Sallow, yes, from hours in the gym and a lifetime under Saturn. They called him "The Baby-Faced Assassin." Watch as he moves in for the kill. Sin City or Albuquerque? Can you remember? Get closer to the flickering image, washed out now in sepia, pixels leached by passing years. You will never see this man again.

3.

What Johnny Tapia accomplished in the ring is nearly as surprising as the fact that he lived as long as he did. Because the truth is, Tapia was past his physical peak by the time he beat Henry Martinez in 1994 to win his first title. From late 1990 to early 1994, Tapia was on a forced leave of absence from boxing. This was not a Muhammad Ali layoff—college lectures and time spent in mosques; nor was it a Mike Tyson layoff—three squares a day in the Indiana Youth Center. No, after Johnny Tapia had his license revoked in 1991 for failing drug tests, it was years of heroin, coke, methamphetamines, homelessness or holding tanks, smokers in Albuquerque dives, gunshots, gutters, and grief. Little by little Tapia whittled himself away. "I didn't have a dollar in my pocket and didn't know where I was," Tapia told the *Santa Fe New Mexican* about his season in hell. "I had nowhere to go, nothing to eat." A decade earlier, another bantamweight—Frankie Duarte—emerged from a skid-row nightmare to thrill delirious crowds at The Forum in Inglewood. They showered the ring with coins when he fought. But Duarte never won a world title. He had seen too many blue hours and way too many yesterdays. Just like Johnny Tapia. But Tapia was made for it, if you can ever figure out what "it" really was.

4.

Johnny Tapia had been killing himself—off and on, now and then, here and there—for years. Addicted to drugs, to prizefighting, to adrenalin rushes, and, finally, addicted to near-death experiences, Tapia was a junkie in a way that most junkies are not. Like a phoenix, he rose from the ashes more often than anyone has a right to. Finally, he got it right. Or Death did. Between his battles with a beckoning grave, Tapia lived inside the ring. Call his sordid life a waste if you want, but for some of us, maybe, it was a gift.

5.

Sadism, whether one admits it or not, is an essential part of boxing. So is masochism. Johnny Tapia took more punches than necessary, perhaps to hear the roar of the crowd, perhaps for reasons altogether darker. He used to wipe his face during combat and lick the blood from his gloves.

6.

"Beatings. That's all there was sometimes. That's how it went. I got constant beatings. Half the beatings I took were for somebody else. There were lots of beatings on everybody, but especially on me. So many beatings, I got used to them . . . I drew the beatings like a magnet and they just made me stronger. And sometimes, to be truthful, it was the only way I didn't feel the pain. The pain of being alone. The pain of being without my mother."

7.

Tapia was diagnosed as bipolar. He suffered from ADD. He was depressed and suicidal. Dysfunction was his God. His mother was viciously murdered when he was eight years old. He was pitilessly abused as a child. His father died before he was born. Like Jake LaMotta, whose father forced him to fight in smokers as a child, Tapia was pitted by his uncles against other children in his neighborhood for the benefit of adult wagering. Albuquerque was a "Target City" in the 1980s—federal grants pour in to fight a drug epidemic that left Duke City morgues overwhelmed with graying dead.

8.

"I can't hear your voice. I can smell you and taste your breath. I can feel you. You're brushing against me. You're gone and I want more of you."
—James Ellroy

9.

John Lee Tapia was born on Monday, February 13, 1967. He liked to say that he was born on Friday the thirteenth, but no one needs poetic license for such a lifetime of tragedy.

10.

October 1991: License revoked after failing his third drug test
April 1992: Charged with threatening a witness in a murder trial
February 1993: Arrested for driving under the influence
Mid-1993: Overdoses on the night of his wedding and is declared clinically dead

July 1994: Charged with trying to sell drugs to an off-duty policeman
October 1995: Weapons felony charges
August 1996: Police arrest rioters during his bout against Hugo Soto
March 1997: Charged with weapons possession in California
June 2000: Shot at during a road rage incident
July 2000: Hospitalized for depression
August 2000: Charge with assault
January 2003: Felony drug paraphernalia charges
December 2003: A drug overdose leaves Tapia on life support
March 2007: Overdoses and slips into a coma
February 2009: Arrested on drug charges
April 2009: Begins sentence at the Central New Mexico Corrections
    Facility
April 2010: Back in jail on drug charges
December 2010: Files for bankruptcy
January 2012: Arrested for DWI after crashing his SUV
May 27, 2012: Dead

11.

"Every man has inside himself a parasitic being who is acting not at all to his advantage."
—William S. Burroughs

12.

"The night she died I saw her taken away. I was eight years old, pounding on the windowpane, yelling for help, but nobody believed what I saw. There was nothing I could do and so she died. And I've been blue ever since. And ever since I haven't known if I should live or die. That's the god's honest truth. That's the only way I can say it. As long as my mother's in heaven, there's a calling for me to go."

Total Everything Now

o, they should know by now that they can't stop this bum-rush."
—Flava Flav

◆ ◆ ◆

"That whole year was crazy," he would recall, more than two decades after the tumultuous events that ultimately led to his shocking downfall took place. In 1988, Mike Tyson traded hand wraps, mouthpieces, and gloves for subpoenas, police reports, hospital beds, prescription meds, and a seemingly permanent spot in the scandal-addled American psyche.

If Andy Warhol was the *ecce homo* of exhibitionism, as poet and novelist Stephen Spender once put it, then Tyson was the "Greed Is Good" 1980s equivalent: more violent, as the accelerated age demanded, and now with a distinctly urban tinge. And, to the prizefighting axioms that had been drilled into his subconscious by Cus D'Amato and Teddy Atlas since he was an oversized teen, Tyson seemingly misappropriated a bit of Aleister Crowley as well: "Do what thou wilt shall be the whole of the law." Even as a self-proclaimed extremist, Tyson went beyond the boundaries of commonplace self-destruction.

Until he was thirteen years old, Tyson lived either in squalor as a vicious juvenile delinquent on the cratered streets of Brownsville, Brooklyn, or behind the walls of foreboding institutions dedicated only nominally to the idealistic notion of rehabilitation. When he was taken under wing by eccentric boxing Svengali Cus D'Amato, Tyson blossomed as an athlete, but he was never able to shake off his ruthless past. When Tyson was a child he lived in abandoned buildings—sometimes without heat or water; he wore the same threadbare clothes so often he earned the nickname "Bummy" from his classmates; he was tormented by bullies and terrified of going to school. His mother was an alcoholic who took up with a series of abusive men. His biological father, a pimp, abandoned the family when he was an infant. Tyson was twelve or thirteen when he entered the Tryon School for Boys in Fulton County, New York. As a preteen, Tyson was not just streetwise, not just a run-of-the-mill urchin specializing in truancy, he was Phi Beta Kappa curbside material. Robbery, assault, pickpocketing, fraud, gambling, and countless back-alley brawls left him with an arrest record that should have earned him a spot on *Scared Straight*.

As 1987 drew to an end, however, Tyson had emerged as the winner of an HBO tournament to crown a single heavyweight champion after years of disarray. Lopsided victories over Trevor Berbick, James "Bonecrusher" Smith, and Tony Tucker had given Tyson possession of every sanctioning body title extant, although a fight with the premier heavyweight of his day, Michael Spinks, remained elusive. In just over two years, Tyson had also developed into a genuine star with the kind of crossover appeal that had been waning among boxers outside of the Sugar Ray Leonard/Marvelous Marvin Hagler/Thomas Hearns axis. His electrifying ring style—which gave him a KO percentage rivaled only by the legendary likes of Rocky Marciano—and his curbside charisma made him an antihero in the age of Morton Downey Jr., Public Enemy, Freddy Krueger, and Rambo. An unrepentant spendthrift, Tyson also reflected the material world of the gaudy and gluttonous 1980s, where nothing succeeded like excess, and his luxury goods sensibility (Gucci, Piaget, Versace, Ferrari) set a template for hip-hop fashionistas.

For the first defense of his unified championship, Tyson was set to face arthritic ex-heavyweight-king Larry Holmes, who had won his title in 1978 and had been inactive since April 1986. As a retiree from the ring, Holmes was enjoying prosperous business ventures in Easton, Pennsylvania, along with the irregular gig warbling with his R&B band. A highlight performance took place in 1987, when Holmes and Joe Frazier squared off at the Sands Hotel and Casino in Atlantic City in a battle of "Singing Heavyweight Champs." From time to time, Holmes would also promote club fights in Easton, where boxing aficionados failed to gather en masse, despite its favorite son being the former heavyweight champion of the world.

Because name recognition is always a variable and valuable commodity in boxing, Holmes had received several lucrative offers for a comeback since retiring. Nearly two years after his last fight, he finally accepted one: from Jim Jacobs and Bill Cayton, co-managers of Tyson. To keep his profile visible over the years, Holmes had targeted Tyson occasionally in the press, issuing mock challenges and questioning the abilities of the fighter soon to be known as "The Baddest Man on the Planet." Now he would get his chance to prove his criticisms were correct.

Although Holmes had been stumbling under the spotlight since the late 1970s, he still craved its defining, if sometimes distorting, glare. Consecutive losses to Michael Spinks were controversial and embarrassing (who can forget the Rocky Marciano jockstrap riff?), and Holmes was distressed by this pitiful coda to his legacy. "I hated the way I lost to Spinks," Holmes told *Sports Illustrated*. "Win 48 and then lose two like that. That's why I came back. One way or another, this time I will retire at peace with myself, and with honor."

Money, of course, also enticed a restless Holmes. A purse of $3 million ensured that his occasional gym workouts, in hopes of keeping creeping middle-age flab at bay, would turn into something more serious: preparation for one of the deadliest punchers in heavyweight history. With his usual paradoxical candor, Holmes never mentioned legacy when he explained his motivation to the *Morning Call*: "I'm fighting for the money and I'm the only one who will say it. It beats 9-5, dammit."

At a public kickoff to announce the fight, Tyson rebuffed Holmes with a street eloquence "The Easton Assassin," once a borderline juvenile delinquent and a noted grouch, must have admired. "Go fuck yourself," he snarled when Holmes extended his hand. In response, Holmes removed a photo of Tyson from a wall in his office dedicated to heavyweight champions and no-showed a subsequent press conference. He also made withering personal comments about Tyson. "I'm going down in history, not Mike Tyson," Holmes said. "He's going down as a son of a bitch. If he do happen to win the fight, down the line, he'll destroy himself."

A churlish Tyson, already revealing hints of the distemper that would mark the second half of his career, brushed Holmes aside almost as brutally as he would in the ring. "If he lets anything like that upset him, then I don't think he's as great a champion as I thought he was," Tyson said. "He said derogatory things about me, that I was a dirty fighter. Then he wanted to forget it. If you don't like me, then I don't like you. Let's never talk."

No sooner did Holmes ink his deal to face Tyson than troubling signs developed. Most apparent was the fact that Holmes trained in secret, without even an open workout for publicity purposes. It was clear that Holmes was hiding something: either his dedication or his form, or, possibly, both.

On January 22, 1988, Tyson and Holmes met at the Convention Center in Atlantic City, New Jersey, on a card hosted by an emerging figure on the boxing scene: Donald Trump. Tyson, in his first outing under his exorbitant HBO contract—seven fights, approximately $27 million—sauntered to the ring in typical minimalist fashion. When the opening bell rang, he practically skipped out of his corner, happy to take part in his favorite pastime: hand-to-hand combat.

For three rounds Holmes stayed out of danger by moving side to side and keeping Tyson at bay with a stiff-arm and the occasional errant right. In the fourth, Holmes suddenly seemed emboldened and began circling the ring on his toes—as if it were 1979 all over again, The Knack, Chic, and Donna Summer dominating Billboard—snapping out his jab with zeal. A crowd of eight thousand roared at this sighting of a vintage Holmes, but Tyson recognized it for what it was: a last-stand bluff. "The people were more excited than I was," he said after the fight. "He let his ego get involved. I thought, 'He's gonna get it.'"

In no time Holmes was on his back, cockeyed, courtesy of an overhand right that dropped him with an echoing thud. Just as he had after suffering thundering knockdowns against Earnie Shavers and Renaldo Snipes in legendary title defenses, Holmes summoned his bottomless courage and wobbled to his feet to beat the count. Dazed, Holmes was ready to topple at the slightest contact, and, sure enough, down he went from a cuffing blow that nearly sent him hurtling through the ropes. Again Holmes beat the count, but the end was as predictable as it was breathtaking. A final barrage left Holmes, crumpled, in his own corner, like the victim of a mugging in a dark alley. After the fight was halted, after Holmes had been allowed to rise from the canvas, after the din of the crowd had subsided, the two heavyweights met at ring center to exchange pleasantries. "You're a great champion, but you still ain't shit," Holmes offered. "You ain't shit either," Tyson responded.

Among the VIPs at ringside for the Holmes massacre—a short list included celebrity stalwarts Jack Nicholson, Muhammad Ali, and Norman Mailer, as well as 1980s footnotes Cheryl Tiegs and Tatum O'Neal—sat Robin Givens, sitcom starlet with a heavily mascaraed eye for the main chance.

Tyson and Givens had already been squabbling for months in an on-again, off-again relationship that boded poorly for future stability. Even so, on February 7, the dysfunctional couple were in attendance at the NBA All-Star Game in Chicago when Tyson impulsively asked her to marry him. Givens agreed, and they left the stadium for a service, of sorts, performed by Father George Clements, who had been portrayed by Lou Gossett Jr., in a TV movie that had aired just two months earlier.

To some, marrying Givens was the spark that set 1988 aflame for Tyson. Givens had a CV that was as much fiction as the scripts of some of her made-for-TV movies were. But ambition? That was real. At fifteen, she was accepted into Sarah Lawrence College, and within a few years of graduation, she had already been featured on TV staples such as *The Cosby Show* and *Diff'rent Strokes*. Her mother, Ruth Roper, had earned her share of infamy by suing Yankees outfielder Dave Winfield for, of all reasons, allegedly giving her a sexually transmitted disease, believed by some to be herpes.

For Tyson, who had exchanged school for a series of reformatories, Givens was a beguiling high-society muse. She was his Daisy Buchanan and he, a two-fisted Gatsby with a volcanic temper and a background that far exceeded that of Jay Gatz for brutishness. But to Givens—and the entire Roper-Givens clan—Tyson was more like the Wild Boy of Aveyron (transplanted to the concrete jungle of Brownsville, Brooklyn), a feral child who had never been properly "socialized." From their middle-class heights, Ruth Roper and Robin Givens looked down on Tyson, sometimes privately, and sometimes publicly, as déclassé.

Gorgeous, if not exactly glamorous (starring in a sitcom such as *Head of the Class* hardly seemed to qualify her for the A-list), Givens was considered a "gold digger" as soon as she entered the gossip columns alongside Tyson. She had already been linked to Eddie Murphy and Michael Jordan, and the media at-large was not nearly as PC as it is now, thirty years later. Today, the concept of a "gold digger" would be an anathema to women across America or co-opted by feminists to advance identity politics. The fact remains that Givens—and her mother—seemed almost transparently devious from the moment they arrived on the scene. None of this neutralizes the fact that Tyson was an unremitting lout, a man whose 1992 rape conviction was only the most severe by-product of his long-standing misogyny. That Tyson mistreated Givens—emotionally and physically—is a matter of record.

For an entire year, Tyson and Givens dominated the pop culture landscape of America—supermarket scandal sheets, New York City tabloids, *People*, and television news magazines—from *Hard Copy* and *A Current Affair* to *Entertainment Tonight*. Their newlywed period was interrupted by the rigors of prizefighting, and that included traveling to the Far East in March for a soft-touch title defense. If Tyson was a star in America, he was, strangely enough, a phenomenon in Japan. Despite its xenophobia, Japan viewed Tyson in near-mythological terms; to the country at large, he was a five-foot-ten Godzilla ready to trample downtown Tokyo. Media coverage for someone who was, after all, a *gaijin*, bordered on over-the-top. Tyson was featured on magazine covers and in newspapers, and he was the subject of a slew of television specials in the weeks leading up to his debut in Tokyo.

Tyson parlayed this inexplicable fame into one of the most lucrative deals of his era. For a reported $9 million purse, Tyson would open the gleaming new Tokyo Dome by facing an opponent of his own choosing. Ultimately, Japanese promoter Akihiko Honda approved Tony "TNT" Tubbs, a former alphabet titleholder whose battles with the bulge were more compelling than his battles in the ring. Within hours, ringside tickets, for a fight that was scheduled to air on national TV, were sold out. It was as if the opponent was irrelevant—all that mattered to the Japanese was getting a glimpse of the Tyson mystique. Tubbs was the 1980s version of Buster Mathis, with a Jheri curl and a taste for controlled substances. Although Tubbs had talent, a lack of discipline and motivation undercut his smooth boxing skills, his snappy jab, and his combination punching. So untrustworthy was Tubbs that Don King hired Jose Ribalta (stopped by

Tyson in 1986) as a standby in case Tubbs showed up in woeful condition. With a paycheck of nearly $1 million at stake, it seemed improbable that Tubbs would pull out with a mysterious injury as he had in 1986, when he sidestepped a title shot against Tim Witherspoon, in protest against his treatment at the hands of King. But not even a $50,000 bonus to come in under 235 pounds could galvanize Tubbs. He weighed in at an unsightly 238 pounds, justifying the nickname US sportswriters had saddled him with years earlier: "Tubby."

During his training camp, Tubbs had already managed to upstage himself by hiring Lou Ferrigno as a consultant. How does someone work out with "The Incredible Hulk" and still enter the ring blubbery from head to toe? Only Tubbs knew the answer to that. And Tubbs had only the usual prefight bluster to offer. "They sure have a lot of plans already set," he told the *Philadelphia Daily News*. "They're just running all over me like I'm not here. I'm just the stepping-stone. I'm the tune-up. I don't even count. Well, they picked a hell of a tune-up messing with me. I'm just about the best of the litter."

In Tokyo, Tyson spent most of his time sequestered in a hotel, avoiding the American press corps as well as his Japanese admirers, who had flocked to see him arrive at the airport and who gathered around him worshipfully whenever he was out on the town. He fell asleep during a screening of *The Last Emperor* and skipped out on a Tina Turner concert within minutes of the opening notes.

Honda may have thought that Tubbs was good for more than a handful of rounds—Tubbs had never been stopped—but as fight morning drew near, a fiasco seemed more and more imminent. On March 16, Richie Giachetti, best known for training Larry Holmes, quit the Tubbs camp. "I can't be connected with a guy who doesn't want to work," Giachetti announced. "This thing won't go four rounds. You know, it's a shame because Tubbs has some skill . . . he could have made this a fight."

In the end, Tubbs did flash his talent—for all of three minutes. At ten in the morning local time, Tyson and Tubbs entered the ring in a cavernous arena whose silence seemed like a reproach to American blood sport customs. Using his surprising mobility and hand speed, Tubbs outmaneuvered Tyson in the first round and even landed a nifty combination. But "TNT" soon fizzled out. In the second, Tubbs, whose jab-and-jiggle style was surprisingly effective, made the mistake of exchanging with Tyson on the inside. Eventually, Tyson landed his trademark right-to-the-body/ right-uppercut combination, and Tubbs, stunned, backpedaled. Like a pit bull, Tyson attacked, once again demonstrating his major selling point: a killer instinct modeled on that of Jack Dempsey. A scalding hook left Tubbs with a gaping cut above his right eye. As blood poured down his face, Tubbs, woozy, went into full retreat. Before long, he was splayed out on the canvas, limbs akimbo, and his trainer, Odell Hadley, was ducking through the ropes to halt the slaughter. It was all over in less than five minutes, but the Japanese crowd seemed content. "I did what I was supposed to do to a guy supposedly out of shape," a nonchalant Tyson said in a post-fight interview.

When Tyson returned to New York, he was greeted with the stunning news that Jim Jacobs, his co-manager, had died. For years Jacobs had lived with a terrible secret: He was suffering from lymphocytic leukemia and living on borrowed time. Only a few trusted friends knew about his terminal disease. His death was a jolt to Tyson, still only twenty-one, and now suffering his second significant loss in less than three years. Cus D'Amato, who had rescued Tyson from a life behind bars, had died in November 1985. What made this blow even harder for Tyson was the fact that his inner circle had conspired to keep Jacobs's illness a secret from him. It left Tyson disillusioned. "I was messed up," Tyson wrote in his memoir, *Undisputed Truth*. "I had known Jimmy for a long time. I had felt that Cus had entrusted me to Jimmy, who was very close to Cus. If Cus was like a father to me, Jimmy was like a brother. So, you can imagine how my grief was compounded when I found out that Jimmy had been suffering from chronic lymphocytic leukemia for over nine years and had hidden his condition from me. What's worse, everyone had lied to me and told me that Jimmy wasn't sick."

(Meanwhile, while Jacobs was being laid to rest in Los Angeles, Robin Givens, now with power of attorney over Tyson, was in New York trying to withdraw money from a Merrill Lynch account that had been set up by Jacobs and Bill Cayton. "Give me my motherfucking money, motherfucker!" she shouted at the executive in charge of the account. Givens was accompanied by her ever-present mother, Ruth.)

When Jacobs died, it left Tyson adrift and opened up a breach with Cayton. It would take an all-star team of psychoanalysts to understand how and why Tyson came to loathe Cayton seemingly overnight. (Jacobs and Cayton had proven themselves to be skillful managers with both Wilfred Benitez and Edwin Rosario. In the 1990s, Cayton, now solo, also did a fair job guiding Tommy Morrison and Vinny Pazienza. His last fighters of note—Jeremy Williams and Omar Sheika—lacked the talent to exploit some of the savvy PR moves he made on their behalf.) Although Tyson was close to Jim Jacobs, he recognized Cayton for his business acumen. At least he did until Don King entered the picture and joined forces with Robin Givens and her mother.

In the years since making a name for himself with "The Rumble in the Jungle," King, former numbers runner, convicted murderer, and perpetual litigant, had solidified control over the heavyweight division in the mid-1980s with a motley crew of interchangeable title claimants who would come to be known, collectively, as "The Lost Generation."

Although King had controlled the heavyweight division for most of the 1980s, he ruled deliberately over numberless widget champions who all had one thing in common: They were contractually tied to King. Such an arrangement meant that King had nothing to lose whenever they fought. This daisy-chain operation guaranteed King a steady income and perpetual access to what had formerly been the most important title in all of sports: the heavyweight champion of the world.

But an X factor, one King could not have foreseen or controlled, entered the equation. With only a year as a pro under his belt, Tyson was, aside from Marvelous Marvin Hagler, the hottest star in boxing. Signed, at the age of nineteen, to multifight deals with both HBO and ABC, Tyson was on the fast track to crashing the heavyweight tournament, despite being a promotional free agent. In Tyson, King was hungrily eyeing the first real heavyweight gold mine since Muhammad Ali in the 1970s. His association with Larry Holmes over the years had been profitable (both above and below board), but Tyson promised untold riches for years to come.

King went to work. To ingratiate himself to Tyson—and to make himself seem indispensable to the troubled heavyweight champion—King set up camp at an Albany hotel, within minutes of his intended mark. The Hilton may not have been comparable to his New York City townhouse or his Los Angeles mansion or even his Ohio compound, but it served his purpose: to draw Tyson under his crooked wing. He was like a Dashiell Hammett character, The Continental Op in *Red Harvest*, playing various factions against each other in the amoral city of Poisonville.

With his overpowering bluster and his con man MO, King convinced Robin Givens and her mother that Cayton was fleecing Tyson. Soon Tyson would sue Cayton to break a managerial contract that, years ago, had earned the approval of the irascible Cus D'Amato, a man with a highly developed sense of paranoia. For the moment, however, Cayton and Tyson worked together, icily, in hopes of finalizing a fight against Michael Spinks, whom many believed was the true heavyweight champion of the world.

When Spinks bolted the HBO tournament in 1987, it was, ostensibly, to take a lucrative out-of-bracket match against Gerry Cooney, who was still trying to cash in on his White Hope dreams—five years after Larry Holmes had violently dashed them. But Spinks, along with his promoter, Butch Lewis, also realized that Tyson was a phenom whose market value would only increase down the line. Facing Tyson, the most dangerous fighter in the world, for the contractual minimum provided by the HBO tourney, was out of the question. Now, after months of grandstanding, wrangling, hand-wringing, and haggling, the fight was set: June 27, 1988. And it was made at the request of Tyson himself. Unlike so many fighters who took center stage in his wake, Tyson prodded his team to make the Spinks fight. It was an insult to his outsize ego for anyone to assume, even mistakenly, that he was reluctant to face Spinks.

Dubbed "Once and for All," Tyson–Spinks would take place at the Atlantic City Convention Center. In the biggest coup of his nascent boxing career, Donald Trump had snagged the superfight of the moment. For a site fee of $11 million, Trump managed to sabotage Las Vegas—then the fight capital of America—and, simultaneously, bring the biggest fight in history to New Jersey. In the mid-1980s, Trump realized that hosting marquee fights could help boost the drop at his Atlantic City casinos. To that end, he overpaid for a pair of Tyson title defenses (against Tyrell Biggs and Larry Holmes), which allowed him a first-rights bid on the Spinks extravaganza. Eventually, Trump would become a short-lived "adviser" to Tyson in that zany spring and summer of 1988, even hosting Tyson and his wife on weekend getaways aboard his yacht. That relationship would crumble, however, when Don King suggested to Tyson that Trump was sleeping with Givens.

For some, the biggest question surrounding this fight was simple: Would Tyson make it to the Convention Center before cracking up? As

"Once and for All" neared, Tyson began to feel the strain of a hectic personal life. (His opponent, Spinks, also took note: "I'm afraid all that has happened to Tyson will just make him meaner.") He was at war with Cayton, his marriage was on the rocks, he was fodder for tabloid papers and television news programs, he was being reprogrammed by Don King, he bickered with his trainer Kevin Rooney (a Cayton loyalist), and he continued drinking and carousing. Before he became the permanent eye of the mass media storm, Tyson had suffered from alopecia areata (spot baldness), triggered by anxiety.

Even a minor fender bender became a firestorm. After Tyson crashed his $180,000 Bentley—a silver convertible—in traffic on Varick Street, he compounded his mistake by gifting the car to a pair of police officers who had arrived on the scene. Tyson simply tossed them the keys and said, "I've had nothing but bad luck and accidents with this car." Bribery, especially public bribery, was, ostensibly, a no-no among the NYPD ever since Frank Serpico testified to the Knapp Commission in 1971. Later, the rumor mill suggested that Givens forced Tyson to lose control of the car when she attacked him from the passenger seat after finding a pack of condoms in his jacket pocket.

As a result of these continuous explosions, both minor and major, Tyson was surlier than ever during the lead-up to a fight. "I hate them all: writers, promoters, managers, closed-circuit, everybody," he told stunned reporters at a press conference. "They don't give a fuck about me, they don't give a fuck about my wife, they don't give a fuck about my trainer, my mother-in-law, my stepmother, my stepbrother, my pigeons. Nothing concerns them but the dollar, so I don't want to hear anything. We're friends, that's bullshit. I don't want no friends, there's no such thing as personal friendships. I can go in the street and fight. I don't need anybody to manage me. It's too late for that stage. All I need is a trainer. I'll go into the street and make a million dollars in a street fight."

Less than two weeks before the fight, Tyson once again made sensational headlines. This time, it was his sister-in-law, Stephanie, a professional tennis player, who publicly shared the gory details of his barbarity. Stephanie Givens gave a shocking interview to Wallace Matthews of *Newsday*. "He's the type of person who feels, he's Mike Tyson, he can do whatever he wants," she said. "He loves to damage things in the house, just for no reason. If he feels like kicking in the TV set, he'll do it.

If he feels like punching a hole in the wall, he does it. Why? I guess he gets bored."

Stephanie Givens also seemingly solidified long-standing rumors concerning domestic violence: Tyson did, indeed, physically abuse his wife. Even before the #MeToo movement, these were explosive charges, but Robin Givens cut such an unsympathetic figure that Tyson remained mostly unfazed. Although he lost a Pepsi sponsorship, he remained a hero to millions across the country, and his impending showdown against Spinks promised to be the most lucrative matchup in boxing history.

While Tyson was struggling with day-to-day strife—even weeping in the arms of veteran reporter Jerry Izenberg on the morning of the fight—Spinks had another problem altogether. He had survived the infamous Pruitt–Igoe projects in St. Louis. He had won a gold medal at the 1976 Olympics in Montreal. He was a veteran of over thirty professional prizefights and had been the undisputed light-heavyweight champion and the generally recognized heavyweight champion of the world by virtue of a pair of wins over Larry Holmes. And yet, Spinks was afraid of Tyson. "A little terror in your life is good," Spinks once said about facing Tyson. But his public jocularity only masked his fear.

A few years ago, Emanuel Steward recounted the visible shambles Spinks was in before the opening bell tolled for him. "I went into his dressing room," Steward told authors John Florio and Ouisie Shapiro. "They couldn't even get him to come out, he was so scared. He was a nervous wreck, really freaking out." For Spinks, it was clearly not just another payday. But his manager, Butch Lewis, made things infinitely worse on fight night when he harangued Tyson and the commission about hand wraps while Tyson was getting prepped for the bout. Such grandstanding was supposed to undermine a fighter psychologically. In response to the manufactured uproar, Tyson punched a hole in his dressing room wall. Tyson, it seemed, was as primed as he had sounded when he spoke to the *Boston Globe* a few days earlier. "I'll break Spinks," Tyson vowed. "I'll break them all. When I fight someone, I want to take his manhood. I want to rip out his heart and show it to him. People say that's primitive, that I'm an animal. If I wasn't in boxing, I'd be breaking the law. That's my nature."

On the night of June 27, the stars—Jack Nicholson, Norman Mailer, Warren Beatty, Madonna, Sean Penn, Jesse Jackson, Leroy Nieman—

flocked down to the boardwalk to bump elbows, hobnob with Trump, and watch Spinks walk a gangplank, of sorts. For Cayton, the night did not begin with much amusement, despite the gala atmosphere: At ringside, a process server delivered a lawsuit from Tyson, who was trying to sever their managerial contract.

An unusually animated Tyson warmed up by throwing lightning-fast combinations and pacing the ring as the celebrities in attendance were announced to the crowd. By contrast, Spinks barely moved. He kept his robe on until the fighter introductions began, as if he was hoping to remain, in a sense, armored for as long as possible. After both fighters were announced, Spinks returned to his corner and knelt in prayer.

The bell rang. Within seconds, Tyson unleashed a blurring combination that forced Spinks to retreat. As Tyson advanced, his bob-and-weave style not only elusive but perfectly coordinated for maximizing firepower, Spinks backed into the ropes. In a flash, Spinks, who had never been down in his career, was dropped by a left uppercut followed by a knifing right to the body. He beat the count and, sure proof that he was disoriented, marched directly into fire. Although he threw his vaunted right hand once, in desperation (he missed), Spinks was a loud target for Tyson, who bored in and landed a blurring left hook, followed up a right uppercut, that flattened Spinks. His head bounced against the canvas, under the bottom rope, like a tombstone knocked off its base by vandals. With his eyes wide yet clearly unfocused, Spinks tried to scramble to his feet, but his nervous system was haywire, and he floundered before pitching through the ropes. By then, Referee Frank Cappuccino had already stopped his count.

It was all over, after only ninety-one seconds. Tyson, now the undisputed heavyweight champion of the world, merely stretched out his arms, gloved palms outward, and gazed into the stunned crowd. This extraordinary gesture of nonchalance was a sharp contrast to the tumult of his life. By annihilating Spinks, never the most convincing big man but still the only other heavyweight in the world that mattered, Tyson reached a peak he was never able to duplicate. In the wake of his crowning achievement— he was the first undisputed titlist since 1977, and now the lineal champion as well—Tyson seemed almost joyless. No one ever seemed less happy after such an explosive win. An angry Tyson announced his (short-lived) retirement after the fight and continued his running battle with the media. "I wasn't very appreciative of what you guys, the reporters, did to me,"

Tyson said at the post-fight press conference. "You tried to embarrass me. You tried to embarrass my family. You tried to disgrace us, and as far as I know, this might be my last fight. . . . I don't like reading that my wife is a whore, that my mother-in-law is a sneaky conniver. And then I read that I'm an idiot. I know it goes with the territory, but it's difficult."

Who would have imagined that, after scoring the most important win of his career, Tyson would be the loser of the biggest upset in sports history only a year and a half later?

In July, Tyson spent most of his time bickering with his wife, making court appearances pertaining to his lawsuit against Cayton, and vacillating on a commitment to face top contender Frank Bruno in England.

But it was what took place in August on a Harlem sidewalk at four-thirty in the morning, just outside Dapper Dan's Boutique, that marked 1988 as an *annus horribilis* for the multimedia ages. That you could find a clothing boutique (catering almost exclusively to hustlers, rappers, and drug dealers) open all night in New York City might come as a shock to current Big Apple denizens, used to a Starbucks on every corner and studio apartments renting for $5,000 per month. Even more surprising, perhaps, to the affluent hordes who have infused the ex-mean-streets with Middle-America mores since the dawn of Y2K would be some of the bespoke wares that were available, such as Kevlar couture. "If you had a real beef, you didn't just wear the bulletproof coat when it was cold out," Daniel "Dapper Dan" Day wrote in his autobiography. "You wore that joint all summer. Bulletproofing became a big business for me."

Some nights, Dapper Dan's also doubled as an after-hours spot, where, invariably, the occasional ruckus broke out. The street brawl between Tyson and Mitch "Blood" Green, which lit up the newswires as well as the informal barbershop talk-circuit also brought Dapper Dan widespread notoriety and the kind of scrutiny that eventually resulted in his undoing.

Possibly the only fighter in history with more mugshots than knockouts, Mitch Green, an ex-member of the Black Spades street gang, was, to put it mildly, deranged. As an amateur, Green won four New York Golden Gloves titles, but he never lived up to his early potential because his interest in the WBC, the WBA, and the IBF could never match his interest in PCP—angel dust. Green was both dangerous and offbeat. He was once arrested for driving with a television set screwed into his dashboard. Like 1920s gangster Legs Diamond, who survived multiple assassination attempts via gunshot and thus claimed the nickname "The Clay Pigeon," Green had been riddled by bullets before he turned thirty. In a unique twist, however, Green once also managed to shoot himself, accidentally, with a homemade zip gun.

Over the years, Green had been stabbed, subdued by a taser, bitten by a bodyguard (employed by Larry Holmes), and brawled with prison inmates, police officers, gas station attendants, and toll booth agents. Although Green went ten rounds with Tyson in the ring in 1986, he barely made an effort in spoiling his way to the final bell. According to Green, the humiliation of earning only $30,000 to face Tyson in Madison Square Garden sapped him of ambition. He blamed Don King for his meager purse, but it was not King whom he encountered by chance on 125th Street nearly two years later.

They met in the sweltering predawn of August 23, when Tyson, along with his friend Walter Berry (an NBA power forward soon exiled to Europe) arrived at the boutique to pick up a custom-made white leather jacket bearing the phrase "Don't Believe the Hype" on its back.

According to Dapper Dan, Green was in the vicinity, wandering the streets while under the influence, when he was goaded into confronting Tyson by neighborhood ragamuffins. "On that particular night," recalled Dapper Dan, "the kids were out front, trying to escape the summer heat, when all of a sudden, they saw Mike Tyson pull up in his Rolls-Royce and walk into the store. . . . The kids knew exactly how to get their entertainment for the night. They ran right to the area where they knew Mitch Green always be at. Sure enough, they found him there and told him, 'Mike Tyson kick yo ass and he around at Dapper Dan's right now.'"

No sooner had Green been heckled by a nocturnal "Our Gang" in Air Jordans than he was stumbling through the door of Dapper Dan's, insisting that Tyson had not beaten the real "Blood" Green. "You didn't beat me," Green hollered. "I had no food. That motherfucker Don King didn't give me no food."

Although Tyson tried reasoning with Green—even getting a reluctant handshake out of him—things degenerated when they stepped out under the streetlights. Unwisely, Green continued haranguing Tyson, who was drunk and operating with a much shorter fuse than usual. Eventually, Green became physical, sparking one of the most infamous extracurricular sports moments in history. "He got into my face and started clawing at me and I looked down and he had ripped my shirt pocket," Tyson recalled in his memoir, *Undisputed Truth*. "That was it. I just walloped him right in his eye. I was drunk and didn't realize that he was high on angel dust so he really wasn't going to hit me back. It was like fighting a ten-year-old. I would drag him all up the street, and he was screaming. He fought me better in the ring than he did that night." The blows Tyson landed that morning—sans Everlasts—left him with a hairline fracture of his right hand.

Indeed, the unsanctioned rematch was as one-sided as Tyson–Spinks had been two months earlier. Dapper Dan was one of several eyewitnesses. "With Mitch on the ground, Mike landed one right hand after another that closed up Mitch's left eye and broke his nose. . . . All this information came out in later reports of the fight, but what people don't know is that after Mike knocked him down, he got on top of Mitch and started choking him out. That's when people jumped in and finally got Mike off of him. 'I'll kill you and your bitch, too,' Mike said before driving away in his car and leaving Mitch bloody in the street."

After getting stitched up in the hospital, Green limped over to the nearest police precinct and swore out a complaint against Tyson accusing him of misdemeanor assault. A few days later, Green dropped the charges in exchange for a guaranteed rematch—in the ring. There was only one condition: Green would have to work his way back into the heavyweight ratings.

In the aftermath of the sidewalk fracas, Green received numerous offers from managers and promoters looking to capitalize on the publicity. "How do you like that?" Green asked. "I'm a hot item right now." But Green was more than just hot; he was radioactive, a man whose impulses overrode everything, even his well-being. For a few weeks, Green was as omnipresent in New York as squeegee men or soapbox preachers in Times Square. Wherever he went, he carried with him a rubbery Gremlins doll fixed up with a dress and a homemade cast on its arm. This grotesque representation of Tyson, whom Green referred to as "Cicely," took a drubbing from Green from borough to borough, but that was the closest he ever got to a rematch.

Less than two weeks after his fracas with Green, Tyson was back in the headlines when he drove his BMW into a tree while in the town of Catskill. It was enough of a collision to knock Tyson unconscious and send him to the hospital, where he could find no rest even in a private room at Columbia-Presbyterian. Robin Givens, her dramatic instincts as sharp as ever, wasted little time in turning his bedside into a photo-op. Worse, down on the street, with a crowd massing around him, was Mitch Green, howling for "Cicely" Tyson. The next day, the front page of the *Daily News* read, in slashing tabloid font, "Tyson Tried to Kill Self." At the time, Tyson denied the assertion, but later he would admit to driving into the tree deliberately for one of the strangest reasons imaginable for the most polarizing athlete in the world: He wanted attention.

With a chest contusion to go along with his damaged hand, Tyson was in no shape to face Frank Bruno on October 22. The fight was canceled, and Tyson spent the rest of the year idle, something his original brain trust would never have allowed. The discipline of several training camps per year kept Tyson focused and out of trouble. Now, however, he was determined to commune with his dark side. Without Cus D'Amato and, now, Jim Jacobs, Tyson began to regress. The short leash Jacobs tried to keep him on was gone, and Tyson was free to run wild.

During the turbulent summer of 1988, Tyson went from edgy sports personality to full-on boor, a joyless hedonist whose dissolution seemed to be an end in itself. He was the youngest heavyweight titlist in history, a sporting phenomenon who dominated the back pages and gossip columns, and yet he was as bleak as Caligula in an Albert Camus play. "I had everything I wanted," he wrote, "but I wasn't happy within myself. The outside world wasn't making me happy anymore. I didn't know how to get it on the inside, because happiness, as I realized later, is an inside job."

For Tyson, fame was not only a means of gate-crashing respectable society but of unleashing his pent-up id. Any travelogue featuring Tyson would have been rated XXX and thus ineligible for, say, an episode of *Lifestyles of the Rich and Famous*, which chronicled the day-to-day adventures of the go-go celebrity jet set of the 1980s. Robin Leach, despite his adventures involving yachts, helicopters, champagne magnums, and Lamborghinis, would have been hard-pressed to keep up with Tyson. And the sexcapades Tyson took part in might have made Hugh Hefner blush. (What was remarkable about his exploits was the fact that he was often on Thorazine during that explosive period. Givens, with the help of a friendly psychologist, had convinced Tyson that he was manic depressive. Before long, Tyson was on medication that often left him sluggish.)

In addition to life as a libertine, Tyson seemed determined to become the baddest man on the planet—not just in the ring, but out of it as well. These aspirations were driven in part by his childhood as a violent gutter-snipe rampaging through the streets of Brownsville in the late 1970s and his admiration for the reckless boxing legends of the past. Jack Johnson, Battling Nelson, Mickey Walker, Harry Greb—all fighters who fought, caroused, and raised hell full throttle. Above all, however, Tyson seemed drawn to the ill-starred career of Sonny Liston, whose mysterious death when he was in his early forties capped off a life of unrelenting stress. Tyson was also a devotee of certain "great men," not the peaceable ones such as Gandhi or Martin Luther King Jr., but the bloody conquerors, despots, and tyrants: Alexander the Great, Hannibal, Genghis Khan, Mao (whose likeness he would eventually tattoo onto his rib cage), Napoleon, and a few select Roman emperors were his nonsporting heroes. These bloody historical figures fed his natural inclination toward megalomania.

Only a few days after checking out of Columbia-Presbyterian, Tyson traveled to Moscow with Givens, where shocking reports of "Iron Mike" terrorizing a hotel came back to America like dispatches from a distant war zone. By then, Tyson was as cavalier about taking his psychophar-maceuticals as he was about money, women, and liquor. Whether Tyson actually needed meds is open to debate (at the behest of Cayton, Tyson received a second opinion, which determined that Tyson was not bipolar), but their use, along with binge drinking, could not have helped his moods.

As if to underscore his headlong rush into chaos, there came another series of headlines. First Tyson scuffled with NBC cameramen while on a morning jog in New Jersey. Then, on September 30, 1988, came the infamous appearance on *20/20* with Barbara Walters, where Givens spoke about the torture of living with her "manic depressive" husband, while a docile Tyson sat next to her on a prop couch. According to Peter Heller, author of *Bad Intentions*, Tyson had taken Thorazine and Lithium before the taping of the show. Givens went on to describe a married life that fell far short of the Huxtables ideal. "He has got a side to him that is scary. Michael is intimidating, to say the least. I think there is a time when he cannot control his temper, and that is frightening to me, and to my mother and to anyone around, it's scary. It's been torture, pure hell. It's worse than anything I could possibly imagine. . . . He shakes, he pushes, he swings. Sometimes I think he is trying to scare me. There were times when it happened that I thought I could handle it, and just recently I have become afraid. I mean very, very much afraid. Michael is a manic depressive, he is, that is just a fact."

A few days later, in a delayed reaction to his nationally televised embarrassment, Tyson, who had been convinced by his cronies that he had been publicly emasculated, erupted at his Bernardsville, New Jersey, mansion, sending Robin and Ruth fleeing in terror. His rampage included hurling a glass at his wife, throwing furniture out of the window, kicking in a television set, and verbally abusing the entire household. It was an outburst that brought the police to the front door. Five days later, Givens filed for divorce, after less than eight months of unholy matrimony.

On October 21, Tyson shocked the sporting world by signing a dubious promotional agreement with Don King, whose sinister reputation had preceded him since the late 1970s, when *The Ring* ratings scandal forced ABC to abandon its United States Boxing Championships. "And then I got caught up with this other piece of shit, Don King," Tyson recalled in his memoir. "Don is a wretched, slimy reptilian motherfucker. He was supposed to be my black brother, but he was just a bad man. He was going to mentor me, but all he wanted was money. He was a real greedy man. I thought I could handle somebody like King, but he outsmarted me. I was totally out of my league with that guy."

At every level in boxing, a subterranean pursuit overrun by the seedy, the shady, and the sleazy, moochers and leeches can be found. When the richest athlete in the world happens to be a prizefighter, however, the scam artists are, inevitably, of a lower grade. But King, the most successful black promoter in history, was something else altogether. Not only did King have the street background that attracted Tyson, he also exploited racial anxiety. Although Tyson was from a slum almost completely devoid of white people, the fact remained that his reclamation from guttersnipe to the richest athlete in the world was engineered entirely by Caucasians. Kevin Rooney, who had a difficult time figuring out which side of his bread was buttered, put the King–Tyson dynamic in a decidedly politically incorrect light. "It's because of his black ghetto, jive jailhouse background," Rooney told *Newsday*. "King is literally putting the con on him with his flash and black talk. See, Mike was in reform schools, but King went to the big house for murder. And the only reason Mike never went to the big house is because of Cus D'Amato. But growing up, Mike looked up to hoods. Now he's looking up to an ex-hood with a legal license. If he falls into that trap, it will be sad."

Tyson may have been out of his league, but he was also insecure, confused, and strangely malleable. He was not even a teenager when he subordinated his identity to the brutal gang code of the Jolly Stompers in Brownsville. After his release from the Tryon School for Boys, Tyson had been indoctrinated by Cus D'Amato, whose free-floating paranoia was combined with fringe-theory life lessons steeped in Freud and street mysticism. At twenty-one, Tyson had been lovestruck and susceptible to the gaslighting of Givens (and his ubiquitous mother-in-law, Ruth). Finally, it was King, with his atomic personality and his rat-a-tat-tat con man chatter, who molded an all-new Tyson, a man now openly, and angrily, espousing victimhood. "They all want something from me," Tyson moaned. "They're all making their living off me. Everybody's got their hand out."

Bill Cayton recognized how King had used his oratorical skills to turn Robin Givens against him. "He was feeding her all these goddamn lies, and she was believing them," he told Peter Heller. "King is a very convincing scoundrel."

In a strange if remunerative nod to racial solidarity, King would go on to fleece Tyson of millions of dollars and, almost perversely, encourage "Iron Mike" to pursue debauchery instead of roadwork. Then Tyson cut the last remaining link to his Catskill past when he fired trainer Kevin Rooney, who had refused to denigrate Cayton and thus was viewed as a traitor. "I'm the fighter, not him," Tyson would later say. "Kevin Rooney was a good trainer, but Cus D'Amato was the one who established me. It's ridiculous for me to pay someone like Kevin Rooney ten percent of my purse when there's no loyalty on his part."

For a man who once wrote, "Instant gratification is not quick enough for me," 1988 could not end soon enough. But Tyson would continue to make headlines in 1989, for everything from court depositions to drag racing to trysts with his estranged wife (during divorce proceedings) to rape accusations to his old standby, smashing television cameras. Even so, his outlook would remain essentially zen. "The way I am is the way I am: high-spirited, energetic, and wild. I'm going to live the way I want to live anyway. I have to live my life. Once I start to change, that's the first sign of failure."

The Windfall Factor

y the late 1980s, the end of the glitziest decade since the Jazz Age, Bert Cooper was at rock bottom. Zealous partying had waylaid his stamina. At times, he popped more tabs on Old Milwaukee cans than jabs in sparring sessions. He swapped speed bags for dime bags—and worse. His mentor, Joe Frazier, had left him, and his reputation in the ring was in ruins after he quit on the stool against a comebacking George Foreman in Phoenix, Arizona, on June 1, 1989.

Bertram Blair Cooper was only a teenager when he begged his father to take him down to Philadelphia from Sharon Hill, where he was born and raised, to train with Frazier, the heavyweight legend still toiling in his gym on North Broad Street. "I was fifteen," Cooper told the *Roanoke Times* about meeting Joe Frazier. "I used the money I earned working at a Hess gas station to pay the fee to work out. His gym was a slaughterhouse. After I started beating up some older guys, Joe started watching me, and then I stopped having to pay."

Billed as the nephew of Frazier—whose true bloodline (Marvis, Rodney, Tyrone, and Joe Jr.) had washed out as pros over the years— Cooper immediately made a name for himself with explosive wins over two former Olympians, Henry Tillman and Willie de Wit, in 1986 and 1987, respectively. Both bouts were aired on CBS in the days when fighters built followings on national television.

No sooner had Cooper begun to make a name for himself, however, than his libertine outlook began to undercut his career. And Frazier, whose disciplinarian attitude was as legendary as his feats in the ring, soon began to sour on his protégé. Frazier cut Cooper loose after the debacle against Foreman. Cooper remained bitter at his childhood idol for years. "When I was a kid," Cooper told writer Bernard Fernandez in 1991, "he used to open up his coat and say, 'Here, kid, take your best shot.' I'd like to take that shot now."

Against Foreman, the luckless Cooper, who refused to answer the bell for the third round, fell to more than just the earthshaking blows of "Big George." In fact, Cooper would later claim that a low-rent conspiracy had taken place in order to sabotage his chances against the aging ex-heavyweight champion of the world. Two sultry women—identical twins, for the love of God—had buttonholed Cooper in the lobby of the Macha Hotel and led him on a seventy-two-hour *ménage-à-trois* binge that left him spent on fight night. Not exactly Warren Commission material, to be sure, but the lurid details are pure Bert Cooper: "I didn't sleep for three days," Cooper told Ken Rodriguez of the *Miami Herald* years after the fight had taken place. "They set me up. I drank about a keg and had some mixed drinks and Long Island iced teas. I did about a quarter ounce of cocaine." Indeed, Cooper tested positive for cocaine after the fight and was docked a portion of his $17,500 purse. To make matters worse, the Arizona State Athletic Commission suspended Cooper in absentia. Cooper, you see, was on a bender across the Grand Canyon State that would last nearly three months, or far longer than any of his training camps.

After the parties were over, however, Cooper entered a rehab center and geared up for an uncertain future. When Cooper returned to boxing a few months later, he renewed his commitment to discipline—in his own fashion, of course—but eventually surrounded himself with a fairground aura that held out little promise of success. His new team included former WWF star Big John Stud; an ex-bodyguard to wrestlers, Jimmy Lee Adams; and a young wild-eyed promoter who nicknamed himself "Elvis."

Even for the fight racket, Rick "Elvis" Parker was beyond the pale. In a pursuit as morally cloudy as boxing, Parker seemed to be the symbolic apex of all its ills. Obese, crooked, obnoxious, drug-addled, erratic, and unscrupulous, Parker personified the subterranean nature of outpost boxing. Away from the neon dreams of Las Vegas and New York City, far from the Klieg lights of national television, prizefighting was a barely regulated netherworld from the Rust Belt to the Bible Belt to the Sun Belt. In high school gymnasiums, bingo halls, VFWs, ballrooms, and armories, in Sheratons, Hyatts, and Desert Inns, the seedy side of a sport that had once been an outlaw pursuit in America flourished. To think of Rick Parker today is to recall some of the lunatic fringe moments of the late 1980s and early 1990s: apartment wrestling, Lobster Boy, Jack Kevorkian, Satanic ritual abuse, adult diaper fetishists, Branch Davidians, Moonie weddings, GG Allin, weeping televangelists.

Born in Missouri in 1955, Parker grew up in a broken home and dropped out of high school when he was sixteen years old. But Parker, street-smart and, in his own devious way, ambitious, would not need a formal education to get where he wanted to go. In 1968, he moved to Lakeland, Florida, where he eventually began his career in flimflam as a pool hustler. After bamboozling the denizens of the Gulf Coast with his Sneaky Pete cue, Parker discovered the joys of door-to-door scamming when he stumbled across a cleaning agent he dubbed Sun-Station. He founded a company with the generic name American Safety Industries and began making serious money by expanding his territory across the country. Parker recruited his sales force from a seemingly endless population of teen runaways and hotheaded ex-cons. In fact, his goon squads—which, in some ways, resembled cults—were modeled on magazine crews, a coast-to-coast phenomenon that eventually sparked a congressional hearing in 1988.

In the early 1980s, Parker branched out to promoting rock concerts, and the nighthawk glamour of hair-metal acts like Ratt and Bon Jovi seemed to stir a desire for a flamboyant lifestyle to go along with his nouveau-riche status.

Throughout his short career as a boxing promoter on the very fringes of the fringe, Parker claimed that it was a chance meeting in 1985 with one of his idols—Don King—that led him into the red light district of sports. King and Parker sat next to each other on an airplane, where, supposedly, the electro-haired humbug encouraged Parker to enter the twisted world of boxing promotion. According to Parker, it was King who kick-started his overriding obsession—winning the heavyweight championship of the world. Parker called his goal "the windfall factor." In 1994 Parker explained its meaning to *60 Minutes*: "Oh yes. The windfall factor. All of your dreams coming true. Millions and millions of dollars, all at one time."

In 1987, Parker, who wore outrageous sunglasses and an even more outrageous red hairpiece as part of his Mid-South Championship Wrestling style, staged some of the earliest George Foreman comeback fights, but he was elbowed out by Bob Arum before the real money started pouring in. Underwritten by sales of his Sun-Station solution, the Rick Parker carny was on the slow trail to nowhere, with only journeyman Tim "Doc" Anderson gaining some notoriety in a losing performance against Foreman in Orlando, Florida. But Parker had one legitimate if war-torn fighter in a reclamation project named Bert Cooper. Although Cooper was a basket case with a spotty record, he had a left hook that could make or break dreams in a nanosecond.

In 1990, Cooper seemed on the verge of reversing his misfortunes. He knocked out Orlin Norris in February to win the NABF heavyweight title and dropped a spirited decision to hard-hitting Ray Mercer six months later on CBS. Over twelve explosive rounds, Cooper showed the heart and determination against Mercer that had been lacking so often since his downward spiral began in 1987. But a few months later Cooper was demolished by a young Riddick Bowe in two rounds. Even against a rising powerhouse like Bowe, then less than two years away from winning the heavyweight championship of the world, Cooper could not keep his impulses in check: Cocaine had been one of the most popular items on his training-camp menu. This time, Cooper tried to patch himself up in Salem, Virginia, where, presumably, the lure of wild nights would be far from his reach.

Chaos and boxing are virtually inseparable, and the route it took for Cooper to reach the biggest night of his life should have been marked with milestones reading SNAFU and FUBAR all the way down the line. In early 1991 the biggest fight in boxing history had been announced: Mike Tyson, still the reigning king of both the box-office and the tabloid headlines, would face Evander Holyfield for the undisputed heavyweight championship of the world. Never mind the fact that Tyson was under indictment on rape charges that would eventually lead to a conviction and a three-year stint at the Indiana Youth Center. What boxing wants, boxing usually gets, and what it wanted more than anything in the early 1990s was the temporary El Dorado of Holyfield–Tyson. But history would have to wait a few years. Tyson suffered a rib injury only weeks before the fight, and Holyfield took a dramatic $24 million-dollar pay cut to face

Italian Olympian Francisco Damiani on HBO instead. Holyfield requested that this downscaled bout take place in his hometown of Atlanta, Georgia, as a gift to his fans. Before Damiani could waddle over to The Omni, however, he twisted an ankle and withdrew, despite the protests of his wife.

Enter Bert Cooper. Less than a month earlier he had battered fringe contender Joe Hipp into submission in Atlantic City. Now, sitting in his mobile home in Virginia, Cooper was shocked to receive a phone call outlining the details for the chance of a lifetime: a short-notice fight against Holyfield for the heavyweight championship of the world. Cooper took the offer—and the reported $750,000 paycheck—only six days shy of the opening bell. "I just had time to shave and catch the plane to Atlanta," Cooper told columnist Jim Murray.

Although Holyfield was the undisputed heavyweight champion of the world, respect was a little harder to come by than he had expected. In fact, Holyfield, twenty-nine, was already seeing his star lose its glitter. First, Buster Douglas took some shine away from Holyfield when he showed up overweight and disinterested for their title fight in 1990. Then, when Douglas nonchalantly listened to the full count after being dropped by a thundering counter right hand, Holyfield saw his title-winning effort diminished even further. The new champion also took his share of criticism for failing to stop geriatric George Foreman in their April 1991 superfight, an event in which the challenger was by far the popular favorite. Now, Holyfield, still undefeated at 26-0, would be facing an unranked journeyman best known for his chaotic lifestyle and a history of dogging it in the ring. No one gave Cooper, a 22-1 underdog with a spotty 26-7 record, a chance. (Cooper would enter the ring against Holyfield with more than just the odds against him. According to Jon Hotten, whose book *The Years of the Locust* chronicles the sordid rise and fall of Rick Parker, Cooper came down with the flu two days before the fight.) Not even the WBC considered Cooper a threat; they refused to sanction the bout, leaving the undisputed champion of the world defending only two-thirds of his titles.

Only Parker, haunted by "the windfall factor," thought Cooper could score an improbable upset. During the short media buildup for the fight, Parker touted his dark horse to anyone who crossed his path. Unimaginatively, Parker even referred to Cooper as "The Baddest Man on

Planet Earth," a sobriquet that belied just how erratic Cooper could be in the ring. But Parker had a serious wish-fulfillment mojo going for him, and the fact that Cooper probably needed a Nyquil/Dayquil co-pack in the corner more than he needed a water bottle could not diminish his hopes. If Cooper could somehow spring the upset, Parker, who had been a laughingstock as a promoter for years, would control the most prestigious title in sports. Overnight, Parker would become a de facto powerbroker—a notion that must have troubled even the strange bedfellows of boxing.

Murad Muhammad, who promoted 1990s heavyweight contender Razor Ruddock, seemed to have an inkling about the potential dark side of a successful Parker run. "The bottom line is if Bert Cooper lucks out," he told Tim Dahlberg of the Associated Press, "look what we have as the undisputed heavyweight champion of the world." Whether Murad was referring to Cooper himself or the misfit team behind him will never be known.

On November 23, 1991, more than twelve thousand fans gathered at The Omni to see Holyfield, their hometown hero, add the punchline to a gag most sporting observers considered to be in bad taste. If Holyfield had entered the fight overconfident, then Cooper gave him no reason for doubt in the first round. "The Real Deal" opened by bouncing on his toes, working behind a sharp jab, and dropping straight rights over the top. With Cooper floundering in front of him, Holyfield unleashed a damaging combination and stepped out of range. A few seconds later, he ripped a left hook to the body that sent Cooper to the canvas in sections.

It was no surprise to see Cooper down so early; wiseguys from one betting parlor to another had practically guaranteed it. But what was surprising was the fact that Cooper survived the follow-up onslaught and returned fire, catching a careless Holyfield with a looping right, and then, as the round wound down, a thudding left hook. Even so, Holyfield appeared virtually unstoppable at midrange, and he battered an onrushing Cooper with combinations in the second. Cooper seemed as overmatched as his critics had feared. Still, brawling with a man trained by Joe Frazier was a tactical error, and it gave Cooper his only chance to win. Even after being outclassed for most of the round, Cooper managed to land a cracking right and a pinpoint uppercut that forced Holyfield to clinch.

Then, in round three, "the windfall factor" nearly became a crashing reality. After being rattled by a fusillade of blows, Cooper grinned at Holyfield and redoubled his assault. A savage right about a minute into the round wobbled Holyfield, and a bloodthirsty Cooper charged after his wounded prey. "My heart skipped a beat," Cooper would later say about the moment when his dreams seemed so close to being fulfilled. "Then it went boom, boom, boom. I said to myself, 'Oh, boy, this is it.'" A follow-up barrage sent Holyfield stumbling around the ring like a man who had just stepped out of a whirligig. When he finally crashed into the ropes, referee Mills Lane jumped in, ruled a knockdown, and began the mandatory eight-count. It was the first time Holyfield had been floored in his professional career. After the count had been completed, Cooper closed in on Holyfield and whipsawed both hands against the groggy champion, who leaned and buckled against the ropes in hopes of riding out the storm. Moments later, Cooper was out of breath and Holyfield suddenly opened up with a cross-fire attack. It was a remarkable turnaround for a fighter who only moments earlier appeared to be on the verge of being stopped. Before the round ended, however, Cooper would again rally, landing two long rights that drove Holyfield back as the bell rang. Both men, groggy, staggered to their corners.

If any bookie had laid odds that Cooper would quit, as he had in the past, after taking his first serious dose of punishment from Holyfield, then he would have gone bust. That night, November 23, 1991, Bert Cooper, high school dropout, son of a minister, professional flop, was dead game. Which is exactly why he came out in the fourth bobbing and weaving, walking into a hail of punches just to land his own thumping shots—hard rights to the body, left hooks to the head—and in the last minute of the round landing a shocking multipunch combination with Holyfield against the ropes. Despite his occasional success, Cooper was taking one barrage after another. It was clear: Holyfield was breaking him down with hooks to the ribs, stiff one-twos, and an unerring right uppercut.

In the fifth round, Holyfield battered Cooper so relentlessly that one of his gloves split open and had to be replaced. A five-minute respite followed while Holyfield had his glove repaired, and Cooper sat on his stool, trying to recuperate from the jackhammer blows he had received. From that point on, Cooper was bone-weary, and the sixth round saw him decelerate with every passing second.

Although Holyfield slowed the pace and picked away at Cooper with uppercuts and body shots, Cooper, at this point, had still managed to land at a remarkable 55 percent clip. Needless to say, Holyfield was even more successful with his connect ratio. No fighter, particularly a heavyweight, can withstand that kind of sustained punishment, and Cooper, little by little, was withering away under the ring lights.

Early in the seventh round, Cooper walked into another corkscrew uppercut. Seeing that Cooper was ready to give way, like a levee against hurricane waters, Holyfield attacked. Again and again Holyfield lashed out at Cooper. Again and again Cooper shook, tottered, and shuddered, but would not fall. With less than a minute to go, Holyfield tore after Cooper with a two-handed cannonade, including numberless upper-cuts that threatened to decapitate Cooper. Although Cooper practiced a version of the cross-armed defense (pioneered by Archie Moore), his variation had a counterintuitive flaw: He only crossed one arm. With his left elbow pointed up to the rafters in a strange chicken wing formation, Cooper left a wide gap through which Holyfield torpedoed one crush-ing uppercut after another. Nine times out of ten a man who is hit with dozens of shots from a world-class heavyweight is going to see the black lights; hear, if from a distance, the ten-count tolling in his ear; feel, in the words of Floyd Patterson, as if he were on a pleasant cloud. But Cooper remained upright throughout the barrage, and only the intervention of referee Mills Lane with only two seconds remaining in the seventh saved him from being seriously injured. "Bert Cooper is a tough guy," Lane would later tell reporters. "But he took a lot of punches. He seemed to have lost the ability to fight back."

In the aftermath of the loss, Parker, cockeyed with rage after seeing his dream destroyed, seethed. "Every conceivable thing that should not have happened to Bert Cooper happened," Parker railed, summing up the life and times of Bert Cooper to *KO Magazine* in 1992. "HBO would not give me the theater to voice my discontent and protest. They turned the power off on me at the press conference. We're not idiots. Bert was robbed of the championship of the world." Counterfactual history is something of a fad in boxing. Enough what-ifs hover over the sweet science to keep Harry Turtledove busy for the rest of his life. In this case, the what-ifs added up to a dream scenario hard to resist elucidating. What if Cooper had had a full training camp? What if Lane had not called for a mandatory eight-count when Holyfield was stunned? What if Cooper had not been ill in the days leading up to the fight? What if, what if, what if—but it was Cooper who ruminated about it all for years to come. "I was one punch away from the heavyweight championship," he said during a press conference to announce a contract signing with Don King a few weeks after losing to Holyfield. "They robbed me, but what can you do? What can you say?" King, creative as usual, simply referred to Holyfield as "The Welfare Champion" and promised a bright future for Cooper.

In one night, Cooper, only twenty-five years old, went from being a trial horse in the Rick Parker circus to a feared contender, which turned out to be a mixed blessing. A higher profile meant more fame and money, two temptations a man like Cooper found difficult to resist. For Cooper, just stepping over the threshold of his trailer door qualified as a potential pitfall. Below him stood no safety net; he was, after all, managed by a man with ties to pro wrestling and promoted by a drug-addled hustler. In no time, it was back to the hinterland circuit, drugs, booze, and partying.

In early 1992 Parker had a new con going: ex-NFL linebacker Mark Gastineau, formerly an All-Pro with the New York Jets in the mid-80s, was now a fledgling prizefighter. Acting on a verbal agreement with a representative of George Foreman, still wildly popular despite losing to Holyfield in April 1991, Parker chose Gastineau as the surest route to "the windfall factor." If Gastineau could build a record of at least 12-0, Parker was told, he would receive a shot at Foreman in a sideshow bonanza for all involved.

But the star of the Sack Exchange was finding it harder to corner the Sock Exchange—even in the gym. So his bouts were fixed. In his pro debut, Gastineau dry-gulched an acrobatic professional wrestler in eighteen seconds and then went on to face civilians and professional dive artists until Parker fatefully matched him with Tim "Doc" Anderson. Although Parker and Anderson had been estranged for nearly two years—Parker had cheated Anderson out of thousands of dollars—Parker ludicrously promised his former fighter half a million dollars to play stuntman against Gastineau. Anderson, however, had other things in mind—namely revenge via double-cross. When Gastineau and Parker showed up at his hotel room just hours before the fight to rehearse the dive routine, Anderson shocked them both by refusing to comply. On June 9, 1992, Anderson smacked the hapless, hopeless, and helpless Gastineau around the ring en route to a lopsided decision win aired live on the USA Network. Parker, whose cocaine addiction had worsened over the years, now saw another dream—or delusion—slip out of his meaty grasp.

By refusing to follow the script, Anderson put himself in the crosshairs of a vindictive sociopath. Six months later, Parker offered Anderson a rematch against Gastineau under the pretext that Gastineau had become a liability: Parker wanted Gastineau knocked off in order to trigger a contractual clause that would prove beneficial to "Elvis." Incredibly, Anderson agreed, and the fight was scheduled to take place on December 3, 1992, in Oklahoma, a state without an athletic commission. Gastineau–Anderson II marked one of the lowest points in boxing history and set off a chain of events outrageous even for the anarchic world of boxing.

Improbably, the nearly talentless Gastineau stopped Anderson in the sixth round in front of a few hundred spectators on a non-televised card. Later, the sickening truth would be revealed: Anderson, whose cornermen never showed up and were replaced by strangers, had been poisoned. After the fight, Anderson collapsed in the dressing room, unconscious. He was discovered hours later by a janitor and taken to a hospital, where doctors suspected that Anderson had, indeed, been drugged.

Whatever he had been poisoned with left Anderson suffering from vertigo and largely bedridden for the better part of three years. Desperate for a cure for his undiagnosed illness, Anderson eventually decided to confront Parker. Without knowing exactly what chemicals had been used to spike his water, Anderson faced a lifetime of suffering. It was Parker who had the answers, and Anderson would get them. They met at an Embassy Suites in Lake Buena Vista on April 28, 1995, and their showdown ended with Parker, who had no idea what kind of toxin had been slipped to Anderson, laid out on the floor, shot eight times, DOA. Anderson was convicted of first-degree murder and sentenced to life in prison without the possibility of parole. But Parker was not a man whose death triggered much mourning. His own sister, Diane McVey, probably put it best when she spoke to writer Robert Mladinich in 2005: "Over the years, there were so many people who might have wanted Rick dead. He wasn't a very nice person, and took advantage of a lot of people. I'm not surprised someone killed him."

Parker was only thirty-nine years old when he died. By that time his old friend Bert Cooper was already hitting the skids hard. Over the next twenty years, Cooper fell out of contention and became nothing more than a palooka, but he also lived a life like a loaded gun. Drugs, prison, religious awakening, and all the madness boxing could offer, which included a slot on one of the first professional boxing cards to take place on mainland China, a KO victory over a bare-knuckle brawler making his pro debut, an early loss in a bizarre one-night heavyweight tournament in Mississippi, and a first-round demolition job of undefeated fraud Richie Melito. Before that fight, representatives from the New York State Athletic Commission had visited Cooper in the dressing room to encourage Cooper to perform his best despite rumors of skulduggery surrounding the fight. Cooper obliged. As recently as 2012 Cooper was toiling under the hot lights in boxing hinterlands such as Winston-Salem, Jefferson City, and Hammond, Indiana.

Years after his unlikely role as überspoiler, Cooper recalled his downward spiral. "I burnt bridges. I spent most of my money, not so much on drugs and alcohol, but just on parties," he said. "People I thought were my friends weren't my friends. I gave them money for cars and things like that and when I needed them, they were gone—zoom—just like that." In the same way, perhaps, that "the windfall factor" disappeared from the tumultuous lives of two men forever on the edge: Zoom, just like that, yes, just like that.

Red Arrow

THE MYSTERIOUS DEATH OF SONNY LISTON

Las Vegas, Nevada, 1970. His life was a firetrap; his days were dry tinder. A small spark here or there—some ash from a cigarette, perhaps—and the whole ramshackle hovel would go up in roaring flames. You could shovel all the sand in the world on it, hose it down with the entire Atlantic Ocean—nothing was going to stop that conflagration.

In the brittle Las Vegas heat—sunstroke conditions—Charles "Sonny" Liston, former heavyweight champion of the world, roamed from one dark quarter to another. He was wandering through a dangerous netherworld, one still two decades away from turning into a tourist trap where outlandish replicas of the pyramids and the Statue of Liberty dotted the landscape. No, during those last lost years of Sonny Liston, the Vegas strip was still dominated by garish neon signs and billboards announcing the names of extinct hotels, burlesque clubs, and casinos: The Dunes, The Thunderbird, The Hacienda, The Flamingo. And behind that gaudy façade was an open city for the lowdown and dirty. Sonny Liston, alas, was in his element.

◆ ◆ ◆

After his two mystifying performances against Cassius Clay/Muhammad Ali—fights that stunned and outraged more than just the sporting world—a disgraced Liston moved to Las Vegas in 1966 with his wife, Geraldine, and embarked on a far-flung comeback that began in Stockholm, Sweden. His setup tour reached a dozen consecutive victories before it finally hit The Strip. Then, in his second fight back in Sin City, the beginning of the end finally closed in on him. In December 1969, roughly a year after working his way back into the heavyweight rankings, Liston was brutally knocked out by his ex-sparring-partner Leotis Martin in a fight aired live on ABC. A piercing overhand right, hard as flak, sent Liston nosediving into the canvas—and into the shadowlands of Vegas hustling. Although he had one more fight—a bloody TKO of valiant Chuck Wepner in 1970—Liston was now on his own in an underworld as aboveground as any in the nation.

Liston—the hulking ex-strikebreaker with a ramrod jab and a left hook as heavy as a derrick—was adrift in a city dominated by wiseguys, grifters, and bad luck. No longer earning big paydays—even the ones creative mob accountants cut into quarter-sized pieces—Liston found himself with cash-flow problems and a threadbare résumé. Unlike his friend and idol Joe Louis, who made a good living as a greeter, Liston was sullen and monosyllabic in public. He was, in fact, underqualified for a cushy Vegas entertainment job. So he hit the dust-strewn streets and returned to his roots. Among his Vegas pastimes were blackjack, hookers, craps, vodka, cannabis, and cocaine. Once in a while, Liston made a cameo appearance in a film or a TV show—*Love, American Style*, for example—or he served as a bodyguard for Doris Day and Redd Foxx. Some of his other job descriptions? Try drug trafficker and enforcer. But this raw atmosphere was nothing new to Liston. Until he earned fame as the heavyweight champion of the world, Liston had known little but poverty and violence.

"I can understand the reasons for my failings," Liston once said. "When I was a kid I had nothing but a lot of brothers and sisters, a helpless mother, and a father who didn't care about a single one of us. We grew up like heathens. We hardly had enough food to keep from starving, no shoes, only a few clothes, and nobody to help us escape from the horrible life we lived." One of twenty-five children born to a vicious tenant farmer, Sonny Liston—who never knew his own birthday but settled on a date of May 8, 1932, for bureaucratic purposes—was raised in a tumbledown shack in Arkansas during the Great Depression. Pulled out of school when he was old enough to work the fields with his father, Liston would remain essentially illiterate for the rest of his life. As a teenager he

ran off to St. Louis in search of his mother. There, Liston became an ineffectual thief and a strong-arm man with a burgeoning rap sheet and little
hope for anything else. Dubbed "#1 Negro" by local law enforcement
officials, Liston was eventually arrested for robbery in 1950 and served
time in the Missouri State Penitentiary. "Jeff City," one of the most dangerous prisons in America, was where he learned how to box.

In 1953 Liston turned pro, and after less than a dozen fights, he wound
up under the control of the Syndicate. Early in his career, it would be
the Midwest combination headed by John Vitale. Then it was the powerful East Coast outfit, where the prizefight subdivision was led by
former Lucchese torpedo Frankie Carbo and his bug-eyed sidekick Blinky
Palermo. Liston would be dogged by mob ties—and the vilification that
came with such shady connections—for the rest of his life. Even after
becoming heavyweight champion, in fact, Liston would live through a
perpetual whirlwind of paddy wagons, gavels, congressional hearings,
ruthless headlines, and witch-hunting state commissions.

In the late 1950s and early 1960s, after cleaning out the entire heavyweight division, Liston vaulted from the sports pages and became a
national op-ed nightmare. To a tense America, Liston was a potentially
lethal combination of Stagger Lee, Jack Johnson, Nat Turner, and Lead
Belly. Liston was the first troublesome African American heavyweight
champion of the civil rights era, a man whose silent contempt and unsavory background unnerved both the Establishment and the downtrodden.
Not even the NAACP wanted him to fight Floyd Patterson for the title. It
was as if Liston—by the sheer force of his inarticulate rage—could somehow single-handedly put a stop to the Freedom Riders, Dr. Martin Luther
King Jr., and James Meredith. Never mind George Wallace, Ross Barnett,
or the Ku Klux Klan—the top contender for the biggest prize in professional sports was a threat to progress. Liston, it seemed, never stopped
being "#1 Negro."

One of the most fearsome heavyweights in history, Liston was ducked
for years by Patterson, whose manager, Cus D'Amato, used the sinister
cabal backing Liston as a smokescreen to avoid the imminent ruin of his
physically and psychologically fragile champion. When Liston belatedly
received his title shot in 1962, he knocked Patterson over like a bowling
pin in less than a round to begin the most unpopular title reign since
the days of Jack Johnson. A year later, Liston repeated his performance,

dropping Patterson three times and leaving him walleyed in 129 ho-hum seconds. Then came the debacles against Cassius Clay/Muhammad Ali, and Liston was a continental pariah. Still, in Las Vegas, where the infamous "Black Book" (known after 1976 as the "list of excluded persons") had been in circulation since 1960, even Liston, dragging shadows as long as Route 66 behind him, was welcome.

Just five and a half years after answering the bell as one of the most famous men in America, however, Sonny Liston, aged anywhere from 38 to 42, was dead. On December 26, 1970, Geraldine Liston left Las Vegas to visit family in St. Louis. When she returned, on January 5, 1971, she walked in on the grim sight of her husband rotting away in their bedroom. Police found a syringe, along with some heroin and marijuana, on the premises. Dennis Caputo, one of the officers in the Liston house that night, described the setting for the documentary *Sonny Liston: The Champ Nobody Wanted*. "I arrived at the scene, was escorted into the bedroom where Sonny Liston was laying on the bed," Caputo said. "There was no sign of a struggle. There were no apparent wounds on his body—that was hard to determine because of the deterioration of the body—but there was absolutely nothing to indicate that Sonny Liston died anything but a natural death."

Later, the autopsy would reveal that traces of morphine and codeine—possible by-products of heroin—were found in his system. But Liston, whose magnificent physique had powered him to the heavyweight championship of the world, was in such an advanced state of decay that it was hard to tell what had really happened to him. Ultimately, the Clark County coroner ruled that Liston had died of natural causes. "This autopsy rules out the possibility of homicide," wrote the medical examiner. Another element, one perhaps obliterated by the decomposition of the body—and one the autopsy did not reveal—was the state of his health leading up to his time of death. In November 1970, Liston had been hospitalized after a car crash, and a few weeks later chest pains forced him into an emergency room. In 1991 Geraldine Liston told *Sports Illustrated* that Liston had suffered from high blood pressure. Could some of these afflictions have contributed to his mysterious death?

Over forty years later, no one knows exactly what happened to Liston. It would take a study the size of the Warren Commission report to gather all the theories—conspiracy and otherwise—put forth concerning his death.

Consider this short list of possibilities: The mob gave Liston a "hot shot"; Liston had a contract put out on him by gambler Ash Resnick; he was murdered by some drug dealers he had double-crossed; a Black Muslim conspiracy cut him down; he was depressed and committed suicide. Of course, the simplest explanation of all—that he overdosed on heroin— seems implausible to most. But is it really such a far-fetched scenario?

Most of those close to Liston swore that he was not a heroin addict. Geraldine Liston insisted that Sonny did not dabble in drugs at all. "He never took any drugs as far as I knew, and I sure knew a dopehead when I saw one," she told *Unsolved Mysteries* in 1995. Davey Pearl, his closest friend during his Vegas exile, repeatedly asserted that Liston never even drank. Conversely, Las Vegas trainer Johnny Tocco told *Flash* magazine that Liston had nothing but a taste for liquor. "All Liston did was drink," he said in 1988. "I know . . . I ran the bar here. Vodka on the rocks was all." But these character references are contradicted by the facts: Liston was a documented user (pot and cocaine) and as far from a clean liver as Geoffrey Firmin was in *Under the Volcano*.

The fact that Liston used cocaine brings up other issues as well. In America, cocaine use in the late 1960s up until the early 1970s was limited. It would be years before the "Champagne of Drugs" would become a chic and omnipresent symbol of the disco era. Drug use before the popularity of mirror balls usually meant amphetamines, morphine, mushrooms, pot, LSD, and horse. Prescription drugs—like barbiturates and tranquilizers— were also abused. The mere fact that Liston was using cocaine during 1970 likely meant one thing only: He was selling it. Simply put, cocaine was too expensive for an ex-pug without a bankroll on the hustle in the bleak city Lenny Bruce used to call "Lost Wages, Nevada."

John Sutton, a former federal narcotics agent, makes it clear in his book, *Thin White Lines*, that Liston was not only trafficking but that he was getting high on his own supply as well. Sutton, working undercover alongside an informant, met with Liston in late 1970. "He related that he just made enough from the coke business to get by, have a little cocaine for his own use and pay a few bills," Sutton wrote. "He had no pension, no money saved, and no real future ahead of him." What Liston did have, however, was plenty of access to drugs.

Over the years much has been made about the intense fear of needles Liston reportedly had. Indeed, it is one of the only consistent aspects of the numerous accounts written about him. This fear, reported by Geraldine Liston and Johnny Tocco, among others, is the main reason why many insist that Liston could not have died of a heroin overdose. How, they ask, can someone so afraid of needles shoot up? No doubt Freud would have had a thing or two to say about the story of a man who protested so much about needles only to wind up dead from a possible overdose. As Nick Tosches wryly noted in his biography of Liston, "there never was a junkie who did not start out afraid of needles." It should also be pointed out that heroin can be snorted, inhaled, or smoked; mainlining is not the only way Liston could have been using.

Finally, you can almost see the progression—common in drug users—from one stimulant to another: liquor, marijuana, cocaine, and then? What next? Is heroin next? And if his wife and his friends were unable to spot reefer, coke, and vodka, what makes the historical record certain that they could spot heroin? Plenty of others, however, did finger Liston as a user. Years after the Liston investigation ended, Dennis Caputo spoke to author Paul Gallender. "It was common knowledge that Sonny was a heroin addict," Caputo said. "The whole department knew about it." In early 1971 novelist Bruce Jay Friedman haunted some of the back alleys of Las Vegas for *Esquire*. One night he ran across one of probably hundreds of shady ladies who had known Liston. "With little prompting, she tells you of an evening which she and Sonny and another white chick sat around and all fixed together," Friedman wrote. "How he had gone from sniffing coke to shooting it and, when that didn't get him off, had moved on to skag and how sad it is." This source seems to indicate that Liston was fairly new to heroin. Or maybe he was simply the joypopping type.

And for every Liston confidante who denies drug use, there are just as many who believe that the former heavyweight champion of the world died chasing the dragon. Hank Greenspun, publisher of the *Las Vegas Sun*, put it succinctly: "The man took an enormous belt and OD'd." Gene Kilroy, publicist, also thought that Liston overdosed. "I think he was using and he overdosed," Kilroy told Nick Tosches. "I think he was depressed because he was running out of money. I think either he did himself in or he accidentally did himself in."

Other theories—like the Black Muslim conspiracy—are much sketchier and need a fairly vivid imagination to pursue. As for Liston crossing the mob somehow, well, Liston had worked hand in hand with the mob for over fifteen years without ever, apparently, kicking. Another fact that points away from a mafia hit is this paragraph from a 1968 *Sports Illustrated* article: "The word has been circulated in Las Vegas that Liston is now square with the mob. Though little was ever proved, it has always been assumed that certain underworld elements were cutting the fighter from the beginning. 'Not long ago he paid his way out of all that,' an insider explains. 'He's clean.'" Add to this the fact that other fighters have openly defied the mob and never suffered from payback. Jake LaMotta and Ike Williams, for example, both testified to the Kefauver Committee about La Cosa Nostra activity in boxing.

Although no one has ever come forward with tangible information on a supposed "hot shot" killing or a La Cosa Nostra hit, somebody did speak up about Liston and his heroin connection. In his book *Las Vegas Babylon*, Jeff Burbank spoke to Mark Rodney, whose father, troubled jazz/con man Red Rodney, aka "The Red Arrow," had a heroin habit in the 1950s that cost him several thousand dollars a week—an astonishing figure for that time. Rodney, a superb trumpet player who had toured with Charlie Parker during the height of the bebop era, spent many years in prison for theft, fraud, and possession. In the 1960s and 1970s, Rodney played for show-room orchestras in Las Vegas, but he remained, at heart, a hardcore junkie.

And he was friendly with none other than Sonny Liston.

From *Las Vegas Babylon*: "According to . . . Mark, who was a teenager in late December 1970, Liston knocked on the door of their Vegas home, smiled, and went with his dad into Red's bedroom. Liston soon left. A few days later, Red told his son that Liston's wife had found her husband's moldering corpse—after he'd been dead for a couple of days—in Liston's bedroom. Red feared that the police investigation would lead to him, but it never did. Red soon skipped town anyway."

For Liston, a man whose life was chaos, perhaps nothing as prosaic as a drug overdose would be accepted as an epitaph. After all, inscrutable signs dominate his death scene: Newspapers and milk bottles left outside his doorstep; a glass of vodka on the nightstand; heroin, a syringe, and a balloon, but no gimmick to double as a tourniquet; a mysterious black powder; a .38-caliber gun sheathed in its holster; track marks on the arms of a man who allegedly suffered from aichmophobia.

Despite the mysteries, contradictions, and unfathomable symbols that surround his death, it seems as if Liston died exactly how it appeared he did—by misadventure with a drug he was still relatively unfamiliar with. No conspiracies, no mob hit, no hot shots—none of that. Whether it was because Liston was new to the joypopping game, or whether he had a pre-existing condition that made his drug use a serious gamble every time he dabbled in it, heroin was a death sentence for him. Combine high blood pressure and a recent hospital stay for chest pains with a cocaine habit and a thirst for vodka, and you have a man playing Russian roulette with five chambers.

"Can you tell me what happened to you, Sonny?" Geraldine Liston cried out during his funeral service. This question has echoed and haunted now for over forty years. Perhaps it will no longer. In the end, then, it appears that Sonny Liston died from an overdose of heroin sold to him by a bebop trumpeter nicknamed "The Red Arrow."

The Dark Corner

Even Jake LaMotta seemed fascinated by his own inner turmoil. LaMotta, "The Bronx Bull," who died on September 19, 2017, at age ninety-five, kept volumes of Freud on his nightstand. He studied the psychoanalysts during the heyday of the Age of Anxiety, when "id," "Oedipus complex," and "libido" became part of the American lexicon. "In New York City in 1946," wrote literary critic Anatole Broyard, "there was an inevitability about psychoanalysis. It was like having to take the subway to get anywhere. Psychoanalysis was in the air, like humidity, or smoke. You could almost smell it." Indeed, the surrealist shaman of the subconscious himself, André Breton, whose movement was indebted to Freud, was based in New York City throughout the 1940s and his acolytes were scattered across the country during World War II: Yves Tanguy, Man Ray, Max Ernst, André Masson.

If LaMotta pored over Freudian texts for self-insight, he would, years later, use the knowledge he had gleaned from *The Future of an Illusion* and *The Interpretation of Dreams* for dramatic purposes. His autobiography, *Raging Bull*, was full of what can euphemistically be described as poetic license. Its main narrative hook—that LaMotta was masochistically driven throughout his career by the thought that he had killed a bookie named Harry Gordon—is probably fiction. In 1962, long before *Raging Bull* was published, LaMotta wrote an article for *True Magazine* delving into his life and career. There, you can find a rough draft of his guilty-conscience-as-textual-generator conceit. After mugging a shop owner (not a bookie as stated in the autobiography) and bludgeoning him with a lead pipe, LaMotta flees the scene convinced that he has committed murder. Before he gets picked up for his crime, however, LaMotta is arrested for attempted burglary and sent to Coxsackie, a harsh reform school in upstate New York. "Weeks went by, and months," LaMotta wrote. "I had that man on my mind all the time I was in jail. When I got out of Coxsackie I just had to pass that shop again. It was a magnet. Passing the shop became a habit. I would slow down my walk, turn my head slightly and look at the desk. One day, when I was doing it for about the hundredth time, I saw him. He was paler than I remembered him, grayer and weak looking, but alive. I stopped and stared, unable to believe it for a moment."

The revised version, in which Harry Gordon pops up like a ghost at a post-fight party, was the controlling element of *Raging Bull*. Guilt, a prime mover in Freud as in Kafka, also a 1940s keystone, is what motivates LaMotta throughout the book. That it may be a literary device takes nothing away from an existence whose torrid days and nights mirrored a career remarkable both for its accomplishments and its pandemonium. No ordeal between the ropes, however, could compare to the all-year-round fracas that was his life.

Today the Lower East Side is just another overpriced neighborhood sprouting chichi bistros and million-dollar condos, but when Jake LaMotta was born there, on July 10, 1922, it was a slum that would have exhausted an army of muckrakers determined to expose its sordid injustices. For many, survival of the fittest and social Darwinism were not just concepts found in textbooks and the novels of Jack London or Frank Norris, but day-to-day realities dispiriting in their banality. LaMotta was a genuine *Dead End Kid*, with a future seemingly all used up before it had even arrived. "When I was eight I was already getting mad at people," LaMotta wrote in *Raging Bull*. "I would clock them for talking to each other because I thought they might be talking about me."

A short stint in Philadelphia did little to improve the family fortunes, and the LaMottas returned to New York City, this time to the Bronx, for decades cultural shorthand for urban blight. In the Claremont section, which features a Park Avenue light-years removed from the opulence its name suggests, LaMotta ran the streets, fighting, stealing, and honing an outlook on life that was as bleak as it was violent.

Under the abusive stranglehold of his father, LaMotta saw his socio-pathic tendencies harden day after day in a childhood that seemed almost wholly devoid of joy. In a sequel to *Raging Bull*, written to counteract the relentlessly grim original, LaMotta described turning to his father for $400 to pay bills for his newborn child. Guido LaMotta handed him a check for ten dollars.

> "Is this all I'm worth?" LaMotta writes. "Ya know, Pop, how soon they forget . . . the good times, the money—all the money I made and I helped everybody. I supported the whole family. And most of all I helped you. What were you, Pop? What the hell were you but a cheap little peddler? You dragged the family from one slum to another and pimped me off to fight every kid in the neighborhood. Did you for-get those nickels and dimes I made you? And this is your answer—a lousy ten bucks. How heartless can ya be? Look at yourself—you're a broken-down old man with nothing but broken memories. . . . What do you want from me—another championship? I'm an old man, too, now. I come to you begging for help, and you give me a kick in the ass like I was still eight years old. Why did you always hate me, Pop? All those beatings, and for what?"

During his stint in reform school, LaMotta spent hours battering his over-stuffed pillowcase in grim preparation for an even grimmer future in the ring. His juvenile-delinquent mates in Coxsackie included future welter-weight contender (and murder victim) Terry Young and, for a few weeks at least, Rocky Graziano, whom LaMotta had known as a boy on the Lower East Side.

After a short amateur career, LaMotta signed with Mike Capriano and soon turned pro. On March 3, 1941, LaMotta earned twenty-five dol-lars for his debut, a four-round decision over Charles Mackley at the St. Nicholas Arena on Columbus Avenue. In the World War II era, when dozens of top-notch fighters were drafted and the ranks of marquee pugs were thinned, LaMotta had a fast track to headline status.

His brutish style generated one nickname after another, as if the sport-ing culture at large was having difficulty coming to grips with what it was seeing. "The Bronx Ripper," "Mister Five-by-Five," "The Atomic Bomber," "One-Man Riot," "Bronx Bull"—LaMotta had a ring style that exhausted the fertile imaginations on press row.

In a few short but violent years, LaMotta would be making $10,000 to $20,000 per fight and headlining throughout the East Coast and the Midwest. Because LaMotta refused to kowtow to the New York mob—then the most powerful organization in boxing—he was forced to take his bloody show on the road despite being a box-office magnet with potential. A championship shot, however, seemed out of reach. First, the middleweight title, then held by Tony Zale, had been frozen for the duration of the war. While LaMotta waited for an elusive title shot, he took part in one of the most famous series in boxing history, against Sugar Ray Robinson. Because of the war, championship opportunities were limited; so, too, were headline attractions who could generate box-office bonanzas. Under these circumstances, Robinson took a risk by facing LaMotta, a middleweight with decided advantages in size and strength, but who was also a hometown peer with a dedicated following. Their fierce rivalry took place over nine years—a time span longer than that of most boxing careers—and lit up New York, Detroit, and Chicago. During the 1940s, LaMotta and Robinson waged war five times.

After losing a decision to Robinson in Madison Square Garden in 1942, LaMotta evened the score a few months later in Detroit, where more than eighteen thousand fans at Olympic Stadium watched him swarm over the future legend en route to a bruising unanimous decision. Jake LaMotta became the first man to defeat the incomparable Sugar Ray Robinson. This win, a shocker when it happened, became a milestone over the years, when Robinson forged a new winning streak, one that lasted until 1951. Robinson entered the ring against Randy Turpin that year with an absurd record of 129-1-2. And the only loss had come at the hands of LaMotta.

In their rubber match, only three weeks later, Robinson won a hairpin decision that left the crowd booing for the rest of the night. Two more grueling decision wins for Robinson—the last in 1945—left LaMotta financially stable but seething about his nemesis. Worse, LaMotta was no closer to a title shot, despite his status as a crowd-pleaser and wins over Fritzie Zivic, Jose Basora, Bert Lytell, Vic Dellicurti, Coley Welch, Bob Satterfield, and George Costner.

Outside the ring, the concept of impulse control seemed beyond his ken. LaMotta physically abused his first wife, Ida Geller, once knocking her unconscious, and believing that she was dead, contemplated whether to dump her body in the Bronx River. He raped a neighborhood girl who happened to be dating his best friend, Peter Savage (born Petrella), the forgiving future coauthor of *Raging Bull*. To break an onerous contract he had signed upon turning professional, LaMotta hurled his manager, Mike Capriano, headlong down a flight of stairs. He repeatedly beat his second wife, Vikki, a teenage bride on par with Priscilla Presley and Myra Gale Brown; then, in a jealous fit of rage, he battered Savage, whom he wrongly suspected of having an affair with Vikki. There is no telling how many nights LaMotta spent staring into the abyss of his tortured psyche. "I was a mean, vicious, and cruel person," he told the *Boston Globe* in 1985.

In late 1947, LaMotta made the fateful decision that would bring him his greatest joy and his biggest regret. After six years as a professional, with the middleweight championship nowhere in sight, LaMotta finally joined the wiseguys he had disdained for so long. Seeing his childhood partner Rocky Graziano, whose career was firmly in the grip of the mob, win the middleweight title a few months earlier must have stirred up the spleen in LaMotta. He agreed to dump a fight against manufactured light-heavyweight Billy Fox in exchange for a title shot somewhere down the road.

LaMotta may have gone on to bit parts in films and even on stage after his career was over, but against Fox, his performance was unconvincing. In the fourth round, an exasperated LaMotta, conflicted to his bones at disgracing the profession that had given him his only chance at distinction, allowed Fox to batter him at will, until referee Barney Felix stepped in. Years later columnist Arthur Daly recalled the fight for the *New York Times*. "A curious pride kept him vertical," Daly wrote. "He was willing to sink low enough to be a party to a fraud, but not willing to sink to his knees."

Fox, a product of the Blinky Palermo fight factory, had a KO record as fanciful as anything you could find in the Sunday funny pages. He had already been stopped by Gus Lesnevich in a bid for the light-heavyweight title a year earlier and now his handlers had determined that there was still some blood money to be tapped from his veins. In addition to the betting coup the LaMotta fix brought them, Palermo and Co. also cashed in on a second title fight against Gus Lesnevich, who stopped Fox in one gruesome round only four months after the debacle at Madison Square Garden. Fox lost more than he won from that point on, and when his career was over "Blackjack" found himself tragically adrift.

By losing to Fox in such an obvious frame-up LaMotta saw his reputation, hardly unassailable in previous years, hit bottom. "I regretted it most of my life," LaMotta would say years later. "But it happened, and I had a good reason for it. All I wanted to do was become champion. I wanted a shot at the title and I finally did after I did what I did. I think I was wrong. It could have ruined my whole life." He was fined and suspended by the New York State Athletic Commission, which could not find definitive evidence of a fix, but punished LaMotta on the pretext of LaMotta entering the ring with an undisclosed injury.

But La Cosa Nostra kept its word. From the bocce courts and smoky backrooms of social clubs, the dons grudgingly delivered—for a $20,000 fee—a title shot to the lone wolf who for years had bared his fangs whenever the Black Hand had approached it.

On June 16, 1949, LaMotta challenged international luminary Marcel Cerdan for the middleweight championship of the world at Briggs Stadium in Detroit. LaMotta was making his eighty-ninth start and was nearly twenty-seven years old, but nothing was going to keep him from achieving his magnificent obsession. "I wanted to be champ, wanted to be champ," he once said. "Dreamed it, wished it, believed it." LaMotta bullyragged Cerdan from the opening bell and whipsawed both hands relentlessly until the *pied-noir* superstar—long past his best but still no easy mark, even that night at Briggs Stadium—retired on his stool, citing an injured shoulder.

In a photograph taken ring center after the fight, LaMotta, belt strapped around his waist, is surrounded by joyful well-wishers (including Joe Louis and Al Silvani). But "The Bronx Bull" appears seething, disconsolate, and moments away from weeping. "The road to the title," he once wrote, "almost broke my heart."

It did more than that. LaMotta, nearly a hundred fights into his career and practically malnourished prior to every bout from making weight, was finished as a world-class professional. He dropped a nontitle bout to Robert Villemain, went the distance against unheralded Tiberio Mitri, scored a miracle kayo against Laurent Dauthuille with only seconds left in a fight he was losing handily, and was reluctant to defend against his nemesis Sugar Ray Robinson. The public despised him. His personal life remained grim. He no longer dedicated himself to the austere protocols of his trade. Vikki LaMotta summed up the championship afterglow in her memoir, *Knockout!* "Well, he was the champ. Why not have a drink. And then another. Which is death for a fighter. Soon, he was losing the motivation to train. . . . He wasn't hungry anymore. The edge was gone."

Finally, on February 14, 1951, a weathered LaMotta faced Sugar Ray Robinson for the sixth and final time. After a fast start, LaMotta, who had tortured himself to make the 160-pound limit, began to flag in the middle rounds. "By the tenth round, my jab had puffed his fat face and I had hit him with quite a few body shots," Robinson recalled. "His punches had lost their zing, but he stood there, wobbling a little, and defied me to put him down." In the thirteenth, a bloody LaMotta was exhausted and Robinson opened up with a barrage that made even hard-edged aficionados in the cheap seats flinch. The gory TKO loss left LaMotta in ruins. Everything for which LaMotta had worked so hard had vanished overnight. Even so, LaMotta continued fighting, losing consecutive bouts to Bob Murphy and Norman Hayes. In 1952, LaMotta moved to Miami, where mixed results—including a TKO loss to Danny Nardico, which saw "The Bull" knocked down for the first time in his career—led him to retire after less than two years on the sunshine circuit.

When LaMotta opened a nightclub in Miami Beach, his ruinous tendencies took over completely. Every night was a bacchanal: LaMotta drank and ate and fucked until he was in a perpetual stupor. As his prowess had diminished in the ring, his brutishness against Vikki increased. Not even divorce proceedings kept LaMotta from physically abusing her every chance he got. LaMotta, then living out of his office, would periodically visit his ex-wife with violence on his mind. One day he strode into her house and, without a word, began assaulting her. "In the past, he'd held something back when he hit me," she told Thomas Hauser. "This time every punch was calculated to disable and cause pain and the punches kept coming. . . . I still cry when I talk about it because I didn't think anyone was capable of hurting me that badly. There was nothing I could do. I was helpless and the punches kept raining down. The fear set in. I thought Jake might actually kill me."

The high life ended when LaMotta was arrested for "aiding and abetting" prostitution in a case involving a fourteen-year-old girl. LaMotta was found guilty and sentenced to six months in prison, where he alternated time spent on a chain gang with stretches in solitary confinement and a brief stint in a Dade County hospital after mysteriously injuring his back.

In 1958, after completing his sentence, LaMotta returned to New York City and soon made scandalous headlines once again, this time by testifying at the Kefauver hearings. In front of a televised audience, LaMotta confirmed what the crowd at Jacobs Beach had known for years: LaMotta had thrown his fight to Billy Fox in 1947 at the behest of La Cosa Nostra. "I never did like Washington. All these oversized buildings and monuments made me feel like some dumb bug crawling around in a pyramid or something. I guess I was as alone as any one guy could get. The middleweight champion of the world was about to admit to the greatest sin in boxing. What a shit feeling—like going to confession for the first time. I was in a cold sweat." There sat LaMotta, his face misshapen by ring war after ring war—splayed nose, scar tissue like stucco crusting his eyebrows—detailing his part in what amounted to a criminal conspiracy.

Post-Kefauver, LaMotta was an exile from his sport, partly because canaries are despised in the underworld (and boxing, it should be noted, was long a part of gangland culture), and partly because LaMotta had been a vile figure for years. "I'm not trying to whitewash myself," he once told the *Boston Globe*. "I was a thief, I threw a fight, I did two terms in jail and I'm lucky I wasn't a murderer. But those rats who run boxing make me look like Little Lord Fauntleroy."

He labeled himself "LaMotta non grata" and was booed on the rare occasions he attended a prizefight; he was snubbed from a retirement ceremony held at Madison Square Garden for Sugar Robinson in 1966; and, mystifyingly, was not voted into *The Ring* Hall of Fame until 1985, despite defining wins over Robinson, Cerdan, and a slew of 1940s hard cases ranging from welterweight to light heavyweight.

New York in the mid-1960s may have been labeled "Fun City," but, for LaMotta, the Big Apple was rotten to the core. He did not have a steady income; he worked his stand-up routine after hours in dingy go-go bars; played bit parts off-Broadway and in the occasional B-movie; he worked as a bouncer in a strip joint; he was a maintenance man in Central Park. A newshawk caught up with LaMotta during those lean years. "My life now, it's a period I'm going through," LaMotta said. "I been a bouncer here for almost two years. I accept it, I don't feel sorry for myself. Don't forget I been in jail, in a chain gang, was put in a box in a hole in the ground. And I been punched silly. So this place is not terrible. I do my job. They don't want me to sit in a window and advertise myself the way Jack Dempsey does in his restaurant down the street. Because here, they ain't sellin' me, they're sellin' tits."

By his own account, it was Robert De Niro who pulled LaMotta out of the depths. In the late 1970s, LaMotta received the rare second act for a prizefighter when De Niro optioned a memoir LaMotta wrote in tandem with his childhood friend Peter Savage and Joseph Carter. The ensuing biopic, directed by Martin Scorsese and released in 1980, brought LaMotta the afterlife denied to so many boxers, whose retirements inevitably end in anonymity, poverty, and senility. Although Martin Scorsese cared little about boxing, he found a haunting theme worth pursuing in *Raging Bull*. "It's a really straight, simple story, almost linear," Scorsese said, "of a guy attaining something and losing everything, and then redeeming himself." This is one of those oddities with which history has never bothered to wrestle. If LaMotta had indeed redeemed himself, it was because of the film itself, which brought LaMotta out of the T&A scene (and a job as a liquor salesman) of a New York City on the brink of disaster. Even while training De Niro to box, LaMotta was arrested on charges of domestic violence. "I made a couple million fighting, I went through everything," LaMotta told the *Washington Post*. "When De Niro came into my life, I was just managing, paying expenses."

LaMotta ultimately outlasted everyone: his opponents in the ring and beyond it; his ex-wife, Vikki; even his past as an unrepentant brute. Poor Billy Fox, in and out of mental institutions for years, vanished from sight sometime in the 1980s. La Cosa Nostra was decimated by the twin forces of globalism and Rudy Giuliani. The surrealists, who thought of themselves as revolutionaries, soon saw their aesthetic co-opted by department stores, advertising agencies, and Hollywood. Yes, even Sigmund Freud, for years revised downward as a quack or a charlatan, has faded. But maybe LaMotta knew what he had to do to endure: "I hypnotized myself so in my self-conscious I believed I couldn't get hurt. And I don't mean believe, I mean believe believe believe. Like in the animal kingdom, they wanted so much to survive, they change."

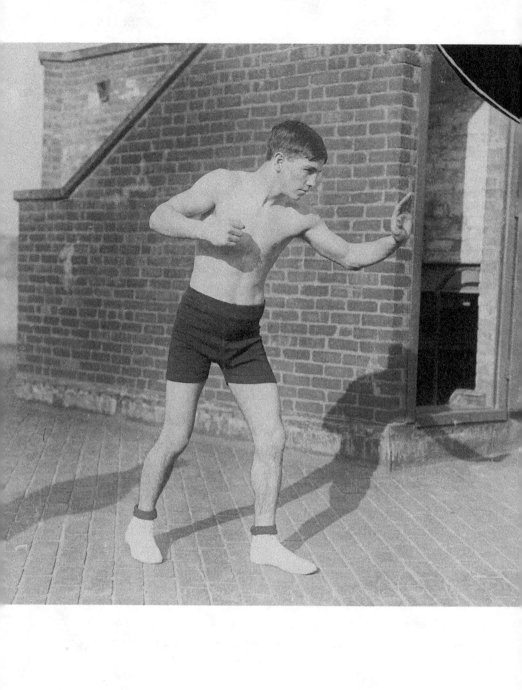

A Young Old Man

AD WOLGAST AND THE REJUVENATOR

I NDIAN MAHARAJAH COMING TO AMERICA TO GET
GOAT GLANDS
—*San Diego Evening Tribune* headline, September 8, 1921, p. 1

◆ ◆ ◆

Like another thunderous product from Cadillac, Michigan, the famous
Shay locomotive, Ad Wolgast tore through the lightweight division for a
few tumultuous years before derailing spectacularly in the kind of tragic
circumstances all too common in prizefighting. If the appeal of boxing
rests on its peculiar ability to dramatize—albeit on a small and unholy
scale—certain bleak cultural touchstones—social Darwinism and the
Nietzschean will to power, for example—then Wolgast can only be exhibit
#1. In his furious life, both in the ring and out, Wolgast resembled nothing
if not a character from a Frank Norris or Stephen Crane novel, natural-
ism personified. Best remembered for his slaughterous free-for-all against
Battling Nelson in 1910, Wolgast also beat several world-class pros from
1908 to 1912, when prizefighting was in its brutal heyday and before his
peak was cut short by the hard logic of the ring.

At sixteen, Wolgast, son of a struggling farmer, left home to eke out a
bootstrap subsistence throughout Michigan. He sold newspapers, shined
shoes, and took on one odd job after another before settling on fisticuffs
as a vocation. In 1907, after compiling a winning record across Grand

Rapids and Petoskey, Wolgast moved to Milwaukee, Wisconsin, where he built a bloody reputation as a relentless brawler with a crippling left hook and a ferocious body attack. Two years later, Wolgast settled in California, the center of the boxing universe after professional fighting had been banned in New York City in 1901.

In Los Angeles, Wolgast raised his profile to a national level with solid showings in a pair of no-decision bouts against Abe Attell and reigning lightweight champion Battling Nelson. If not for the swaggering shadow of Jack Johnson, who dominated headlines from coast to coast, Oscar "Battling" Nelson would have been the most popular fighter of his era. Nelson, who underestimated Wolgast before their first fight in July 1909, sneered at the cocky upstart every chance he got. Finally, seven months after their first encounter, Nelson agreed to meet Wolgast again, this time with the title on the line.

To skirt laws against "fights to the finish," promoter Sid Hester scheduled Nelson–Wolgast for a preposterous forty-five-round limit, knowing full well that the final bell would never ring. What Hester did not know, however, was that Nelson and Wolgast would fight so savagely and for so long. On February 22, 1910, Battling Nelson and Ad Wolgast took what Theodore Roosevelt called "the strenuous life" to grisly extremes in Port Richmond, California. When they met at ring center for final instructions from referee Eddie Smith, Nelson more than justified the nickname "The Abysmal Brute" that Jack London had given him. "Let everything go," he snarled. "No fouls." Never one to shy away from a brouhaha, Wolgast enthusiastically agreed, and the stage was set for one of the most famous bloodlettings in boxing history.

What Wolgast and Nelson produced in Port Richmond, California, was not, in retrospect a sporting event, but a gruesome reminder of how often the line between a blood sport and bloodlust was crossed during an era when mercy was an underdeveloped concept in boxing. As exemplars of rugged individualism, neither man believed in the concept of *sprezzatura*, and toe-to-toe struggles were what they craved for existential affirmation. Anything else would have been bad faith. For Wolgast and Nelson, the ring was a proving ground that transcended athletic mores. It was a way of life and, to them, acted as a correlative to frontier values such as honor and pride.

Both men tore at each other from the opening bell, with Wolgast, six years younger, getting the early edge. After a few rounds under the raw

sun, Nelson, already bleeding from his nose and his mouth, sported purplish lunettes above each cheek. As the fight progressed, his eyes swelled
shut completely, and he found himself tottering on the verge of defeat.
Still, Nelson would not yield. In the twenty-second round, Nelson dropped
Wolgast with a right cross, but Wolgast was as tough as an arrowhead,
and he resumed battering the champion from one end of the ring to the
other. Finally, in the fortieth round, Nelson, nearly blind and splattered
with his own gore, could only paw feebly at the air. Smith finally intervened, hours after the combatants had first touched gloves and long after
the squeamish crowd had called for pity.

"Why say anything else?" Wolgast asked after his struggle against
Nelson. "Just say I am the strongest man ever to put on gloves." Indeed,
Wolgast was strong enough to defend his title at a pace that far outstripped
his predecessor. Among the notable fighters Wolgast faced during his title
reign were Frankie Burns, Joe Mandot, and Owen Moran. His melee against
"Mexican" Joe Rivers on July 4, 1912, was such a spectacular disaster that
it gave Wolgast a *succès de scandale* to go along with his already legendary
title-winning effort against Nelson. Against Rivers, a Los Angeles native,
Wolgast reveled in the ferocity of hand-to-hand combat, what reporter
Lester Bromberg once called his "magnificent obsession." Bruised and
bloody, Wolgast was trailing on points when he cornered Rivers against
the ropes in the thirteenth round. There, the two fighters unleashed simultaneous punches—Rivers a slashing right to the jaw and Wolgast an arcing
left hook below the belt—that sent both men crashing for a double knockdown. With Wolgast on top of Rivers, referee Jack Welsh began tolling
the count, and at some point before reaching ten, he helped Wolgast to his
feet. An outraged crowd, soon primed to rush the ring, watched as Rivers
was counted out for a knockout loss. (In the chaos that followed, Welsh
managed a stealthy escape that would have made a Pinkerton proud.)

To Wolgast, his close call against Rivers was just another example of
his iron will. "Double knockout, hell," he said after the fight. "I was just
too strong for him. Put it in the paper, none of them can take a beating
like Wolgast." But less than six months later, Wolgast was an ex-champion
already making his shaky way to a bleak and black future that lay ahead
of him. On November 28, 1912, he took a terrible beating at the hands of
Willie Mitchell in Daly City, California, before fouling out in the sixteenth
round.

Although Wolgast was still only in his midtwenties, the ultraviolence he demanded between the ropes was beginning to affect him. In those days, boxing was far less charitable than it is now. Referees were less merciful, gloves were smaller, and rounds went far beyond reasonable limits. Little by little Wolgast was disintegrating—both personally and professionally. His brittleness, at odds with a ring style rooted in brutishness, was a dark premonition of his ultimate fate. Over the course of his unruly career, Wolgast had been stricken by appendicitis, ptomaine poisoning, and pneumonia. He broke his wrist, broke his thumb, and suffered fractured ribs as well. Although he was still a box-office attraction—due to his dead-game attitude—the losses began to mount. More than once he broke an arm during a fight. Between 1913 and 1916, Wolgast struggled against one opponent after another. In 1915, Wolgast was pummeled by Leach Cross en route to a TKO defeat in New York City. What made this loss unusual is the fact that Wolgast entered the ring with a black eye and a strip of plaster above his brow. The New York State Athletic Commission suspended Wolgast for six months, ostensibly for being beaten to a pulp before the opening bell.

By 1917, Wolgast was in a Milwaukee psychiatric hospital for what was euphemistically called a "nervous breakdown." In truth, he was already suffering from dementia pugilistica. In and out of institutions for over a year, Wolgast was eventually released from a hospital in 1918. To the dismay of the press, he resumed fighting in the Southwest and California, where he took more punishment from an assortment of second-raters. Eventually, Wolgast would need medical care, but the kind of treatment he received would wind up in a "stranger than fiction" file.

After World War I, when the blood-drenched trenches of Verdun, Passchendaele, and Warlencourt familiarized the globe with both shell shock and mass mechanized slaughter, America, naturally, turned to whoopee in response. Indeed, even with Prohibition looming over the country, the nascent Jazz Age introduced the fox-trot and hedonism as national pastimes. And all that adolescent vigor produced an unusual cultural by-product: the new cottage industry of rejuvenation as peddled by numberless quacks. Old medicine-show standbys such as swamp root, snake oil, and sarsaparilla were joined by miracles such as Worm Candy, Pepsin, and Vim-O-Gen. These mock remedies, sold as cure-alls for everything from fatigue to impotence, often contained liquor, cocaine, and laudanum. They may not have had much medicinal value, but they certainly packed a wallop.

While the American Medical Association was still in the midst of professionalizing healthcare through state licensing boards and a public crackdown on charlatans, rogue doctors (often with degrees purchased from diploma mills) continued hawking magic powders and elixirs anywhere from gleaming office suites to the backs of covered wagons. In 1905, "The Great American Fraud," a series of articles by prominent muckraker Samuel Adams Hopkins, exposed the sham snake-oil enterprise—a peculiar free-market success even in the lauded land of opportunity. "Gullible America will spend this year some seventy-five million dollars in the purchase of patent medicines. In consideration of this sum it will swallow huge quantities of alcohol, an appalling amount of opiates and narcotics, a wide assortment of varied drugs ranging from powerful and dangerous heart depressants to insidious liver stimulants; and, far in excess of other ingredients, undiluted fraud."

Then, like something out of *The Island of Dr. Moreau*, animal transplants via tissue grafts suddenly became part of rejuvenation mania. Already something of a story in Europe, where French surgeon Serge Voronoff had been experimenting with monkeys, the bizarre act of surgically inserting animal glands into scrotums promised to reverse aging and give men new life in the bedroom. In America, the most famous fraud of all was Dr. John Brinkley, who wisely swapped monkeys—exotic animals to most—with goats, a common presence on farms across the country. Brinkley, a dedicated con man who began his bunco career in a traveling show before becoming an "electric medic," triggered an entire subindustry of goat-gland peddlers at the dawn of the flapper era. Seemingly overnight, rejuvenation clinics opened in one city after another.

Wolgast, only thirty-two in 1920, was now a physical wreck and as desperate as any septuagenarian hoping to recapture his libido. So he did what so many easy marks had done since the rejuvenation fad began a few years earlier: He went to see "The Goat Man." In June 1920, Wolgast underwent surgery in a Los Angles clinic. His "doctor," P. Livingstone Barnes, pronounced the operation a success. "Wolgast has been completely restored to health," he said. "He is normal now and his muscles are in excellent condition. . . . His memory, once shattered so that he could not remember names, dates, places, or conversations, is again normal and I see no reason why Wolgast cannot come back."

Even for such a permissive age, the fact that Wolgast could fight again after having been institutionalized was astonishing. But Wolgast insisted his comeback would be different. After all, he had modern science in his corner. "I am no longer an old young man," Wolgast announced, "and since this operation, I have the physique and qualities of one in his early twenties."

On September 6, 1920, only a few months after his operation, Wolgast took part in his last fight, a desultory draw against Lee Morrissey in San Bernardino, California. "The crowd booed the one-time champion and he left the ring almost in tears," reported the *San Diego Evening Tribune*. "He refused to comment at the end of the bout whether he still favors goat glands."

Wolgast, whose record stands at 60-13-17, with dozens of no-decision bouts, never fought again. Now a shambling mess, he was taken in by Jack Doyle, a friendly promoter who allowed Wolgast to live on his compound and train, in his own delusional way, in his gym. A few years later, however, Wolgast was so far gone that Doyle had him committed to Patton State Hospital in San Bernardino. From 1927 to his death nearly thirty years later, Wolgast was confined in a succession of institutions and was largely forgotten.

Almost fittingly, violence brought Wolgast back into the headlines in 1949, when two sadistic employees of Stockton State Hospital assaulted the "Michigan Wildcat." It was like something out of a Hollywood noir—Wolgast, enfeebled, scrawny, and now in his sixties, abused by sinister orderlies. The beating Wolgast took left him hospitalized, then bedridden for the remaining years of his life. No longer would he shadowbox in the hospital corridors, where he had continued "training" in a haze for a phantom bout with his greatest nemesis—Battling Nelson. When he finally died, on April 14, 1955, it must have been a mercy, one of the few a man as proud as Wolgast was likely to accept. Oh, yes, it must have been a mercy.

The Lightning Within

TONY AYALA JR.

"I t's a fucked-up world, but it's all I've got."
—Jack Henry Abbott

◆ ◆ ◆

Tony Ayala Jr., was only a teenager when he quickened one pulse after another in living rooms and grimy gyms across the country in the early 1980s. For the average fan sunk in an overstuffed couch knocking back a Pabst or Budweiser, Ayala was a ferocious competitor looking to win at all costs. For those with an IBM Selectric, WordStar, or even a Commodore 64, Ayala represented the dark side of boxing, one that has its own twisted appeal: the blurring of margins between blood sport and bloodlust.

◆ ◆ ◆

For a time in the mid-1970s, the Ayalas were San Antonio boxing. Mike, Sammy, and Tony all won National Golden Gloves titles. But Tony Ayala Sr. went beyond the stereotype of the strict disciplinarian. He pulled his children out of school to concentrate on uppercuts and hooks. To hell with textbooks, to hell with science, history, biography—the Ayalas were homeschooled in violence and machismo. "Dad might squeeze my thigh or Sammy's or Mike's and say, 'willpower,' and see how much pain we could take," Tony Ayala Jr., told Phil Berger of the *New York Times*. "Once he lined us up and gave us each a bite of raw jalapeno pepper to see if we were man enough to stand the burning it caused in our mouths. Mike ran to the bathroom but me and Sammy stayed the course. The thing about my father, though, is he wouldn't ask us to do anything he wouldn't do first. He'd eat jalapeno pepper before making us try it. And same with the pinching. He'd have us pinch him hard as we could. 'See that,' he'd say. 'Now it's your turn. Men don't cry. Willpower. Willpower.'"

◆ ◆ ◆

Ayala Sr., berated his sons, lashed them occasionally with jump ropes, drove them from tournament to tournament across the parched state in a weathered station wagon, under the broiling Texas sun. He was the dour, domineering patriarch of a family raised in poverty in a San Antonio neighborhood called "Browntown"; he was a hard-bitten ex-Marine born during the Great Depression, a man forever estranged from fighters, friends, and family. In the end, none of his world champions would bear the name Ayala. There was Jesse Benavides, Gaby Canizales, and John Michael Johnson.

◆ ◆ ◆

"One time my oldest son said, 'Where were you when all these things began?' My wife and I sat down. When you don't have an education, and your income is low and you have to pay the rent and you've got kids, you hold many jobs. I washed cars, changed tires, worked in restaurants. I used to go to the farms and buy fresh eggs and sell them out of my pickup on the West Side. I was always working. That's where I was. I wish I could have brought them up in a better neighborhood. I used to go to the city council and plead with them. But it wasn't until rich kids on the North Side started using drugs that they got excited. Then we had a war on drugs."
—Tony Ayala Sr., quoted in *Texas Monthly*

◆ ◆ ◆

He never looked young. There was the moustache, the thick sideburns, the already-receding hairline. Then, of course, there was the hard look in his eyes, disarming for someone who should have been thinking about his prom night or a summer job stocking shelves. He had already seen too much. He had already done too much.

◆ ◆ ◆

Ayala was as precocious as he was vicious. At fourteen he reportedly pushed feared José "Pipino" Cuevas to the brink during a sparring session. At sixteen, he was a National Golden Gloves champion. At seventeen, he was featured in the *New York Times*. At eighteen, Ayala merited a *Sports Illustrated* profile. And then there was the accelerated dark side, adult vices in a boy who still ate Alpha-Bits or Trix cereal. At thirteen, he began drinking, smoking weed, and shooting up heroin. He was already on his way as a scofflaw: a slew of traffic tickets at an age when Huffy bikes are the norm. He is fifteen when he commits his first assault. In the restroom of a drive-in movie theater he attacked an eighteen-year-old college student. Ayala battered her in a rape attempt so violent it left his victim with a ruptured bladder. He avoided prison by paying $40,000 in restitution to a woman whose medical bills were staggering. Then came a break-in, when Ayala claimed he was drunk and had entered the wrong house. In fact, Ayala had slipped into this home, via an open window, to find more prey for his dark hunger. Although the charges were dropped against him (after another payment), Ayala was forced to enter rehab or face revocation of his probation. At the Care Unit Hospital in Orange, California, Ayala continued to drink and mainline: detox is no match for "Torito." After nearly a month in California, Ayala moved to West Paterson, New Jersey, in hopes of leaving his past behind.

◆ ◆ ◆

"For the second time in twenty-four hours, shotgun blasts struck the vacant home of Tony Ayala Jr. Ayala, the undefeated junior-middleweight fighter who is scheduled to begin treatment Wednesday in California for emotional and drinking problems, was not home early Monday nor shortly before midnight Monday when neighbors reported buckshot being fired at his house."

—The Associated Press

◆ ◆ ◆

"At seven or eight or nine, I was the victim of another person's sickness. It lasted a year or two. I spent many years denying and chasing it away. I can't give you a lot of details. I know who the person was and what he did. Most of the details I chased out of my mind. I guess it was my way of surviving those years. As a child, I blamed myself for what happened. What happened to me, I thought, happened because I was bad and ugly, not man enough. That mentality grew as I grew older."
—Tony Ayala Jr., to *Boxing Illustrated*

◆ ◆ ◆

His only opportunities for glory in the ring appear and disappear almost simultaneously. In 1982, Roberto Durán loses a tune-up bout before he is scheduled to fight Ayala. At the time Durán drops a decision to British import Kirkland Laing, Ayala is in a rehab facility, drinking and doping his way through counseling. Then a $750,000 payday to challenge Davey Moore for the WBA junior-middleweight title slips through his grasp when he rapes and terrorizes a schoolteacher on January 1, 1983.

◆ ◆ ◆

"The circumstances of this crime are certainly one of extreme violence and depravity. Mr. Ayala is a definite threat to society and especially the women in our society."
—Judge Amos C. Saunders

◆ ◆ ◆

In seeing his career cut short before he was twenty years old, Ayala becomes a myth. According to some, he was on his way to steamrolling Sugar Ray Leonard, Thomas Hearns, Durán, and Marvin Hagler. But the truth is Ayala was on the Lou Duva plan, the same one Bobby Czyz was on: he preyed on the frail, the pale, the sometimes quailing. His best win was a TKO over Steve Gregory. Duva was an uncanny matchmaker, overpaying mediocre alphabet-soup contenders to move his fighters into position for mandatory challenges. But Ayala mauled his opponents with an uncommon ferocity that recalls Durán at his peak. He spit on Jose Luis Baltazar after scoring a knockdown. Against Robbie Epps, Ayala kept punching after the referee had already stopped the fight. Knocked down by Mario Maldonado, Ayala, like Aaron Pryor, shouted at his opponent, returned fire after beating the count, and won by kayo a few rounds later. He was a fearsome body puncher with a natural left hook and thudding power. He forced a frenetic pace in the ring and rarely decelerated. What separated Ayala from the average pressure fighter, however, was a knack for slipping punches on the way in. This "Torito," who was elusive at times, occasionally played the matador.

◆ ◆ ◆

On August 20, 1999, Ayala returned to the ring after sixteen years in prison. The Freeman Coliseum was sold out. Pay-per-view sales were brisk. Ayala earned $200,000. Less than a year later, he was stopped by veteran Yori Boy Campas after eight rounds of brutal hand-to-hand combat. Ayala, distraught, cried out "I'm sorry! I'm sorry!" while on his stool. In a few months he would be shot by a young woman whose house he invaded. Incredibly, he received probation for his latest infraction. But Ayala was condemned to a freedom he could not endure. In 2004, Ayala, after several infractions, was sentenced to prison for violating his probation. For ten years he denied interview requests. Not long after his father died, in 2014, Ayala was released and headed back to the Zarzamora Gym, back to San Antonio, back to where the beginning of the end began.

◆ ◆ ◆

"Like God. I would imagine it's the closest thing to being like God—to control somebody else. I hit a guy and it's like, I can do anything I want to you. I own you. Your life is mine, and I will do with it what I please. It's a really sadistic mentality, but that's what goes on in my mind. It's really evil—there's no other way to put it. You have these other fighters, and they'll never admit to that: 'Oh it's a sport and I'm just trying to win my fight.' Well you're winning at the expense of somebody else's health.

You're trying to beat this person into submission. It's the only way I know how; I step into that dark most evil part of me and I physically destroy somebody else, and I will do with them what I want."
—Tony Ayala, to John Albert

◆ ◆ ◆

In the ring, Ayala was hemmed in by the ropes. For more than half his life, he was trapped behind bars. The rest of the time? He was locked inside himself. There was no other place in this world for Ayala, it seems, but a boxing ring, a cellblock, a mahogany box. Ayala went from the Freeman Coliseum and Caesars Palace and the Convention Hall in Atlantic City to one bleak institution after another: Bayside State Prison, Passaic County Jail, Trenton State Penitentiary, Rahway, Sanders Estes Unit. Finally, the M.E. Rodriguez Funeral Home on Guadalupe Street in downtown San Antonio.

◆ ◆ ◆

On May 12, 2015, Ayala died of a heroin overdose. He was found dead at the Zarzamora Street Gym, where he began his shocking comeback in 1999.

◆ ◆ ◆

"After I fought, I always spent a lot of money. I'd go through five grand in four or five days. I'd go the week burnt out, and my dad would find me and take me home. I would dry out, then fight; and the process would be repeated. I was feeling very guilty. I felt like a real sneak. If they only knew. You start to live with guilt, and it starts catching up to you. People have no idea of what it was like. I stuck the barrel of a gun in my mouth. My wife had left me. I was playing with a loaded .22 with a full clip. Just stuck it in my mouth. Some people will be sad I didn't do it."
—Tony Ayala Jr., to Arlene Schulman

◆ ◆ ◆

"You shall live by inflicting pain." Mark Strand.

◆ ◆ ◆

Even as a child, I knew you were going to fight at the Armory, along with Davey Moore and Alex Ramos, only a few blocks away from where I lived. My uncle mentioned that one day. The following year, my father took me by the hand to cross the Grand Concourse and then down Kingsbridge to stop at the newsstand on Creston, where the racks popped out like beacons even with the sun blinding overhead. Starlog, Circus, Ellery Queen, Cinefex, Omni, Fangoria. *Then* KO, Boxing Scene, The Ring. *That day, it was you on the cover before your newest sin. A dollar fifty, a dollar seventy-five, maybe, to learn, appalled, all about the lightning within.*

No Exit

THE STORY OF EDDIE MACHEN

Perhaps he crossed the path of a black cat once too often or was given to recklessly overturning saltshakers. Whatever he did, Eddie Machen, a top heavyweight in the late 1950s and early 1960s, was the personification of bad luck in a business—prizefighting—where bad luck is an accepted occupational hazard. A naturally gifted boxer, Machen had a habit of bringing more than just his gloves into the ring; he also dragged with him the kind of bad juju common to characters in a Cornell Woolrich novel or a particularly bleak film noir.

Eddie Machen was born in Redding, California, on July 15, 1932. During the midst of the Depression, Redding was an anomaly: a boomtown—or at least as close as you could get to one in those lean days. The construction of the Shasta Dam, which began in 1938, nearly doubled the population of Redding and brought in its wake a blue-collar workforce as well as the rough-and-tumble atmosphere typical of hard laborers during difficult times. Machen was one of six children. His father was a mail carrier and his mother was a housewife. Somehow lower-middle-class prosperity did not appeal to Machen; he soon dropped out of high school to pursue other interests: among them boxing and its ugly stepsister, trouble. His amateur career lasted all of three fights before he was arrested for armed robbery in 1952. Machen spent three years in prison. "I went in as a kid," he told the *Saturday Evening Post*. "I came out grown up, determined never to be jailed again."

After being released from prison in 1955, Machen fought ten times for Lee Hughes before hooking up with San Francisco fight manager Syd Flaherty (who by then had Carl "Bobo" Olson under his wing) and setting off on one of the most perplexing heavyweight careers in boxing history.

With power in both hands but a strange reluctance to use it, Machen employed his superb defensive skills to fluster opponents and spectators alike. "Cautious Eddie," as he was known, defeated several tough customers on the way to a 24-0 record, including Nino Valdes, Johnny Summerlin, Howard King, Bob Baker, John Holman, Tommy "Hurricane" Jackson, and weathered ex-light-heavyweight champion Joey Maxim. Poor Valdes needed smelling salts after Machen was through with him, and Jackson took such a beating that he was never the same again. After little more than a year as pro, Machen was already a top contender generating significant buzz.

In April 1958, Machen struggled to a draw with skittish jab artist and top contender Zora Folley. This fight, dull enough to ward off fans for the rematch two years later, was an early sign that for all of his natural talent, something in Machen was missing. But it was his disaster against Ingemar Johansson in September 1958 that seemed to define the rest of his up-and-down career. A crowd of more than fifty-five thousand watched as Johansson dropped Machen three times in the opening round to score an effortless stoppage. The right hand that initially capsized Machen was uncorked with such quickness as to seem nearly invisible. But its force was undeniable. "Later," Machen told the *Los Angeles Times*, "I studied the films, looking for my mistakes. I ran it time after time, but it was just a case of getting nailed right on the chin." The second knockdown was just as heavy as the first, and Machen rose like a man with vertigo. With less than a minute to go in the round, Machen was battered to the canvas and out onto the ring apron in his own corner, where his seconds rushed in to halt the slaughter. In a surreal image—and one that is a stark reminder of the clinical brutality of boxing—referee Andrew Smyth continued the ten-count while Machen was being frantically aided by his cornermen.

Before his loss to Johansson, Machen was unquestionably avoided by reigning champion Floyd Patterson. As Arthur Daley put it, "In 1958, the super-cautious Cus D'Amato, the proprietor of Patterson, kept ducking Machen just as he ducked most of the top heavyweights, charging they were all under the sinister control of the forces of evil." While D'Amato seethed against the wickedness of man from rickety soapboxes, the heavyweight championship went through the ignominy of having Pete Rademacher and Tom McNeely contest it in spectacles closer to pratfall conventions than prizefights. In his never-ending jihad against unholy forces in boxing, D'Amato frothed over Sid Flaherty, who, like most fight managers, maintained a working relationship with Jim Norris and the IBC. This flaw, one that brings to mind the poor in medieval Europe accused of witchcraft due to an unsightly mole or an affinity for cats, was enough to demonize Machen.

Behind all of his righteous bluster, D'Amato was merely trying to protect his fragile champion, whose chin made tin resemble titanium. In eleven Patterson title fights from 1956 to 1963, over forty knockdowns were scored, with Patterson suffering at least fifteen of them. Years later, Patterson, the most dignified of fighters, was embarrassed at being protected, and when the world demanded that he face Sonny Liston, Patterson insisted that the fight be made. Public demand, unfortunately, never reached those heights for Machen. (In 1964 Machen finally got to meet Patterson, but by then both fighters had seen better days. Machen lost a tepid twelve-round decision to the former two-time champion in Sweden.)

After seven easy comeback wins, Machen seemingly put the Johansson catastrophe behind him and signed to face Zora Folley again on January 18, 1960, in San Francisco. He was outboxed by Folley in their dreary rematch, and as if to underscore just how hard hard luck can be, the fight was a financial bloodbath for Machen as well. In the end, Machen, who was to pay Folley $15,000 out of his own purse, wound up $270 in the hole that night and did even further damage to his reputation with an uninspired performance. "Referee Vern Bybee," reported the *New York Times*, "proved to be the busiest man in the ring last night. . . ."

On September 7, 1960, Machen got another shot at the big time when he faced Liston in a nationally televised bout from Seattle. Machen looked dreadful dropping a twelve-round decision against "Night Train," then considered the uncrowned heavyweight champion of the world. "Machen simply would not fight," wrote Harry Sanford. "Instead, he got on his bicycle and ran for twelve rounds, save when he would tackle, grab, hold, shove, and pull at Liston, who stalked him all the while, trying to land the big punch, a punch that did not come." After the fight, Machen revealed that he had injured his right arm sparring against Willi Besmanoff and that he fought Liston at a serious disadvantage. Like most fighters who enter the ring injured, Machen needed the money. "With two hands I can take him," he said ruefully. Once again, "Cautious Eddie" had come up short in an important bout.

Less than a year after the Liston fight, Machen was outpointed by crafty NBA light-heavyweight champion Harold Johnson in Atlantic City. From then on Machen became more inconsistent. Once in a while he would still spring an upset (as in his impressive decision over undefeated Doug Jones) or post a solid win (as in his destructive knockout of Mike DeJohn), but he was fighting less frequently, and soon money would become an increasing worry. "It got so bad I took a job as a bouncer in a night club," Machen told the *Saturday Evening Post*. "The Number One challenger shouldn't have to hold down a job. That's for when you're on the way up. And it's just asking for trouble—all those guys with a few belts in them thinking you don't look so tough." He seemed uninspired fighting to a stalemate with Cleveland Williams in July 1962, and once again drew criticism for his performance. Despite his spotty results, however, Machen was named number-one contender the following October. But he would never get a chance at the title. In fact, it would be over a year before Machen fought again.

Over the years Machen struggled variously with the ups and downs of prizefighting, as well as with marital difficulties, alcohol, lawsuits, and depression. Soon he began to give beneath the strain. On December 12, 1962, Machen was discovered sitting in his car on the shoulder of the Cummings Skyway by a police officer. The despondent fighter had a gun and a suicide note in the vehicle with him; presumably, he intended to put both to use. Machen was arrested and taken to the psychiatric ward of Napa State Hospital. His wife told the Associated Press that Machen "had been disturbed over money matters and failure to get a fight. He was trying very hard to get a fight with anyone. Fighting was his profession and he wanted to work at it. He was worried about family finances."

Over the next few days, Machen made headlines for his harrowing behavior in the psychiatric ward—twice attacking hospital staff and having to be restrained by tranquilizers and straitjackets. After a brawl with seven hospital attendants, Machen was declared "schizophrenic." Machen spent the holidays at Napa State Hospital, and after showing improvement was transferred to a private clinic at the request of his family. Within a few weeks, he was discharged.

Incredibly, and unlike his institutionalized contemporaries Johnny Bratton and Johnny Saxton, Machen returned to the ring on September 16, 1963, less than a year after being committed, and scored a sixth-round knockout over Ollie Wilson. He did not, however, return to the ring with what might be considered a rosy outlook. "What do I have to show," he lamented, "for all my years as a ranking heavyweight? Nothing."

Three more tune-ups followed the Wilson fight before his disappointing flop against Patterson in Sweden. At thirty-two, with nine years of adversity behind him, Machen could have been forgiven for thinking that his chances at a world championship were gone and with them his days as a topflight heavyweight. But if the topsy-turvy world of prizefighting specializes in anything, it is Absurdity, with a capital "A." When Muhammad Ali was stripped of the WBA portion of his heavyweight title for facing Sonny Liston in an immediate rematch, Machen was paired off against contender Ernie Terrell to fill the "vacancy." After years of unsuccessfully toiling for a shot at the title, Machen suddenly found himself ironically being handed one for a fugazi belt no one would respect. Still, it was an opportunity for a paycheck and the possibility for bigger fights down the line. Unfortunately, "carpe diem" was not a concept Machen ever seemed to fully grasp. He underperformed on the big stage yet again, losing an eyesore of a decision to Terrell on March 5, 1965, in Chicago. "It was difficult for the spectators to stay awake," wrote Lew Eskin in *Boxing Illustrated*.

By now it was clear that Machen would never live up to his potential. It was also clear that strange things would never stop happening to him. After the debacle with Terrell, Machen went on to lose on points to Karl Mildenberger in Germany, in a match where referee Gerhard Seewald was replaced in the seventh round for incompetence and, more likely, favoritism. The contest itself was described by the *Chicago Tribune* as "a slow, dull fight," and Machen returned to America further dispirited.

As if fed up by his own tedious fights, Machen soon turned in some exciting—if uneven—performances in Los Angeles, uncharacteristically brawling with Manuel Ramos, Joey Orbillo, and George "Scrap Iron" Johnson. His most notable fight—and most impressive victory—during this strange fit of temper was a bruising split-decision nod over a twenty-year-old steamroller named Jerry Quarry. But after being shredded by a young Joe Frazier in ten rounds in November 1966, a declining

Machen became little more than a stepping-stone, losing his last two fights to Henry Clark and undefeated Boone Kirkman. Machen announced his retirement after being stopped by Kirkman. His final career record was 50-11-3.

After retiring from boxing, Machen, who had declared bankruptcy in 1966, worked as a bartender and a truck driver before settling as a longshoreman. He also began behaving erratically again. In 1966 he was arrested for a drunken café brouhaha and once more in 1968 for a roadside brawl with a policeman who needed mace to subdue the former heavyweight contender. Financially unstable, newly divorced, bitter at his fortunes (or, better said, misfortunes) in the ring, without the fame prize-fighting brought him, Machen found himself battling depression once more and turned to psychiatrists for help.

On August 8, 1972, Machen was found dead, in his pajamas, after falling from his window in the Mission District of San Francisco. Whatever hex he suffered from persisted until his last moments: Machen lived on the second floor, and where most might suffer broken limbs, fractures, or concussions from a two-story drop, the former number-one heavyweight contender died from a ruptured liver. There has always been an air of mystery surrounding the actual circumstances of his death—was it suicide or an accident? His girlfriend at the time, Sherry Tomasini, told officials that the troubled ex-boxer was prone to sleepwalking. Machen suffered from insomnia, a common by-product of depression, and often took pills to help him sleep.

It is hard to imagine anyone thinking a fall from a second-story window would prove fatal; perhaps Machen was performing some sort of subconscious wish fulfillment when he stepped into oblivion that night. Perhaps he felt he had nowhere to go. "I was a fighter for almost 13 years," he once said. "It was hard for me to walk into something else after all that time." Machen was forty years old when he died.

One Long Season in Hell

ON MICHAEL DOKES

ow he always believed—what madness—that cheat who
said: "Tomorrow. You have plenty of time."
—Cavafy

◆ ◆ ◆

Once, during his prime, he would toss red roses to the women seated
at ringside for his fights. But that was another lifetime ago. Michael
"Dynamite" Dokes was light-years removed from those carefree days
when he died of liver cancer at a hospice in Summit County, Ohio, on
August 12, 2012. Dokes was fifty-four years old, a short-lived champion,
and a charter member of "The Lost Generation" of 1980s heavyweights,
a grim cast of characters marked by misfortune and tragedy.

For years, Dokes lived a life as bleak and as dark as a late Goya, *Saturn
Devouring His Son*, perhaps, or *The Fates*. Like all fighters, however,
Dokes had simple dreams that would never come true. "There are many
things that I would like to do in my life," Dokes told *Boxing Today* in
1982. "I'm very interested in real estate and the stock market. I enjoy
designing clothes. I have a whole life ahead of me. I plan on spending two
or three years as the heavyweight champion of the world. After that, I can
pass it on with dignity and continue living and growing as an individual."
Such small wants, and yet, they were impossible.

Michael Dokes was born on August 10, 1958, in Akron, Ohio. A gifted all-around athlete, Dokes played football and basketball and ran track. But what he really excelled at was boxing, and Akron followed his every move as a teenage prodigy. How talented was Dokes? As an amateur, he won a National AAU title and a National Golden Gloves title. At fifteen, he was sassing Muhammad Ali. At seventeen, he had to settle for a silver medal at the Pan American Games when he lost a decision to Olympic legend Teófilo Stevenson. Even before he gloved up against Stevenson, Dokes had already been featured in *Sports Illustrated*. By the time he turned pro in 1976 (a second-round KO over Al Byrd in Hollywood, Florida), Dokes was considered a future star.

But it took six years for Dokes to land a title shot. "It seems like I've been fighting forever," Dokes said in 1982. "I'm not impatient. I just know that I'm ready right now." Lost among the disastrous heavyweight stable of promoter Don King, Dokes ran his record up to 25-0-1 but remained in limbo until he became the mandatory contender to a journeyman champion named Mike Weaver.

On December 10, 1982, Dokes scored a knockdown within thirty seconds of the opening bell and stopped Weaver in just over a minute to capture the WBA title in Las Vegas. But the biggest win of his career was overshadowed by the panicky actions of referee Joey Curtis, who stopped the fight before it ever really got started. After a scrum between corners—and with an enraged crowd at Caesars Palace chanting "Bullshit! Bullshit!" and "Don King sucks! Don King sucks!"—Dokes left the ring without even being announced champion. Weaver insisted the whole affair was a fix, and the press sniffed out skulduggery in every possible corner. No matter. Dokes soaked himself in a bathtub full of champagne after his victory party, prefiguring the excess that would eventually ruin his career. Years later, Dokes would estimate that his bubbly bath had cost around $20,000.

There is no jet set as low-rent as the prizefight jet set, and Dokes was soon off on one merrymaking junket after another, surrounded by the leeches that would eventually drain his blood and end up sucking at the marrow. "Once you get into that life and get that kind of money . . ." Dokes haltingly explained to the *Akron Beacon Journal* in 2010. ". . . last night we were talking about the people we were around—the toughest gangsters, the biggest entrepreneurs. It was probably more than we probably should have been biting on at the time, but I was just caught up in it."

In boxing, the enemies of promise are numerous: entourages, managers, promoters, injuries, other fighters. But self-destruction ranks up there with the best of the worst, and Michael Dokes had a talent for dissipation second to none. Soon, Dokes began to look sluggish in the ring as well as outside of it. His downfall was reminiscent of how Mike Campbell in Ernest Hemingway's *The Sun Also Rises* described going bankrupt: "Gradually, then suddenly."

As partial heavyweight champion (alongside the far more established Larry Holmes), Dokes had an undistinguished title reign even by the low standards of the "greed is good" decade. And Dokes began to realize it as much as anybody. "I had attained the most coveted prize in boxing, yet I still was not happy," he told *Newsday* reporter Wallace Matthews in 1989. "I thought everything would be great, but there was nothing but dissension and jealousy in my own camp. I was so let down, so hurt. At that point, I said, 'I'll fix everybody.' I started to escape by the use of drugs. Before I knew it, it became the number-one priority in my life."

A rematch against Weaver ended in a draw, and on September 23, 1983, Dokes was flattened before a sparse hometown crowd in Richfield, Ohio, by Gerrie Coetzee. Dokes never had a chance. He entered the ring at the Richfield Coliseum cross-eyed on cocaine. Coetzee, whose brittle right hand had undergone surgery more than a dozen times, made his limitations count against a zombified Dokes, scoring a KO in the tenth round. With "Dynamite" still out of sorts on the canvas, Don King ducked through the ropes, stepped over a woozy Dokes, and led the congratulatory charge for the new champion, the first white heavyweight titleholder since the days of Ingemar Johansson. Even in his fifties, King was a spry, spry man.

And just how did King—ex-numbers-runner, showman extraordinaire, two-time murderer, and master of the malapropism—affect Dokes? In the early 1980s, the electro-haired promoter had a virtual lock on the heavyweight division as well, it seems, as the souls of the men whose careers he moved at whim on a sinister chessboard of his own design. "Don King hurt me," Dokes once confided to Jack Newfield. "One time I went to Cleveland to ask Don for some money when I was in a jam with the IRS. He said he didn't have any money and I started to cry. I loved that man. I looked up to him like he was my daddy. I even tried to comb my hair so I could look like him. And he had this big mansion, and millions of dollars, and he wouldn't help me out just a little. I became suicidal, close to a nervous breakdown. And I was still doing drugs all the time."

But Dokes was not the only heavyweight who found himself drawn and trapped by a master manipulator whose business sense had been honed by a lifetime of hustling. With the exception of Larry Holmes, no one got away from the dark side King seemed to represent. From Dokes to Trevor Berbick to Pinklon Thomas to Tony Tubbs to Jeff Sims to James "Bonecrusher" Smith to Tim Witherspoon to Greg Page to James Broad to Mike Tyson—all of them sent spiraling into drugs or prison or murder or obesity or injury or privation. Like some sort of creepy fairy tale, King even imprisoned his fighters on a compound in Ohio. "Oh, man, did I hate that training camp," former two-time heavyweight titleholder Tim Witherspoon told Jack Newfield. "Being there was like being back in the ghetto. The mentality put most of the fighters back into a not caring situation. The fighters didn't have money. There wasn't a hundred dollars between us. We knew Don was charging us for staying there. The morale was real low. There was drugs floating all around the camp. It was just like being back in Philly. . . . That camp messed us all up. That's where we became the lost generation of heavyweights, that's what I call us."

This is how Richard Hoffer once described the 1980s heavyweight scene as controlled by King: "Such a monopoly, and that's what it was, guaranteed him the most important title in boxing, no matter who won or lost. There was little anxiety on his part, watching one King fighter batter another. Who really cared who won or lost? Sadly, as it turned out, not even his stable of fighters cared very much; as a group they had become so demoralized over their enslavement that defeat, and the possibility of freedom, had actually become cause for celebration in some cases."

But losing to Coetzee sent Dokes headlong into oblivion. From 1984 to late 1987, Dokes spent more time in prison, rehab centers, and on police blotters than in the ring. Dokes swapped abbreviations like NABF and WBA for SWAT and AA. Cocaine was his lodestar. Alcohol, women, parties, and marijuana also guided Dokes through a permanent American midnight. He used so much dope that he was once charged with trafficking.

In 1987, a SWAT team crashed his Las Vegas home expecting to find a kingpin like Frank Lucas or Nicky Barnes inside and an arsenal to match.

Instead, they found Dokes, a one-man gang of personal use. "I just poured it out until I thought it was enough," Dokes told Wallace Matthews. "If you could picture buying a bag of flour, putting a piece of paper on the floor, and just pouring it out until you had what you thought was enough, that's what I did. I didn't scale it out, I didn't measure it out or nothing. I just started pouring." It was one of several misunderstandings Dokes would have with the law during the mid-1980s, before his comeback, before his last pathetic shot at the heavyweight title, before he almost beat his girlfriend to death and paid for it by spending nearly a decade behind bars.

F. Scott Fitzgerald once wrote, "There are no second acts in American lives," and boxing tries its damnedest to make sure that sentiment is true ninety-five percent of the time. Incredibly, Michael Dokes almost made the five percent bracket when his comeback, begun in late 1987 after a forty-seven-day stretch in the Clark County Detention Center, led to a high-profile fight with Evander Holyfield in 1989. Holyfield, undefeated and only eighteen months from winning the undisputed heavyweight championship of the world, was all that stood in the way of Dokes and the kind of redemption all too rare in boxing.

On March 11, 1989, Holyfield and Dokes savaged each other in a minor classic at Caesars Palace. In preparing for his biggest challenge in years, Dokes had flayed his war-torn body to its absolute peak for one last chance at an honest future. Once a nimble dancer in the ring, Dokes had lost his legs by the time he faced Holyfield, but he still had his hand speed, those blistering combinations, and a raging desire to win. "I was willing to put out whatever it took to overcome," Dokes said after the fight. "It was disheartening to see it slip away from me."

It was the best performance of his career, but Dokes was simply not fresh enough to beat Holyfield. Although only four years separated them, it might as well have been a generation for Dokes, who was thirty at the time but had long ago yielded his natural gifts to the night.

"There were moments during their heavyweight bout last Saturday night in Las Vegas when Evander Holyfield and Michael Dokes looked like two men trying to knock down mountains," wrote Pat Putnam for *Sports Illustrated*. Dokes ripped shots to the body, doubled his left hook, and forced Holyfield to trade in close. But Holyfield responded with just as much fury, and Dokes seemed to be slowing down with each passing second of barbarism under the lights. Holyfield fought through so much pain, he later admitted, that he had begun to doubt his calling as an athlete midfight. Dokes finally succumbed to superior firepower in the tenth round, his dream now as limp as his rag-doll body in the ring. It took nearly ten minutes for Dokes to rise from his stool.

A little over a year later, Dokes was flattened—as still as winterkill—in the fourth round by a left-hooking power puncher named Donovan "Razor" Ruddock. It was not a fight for which Dokes was prepared. Not only was Dokes nineteen pounds heavier than he had been against Holyfield, he had also been arrested for possession only a few months before he was to answer the bell against the dangerous Ruddock. Doctors stormed the ring before referee Arthur Mercante Jr., could finish his gratuitous count. Dokes remained on the canvas, unconscious, for something close to forever. "Maybe it's time to consider doing something else for a living," Dokes later said in his locker room. It had taken him an hour to regroup and face the press. Although he recovered and kept fighting—going through the motions against stumblebums for what amounted to pocket change—Dokes was finished as a contender.

Incredibly, after nearly three more years, Dokes somehow managed to qualify for a title fight—his first since 1983. How the New York State Athletic Commission allowed Dokes to face undefeated Riddick Bowe in such a ghastly mismatch remains a mystery even now, almost two decades later. On February 6, 1993, Bowe trampled a burnt-out Dokes in less than a round before a crowd of more than sixteen thousand at Madison Square Garden. No longer the prodigy of the late 1970s, no longer even the wilted but dedicated pug who pushed Holyfield to the brink in 1989, Dokes looked tired, faded, gray. Dokes had as much business being in the ring that night as Charles Oakley or John Starks, and his baffling training methods inspired the rare snarky headline from the *New York Times*: "The Dokes Diet Program: Eat, Eat, Eat." There was nothing left of him as a fighter that night. Maybe there was nothing left of him as a man.

With his $750,000 paycheck, Dokes invested in a restaurant, and bought a few racehorses and watched them charge from the gate down in Florida. But he soon became restless and returned to Las Vegas to renew his "Sunglasses at Night" routine. In 1998 Dokes brutally assaulted his girlfriend, and in early 2000 he pleaded guilty to attempted murder, second-degree kidnapping, and battery with intent to commit sexual assault. No longer the high roller with an entourage, Dokes was appointed a public defender and was given a ten-year sentence.

When he was released from prison in 2008, Dokes settled in Sin City once again, making a living of sorts by signing autographs and making appearances, but he returned to Akron in 2010, back to where he first put on gloves as a twelve-year-old boy at the Firestone YMCA. Michael Dokes, who fought from 1976 to 1997, finished his career with a record of 53-6-2, with thirty-four knockouts.

The flamboyant personality of thirty-five years ago has long been forgotten. The man who tossed red roses at the crowd before his fights, the man who cooked like a gourmet chef, the man who designed and sewed his own clothes—none of that seems relevant now. But for the fighter who once told *KO Magazine*, "I found out once you get past the clouds, you don't see no angels," it may be best, after all, to remember him for these few quirks and to forget the squandered promise, his heinous crime, that one long season in hell.

Lightning Express

THE QUICK RISE AND EVEN QUICKER FALL OF AL SINGER

"**A** man cannot jump over his own shadow."
—Yiddish proverb

◆ ◆ ◆

Of all the Jewish fighters regarded as potential heirs to Benny Leonard in the late 1920s—a shortlist that includes Solly Seeman, Ruby Goldberg, and Sid Terris—only Abraham "Al" Singer actually managed to win the lightweight title. For a while, Singer even fought under the imprimatur of "The Ghetto Wizard." Today Singer is little more than a historical footnote, regarded as lightly, perhaps, as Jimmy Goodrich or Rocky Kansas, but at his peak, from 1928 to 1930, Al Singer was a bona fide sensation.

"It makes no difference who he fights," Madison Square Garden promoter Jimmy Johnston once said, "a bum off the streets or the champion, we will sell out." Indeed, Singer, who fought sixty-five of his seventy-three bouts in New York City, was one of the greatest attractions ever to step into a Big Apple ring. Some of the box-office numbers are astonishing. Both of his fights with ferocious Roaring Twenties hangover Bud Taylor drew 20,000 spectators; 19,000 watched him decision Stanislaus Loayza; and 21,630 amassed for his first brawl with Tony Canzoneri in 1928. Even bouts with less distinguished figures overworked the turnstiles: sellout crowds gathered to see Singer outpoint Davey Abad and annihilate

Jersey City hero Young Zazzarino. Those were heady days for Singer, "the next Benny Leonard," but they did not last for long.

Born in New York City on September 6, 1909, Al Singer spent his early years on the Lower East Side before his father, a successful businessman, moved the family to Pelham Parkway in the Bronx. Unlike most fighters of his era, Singer did not turn to boxing out of poverty or hardship. While still in high school, the athletic Singer was apprenticed to a diamond cutter but found that fame—the kind that drew the ladies as well as a certain glamorous notoriety associated with speakeasies and tommy guns—came easily with his natural talents: remarkable speed and a concussive right cross. Singer turned pro in 1927 as a featherweight under the guidance of Hymie Caplin and Harry Drucker.

His first bout, for which he was paid seventy-five dollars, was a third-round knockout of Jim Reilly on July 2, 1927. Over the next two years, Singer fought nearly fifty times, lighting up local clubs and arenas from the Ridgewood Grove in Brooklyn to Madison Square Garden on Eighth Avenue. Not since the days of Ruby Goldberg had there been so much ballyhoo over a Jewish fighter. Singer spit out combinations with the speed of a Chicago typewriter, snapped a sharp staccato jab, and stepped around his opponents with the swiftness of a champion jitterbug. Outside the ring his cocky attitude and dark looks created a stir among the ladies, Jew and Gentile alike. Apart from a few early points losses (typically avenged in rematches), Singer resembled *The Spirit of St. Louis* reincarnated in trunks and gloves. In fact, whispers concerning the ease with which some of his opponents were being outstripped soon began to echo.

From the beginning, Singer was haunted by the shadow of the underworld. "I always fought to win, and I thought the other guy was out to do the same thing," he told Stanley Weston. "Sure the mobs were around then. Every tough guy had his fighter. Just like he had a moll and diamonds. It was the style. But nobody ever asked me to 'dump' one or to make a deal."

If nothing else, Singer seems to have cornered the "guilt by association" market. Harry Drucker, for example, was a member of a small but lethal crew of stickup artists and gangland kidnappers. On October 7, 1927, in something out of the pages of *Black Mask*, Drucker was taken for a one-way ride by two overcoats posing as detectives. With his partner gone the way of Judge Crater, Caplin now assumed full managerial duties for Singer. Caplin also had a habit of traveling under partly cloudy moral skies. His brother, immortalized by Herbert Asbury in *The Gangs of New York*, was the notorious mobster Nathan "Kid Dropper" Kaplan, and Hymie himself was eventually sentenced to a stretch at Auburn State Prison in 1941 for grand larceny. Singer also spent many nights hobnobbing with notorious mobster Champ Segal, and several of his fights were accompanied by the kinds of dark rumors all too common during an era when Owney Madden, Legs Diamond, Al Capone, "Boo Boo" Hoff, Waxey Gordon, and Dutch Schultz all owned fighters.

By 1929 Singer was a rated contender as well as a supernatural gate attraction. His thrilling toe-to-toe draw with Tony Canzoneri in December 1928 established "The Bronx Bronco" as a legitimate star in the making, and consecutive wins over Bud Taylor, "The Terror of Terre Haute," boosted his popularity as well as his bankroll. Singer would go on to earn over half a million dollars in his career.

On April 19, 1929, Singer suffered an eye injury during a match with former amateur standout Patsy Ruffalo in Detroit, but, in keeping with his rambunctious ways, decided to keep a May date with crude Filipino slugger Ignacio Fernandez at Madison Square Garden anyway. Ten thousand fans watched in horror as Fernandez mauled their hero, an overwhelming favorite, in three sadistic rounds. "Singer toppled face forward," wrote James P. Dawson of the startling KO, "rolled over and was counted out." Singer, the only quality fighter Fernandez managed to defeat in a career that spanned more than eighty fights, stubbornly entered the ring that night with impaired vision, unable to decline the temptation of another sizable purse. It would be a mistake that Singer would never really overcome. Eye trouble would haunt the remainder of his career.

Singer was back in the ring less than a month after his first knockout loss and regained his momentum with a win over tough Carl Duane at the Starlight Park in the Bronx, and a quick demolition job of ex-featherweight-champion Andre Routis at Ebbets Field. These fights set up a match with Harlem-based Cuban Kid Chocolate, one of the true wonders of boxing in the 1920s and 1930s. Chocolate, box-office gold in New York City at the time because of his smooth boxing skills and free-wheeling lifestyle, entered his match with Singer sporting a gaudy 40-0 record. In August 1929 nearly fifty thousand spectators jammed the Polo Grounds and coughed up a gate just shy of a quarter of a million dollars to see "The Bronx Bronco" and "The Cuban Bon Bon" mix it up. After twelve rounds Chocolate, as slick a boxer as one will ever see, earned a slim decision disapproved of by the zealous crowd.

The fight was close enough to earn Singer a title shot with lightweight champion Sammy Mandell. But first, Singer would have to try to even the score with the only man to knock him out: Ignacio Fernandez. The rematch was set for May 23, 1930, at Madison Square Garden. In the days leading up to the fight, rumors were so thick that James Farley, New York State Boxing Commissioner, visited Fernandez in his dressing room prior to the match to warn the Filipino against any shenanigans. Singer went on to score a decision over Fernandez and was granted a shot at the lightweight title, then held by Sammy Mandell.

Mandell, trained early in his career by legendary Jack Blackburn, was a skilled boxer whose four-year title reign included decisions over Jimmy McLarnin and Tony Canzoneri. He was the first solid lightweight champion to emerge in the fallow wake of Benny Leonard, eclipsing the modest talents of Jimmy Goodrich and Rocky Kansas with ease. By the time Mandell stepped into the ring with Singer, however, he had not made the lightweight limit in nearly a year and had defended his title only four times since winning it from Rocky Kansas in 1926. Still, it seemed curious for oddsmakers to install such a respected champion as a three-to-one underdog.

On July 17, 1930, a crowd of 27,742 gathered at Yankee Stadium to see if the odds could be bucked. They could not. The fight, in fact, might as well have taken place in an abattoir. Apart from shaking hands during prefight instructions, "The Rockford Sheik" never managed to lay a glove on Singer—he never got the chance. Within thirty seconds of the opening bell, Singer caught Mandell with a left hook to the chin that dropped Mandell to the mat. Mandell rose quickly only to be dropped again by a quick flurry of rights and lefts. Once more the brave champion staggered to his feet and once more Singer bowled him over with a fusillade of punches. Mandell, although by now completely blotto, somehow beat the count of referee Arthur Donovan and was allowed to continue despite being little more than a swaying target. Finally, Singer, with a sinister grin, ended matters concussively with a perfect overhand right that sent Mandell spinning into a macabre pirouette before he finally crashed flat on his back where he listened to the count of ten with faraway eyes.

"On the fourth and final knockdown," wrote James P. Dawson, "the Yankee Stadium was transformed into a veritable bedlam. Hats flying in air, newspapers and programs tossed aloft, canes waving, husky throats booming, all mingled in a greeting for the new champion." It was all over in one minute and forty-six seconds. Al Singer, not yet twenty-one, was now the lightweight champion of the world. But not everyone was impressed.

"It would only be keeping the record straight to say that this fight," wrote Westbrook Pegler, "like all other important prizefights in the New York ring nowadays, was preceded by rumors that Mandell was certain to lose and that his manager Mr. Kane had been voted a block of stock in Singer to compensate for the loss of his income from Mandell." To make matters worse, Mandell soon emerged with a cloak-and-dagger tale worthy of Agatha Christie or Eric Ambler: He had been, he insisted, poisoned before his match with Singer. This kind of skulduggery has occurred before in the often-lawless world of boxing, but was it really such a shock to see Singer obliterate a fighter who had entered the ring with the wear and tear of ten years and nearly 150 professional fights? "I guess inactivity had a lot to do with it," Mandell initially stated. "Inactivity and not fighting regularly at the weight." That sounds reasonable enough, but much of the press remained unconvinced. Pegler has the last word: "Mandell was a setup and any fairly aggressive lightweight would have knocked him out as easily as Singer did that night. Such things have happened before, but the most curious factor in this case is that all the leading gamblers in the Broadway delicatessen district were overwhelmingly confident long before ring time that the championship would pass to Al Singer."

For his next fight, Singer brazenly demanded, and received, a match against dangerous Jimmy McLarnin, the dynamic welterweight who had earned, as Bert Sugar aptly put it, "almost permanent possession of any and all Jewish fighters." Jackie Fields, Sid Terris, Ruby Goldstein, and a geriatric Benny Leonard on the sad comeback were some of the brilliant box-fytehs who were knocked out by McLarnin. Singer—and Hymie Caplin, of course—knew that a bout with the wildly popular Irishman would guarantee another blockbuster payday. They were right. For this nontitle tilt, Singer would earn $33,341—an outrageous fortune during the depths of the Depression. What Singer could not know at the time, however, was that Jimmy McLarnin, one of the greatest little men in the history of boxing, would effectively end his career.

On September 11, 1930, Singer and McLarnin faced each other at Yankee Stadium. For two rounds Singer did his best Benny Leonard impression and smoothly outboxed an onrushing McLarnin. Within a minute of the opening bell, in fact, Singer dropped the "Baby-Faced Assassin" to his knees with a hard right cross, and nearly thirty thousand fans in the Bronx erupted simultaneously. Could this be it? Was Singer going to be the one to put an end to the Irish hex? McLarnin rose quickly, and the two matinee idols, both among the top draws in boxing at the time, slugged until the bell. In the second round, McLarnin outworked Singer to the body and sent the lightweight champion into retreat with sharp combinations. At the sound of the bell, Singer returned to his corner with a small cut over his right eye.

In the third round, Singer began to exchange with McLarnin in an effort to get respect. What he got instead from McLarnin was a thudding left hook and a whipping right that caught him square on the jaw. Singer went down as if smacked with a quarterstaff. "He hit me a right on the chin and I fell so hard, I actually thought my neck was broken," Singer told *Boxing & Wrestling* in 1955. "I am not fooling. I thought my neck had snapped." So, apparently, did McLarnin. Halfway through the count, McLarnin, no doubt believing his opponent was through for the night, executed his traditional handspring in a neutral corner; when he popped to his feet again an instant later he saw Singer, who had managed to beat the count, charging forward, ready to swap more leather. The Irishman obliged, dropping Singer for ten with a final crippling left. It would take nearly four more years before Barney Ross, the last great Jewish fighter, broke the incredible McLarnin jinx. By then Al Singer would be washed up.

Despite his loss to McLarnin, Singer was still a relatively hot commodity when he signed to face popular Brooklynite Tony Canzoneri in a rematch of the bout that had first brought Singer fame. On November 14, 1930, Singer stepped into Madison Square Garden before sixteen thousand fans to defend his title for the first time. Much had changed, it seemed, since Canzoneri and an inexperienced Singer fought to a draw in 1928. For one thing, Singer was damaged goods; for another, perhaps more importantly, Singer and Hymie Caplin were now on the outs. Canzoneri, the former featherweight champion and ex-bootblack, was coming off of a shellacking at the hands of Billy Petrolle in September. In addition, Canzoneri had not scored a knockout in seven consecutive fights leading up to the Singer match. The lightweight champion was tabbed a three-to-one favorite. It took sixty-six seconds for Canzoneri to make a schlemiel out of Singer and the oddsmakers. After staggering Singer with a right, Canzoneri connected with a left hook that dropped the lightweight champion flat on his face. Singer remained motionless until the count reached seven, and then he stirred himself into a drunken rendition of "The Crawling Baby Blues" before nearly rolling out of the ring as Referee Johnny McAvoy reached the count of ten. Only twenty-one years old, Al Singer, who had won and lost the lightweight championship in a total two minutes and fifty-two seconds, was through.

Like the Mandell bout, the Canzoneri debacle baffled many. Dan Parker, irascible muckraker for the *New York Daily Mirror*, claimed that Singer laid down to spite Hymie Caplin. Talk of a betting coup was rampant. A few months after the upset, an incident occurred that, in retrospect, might shed some light on the whole affair.

In March 1931, Singer and Caplin met by chance in a Madison Square Garden office when things got out of control. According to reports, Singer demanded $20,000 that Caplin had "cheated" him out of. Before Caplin could protest, Singer socked him on the jaw. A melee broke out involving Singer, Caplin, a paperweight, Louis Singer, trainer Moe Levy, Garden matchmaker Tom McArdle, and two cuspidors. Caplin came out of the rumpus with a split lip and Singer with a shiner, courtesy of a well-aimed paperweight. "I never cheated him out of a cent," Caplin told the newswires. "In fact, I made him a champion and made him wealthy. He's just an ingrate. The fact that he grabbed those spittoons shows how much courage he has. If I managed him in a comeback I'd be afraid to match him with a good fighter even if they agreed to let him use the spittoons."

Caplin sold his interest in Singer to French manager Leon See, ignominiously known as the man who introduced Primo Carnera to the world, and Singer began a comeback. Five easy wins followed, including a knockout over "Cannonball" Eddie Martin, before Singer faced rugged ex-featherweight champ Battling Battalino. On December 11, 1931, Battalino—on the rampage as usual—hammered Singer in two grisly rounds. James P. Dawson described the slaughter: "Singer left himself open, when Battalino overtook him in flight, to a left and right to the jaw, and the Bronx lad went down, floundering on the ring floor as he reached blindly first for referee Haley and then for a ring rope that was beyond his grasp, to pull himself erect." Singer promptly retired.

For the next four years Singer worked at a variety of jobs—café owner, salesman, real estate entrepreneur—before the restlessness that often afflicts ex-prizefighters settled on him. Singer mounted the obligatory failed comeback and finally hung up the gloves for good in 1935. His final record was 62-9-2.

During World War II Singer was stationed in Camp Upton, where he taught fitness and gave occasional boxing exhibitions. Eventually, he was declared physically unfit for service and was discharged. The reason? He could barely see out of his right eye, the same one damaged by Patsy Ruffalo in 1929. Al Singer died of a heart attack in New York City in 1961. He was fifty-one years old.

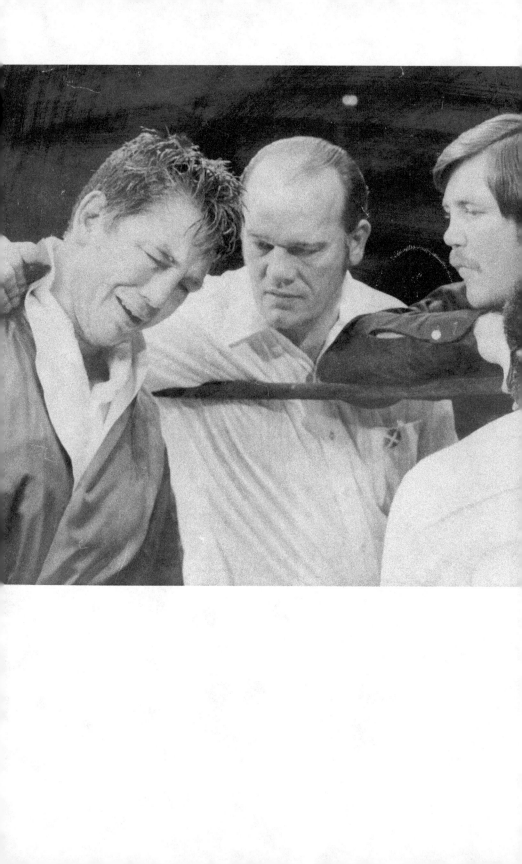

Lived Forward, Learned Backward

MIKE QUARRY AND THE "QUARRY CURSE"

o one who saw the crushing blow would ever forget it; Mike Quarry, however, would never remember it. Quarry, a perennial light-heavyweight fringe contender throughout the 1970s, and a minor celebrity overshadowed by his more famous older brother, Jerry, was undefeated when he challenged Bob Foster for the world title on June 27, 1972. That was the night his dreams were shattered instead of fulfilled. It was also a night that would become part of the "Quarry Curse."

His family, made up of hard-bitten scrappers from Arkansas on one side and Oklahoma on the other, was a sprawling, brawling clan that personified dysfunction. Wherever the Quarrys went, some sort of ruckus—usually involving knuckles—was sure to follow. In the tumultuous history of boxing, not even the Conns (who once rumbled with their prospective in-laws at a wedding) could match the Quarrys for general pandemonium.

Jack Quarry was raised during the Great Depression and his early life was as strenuous as the circumstances that surrounded it. A restless bully who aborted an amateur career as a boxer because of psoriasis, Jack grew up in labor camps in Northern California after his family had abandoned the parched scrubland of Oklahoma. Essentially, Jack was part of the Dust Bowl, whose participants were immortalized (and slightly romanticized) by John Steinbeck in *The Grapes of Wrath*. (They were also ridiculed by Roman Polanski in *Chinatown*, when Jack Nicholson kicks an oafish farmhand in the groin and punctuates the assault with a cry of "You dumb Okie!")

By his midteens Jack was riding the rods and scrambling in hobo jungles, just as Jack Dempsey had done twenty years earlier. "When I was fourteen," he told *People* magazine, "I chopped cotton for one dollar a day in Roswell, New Mexico. You could go out on Sunday and fight three rounds for three dollars—that was three days' work." After marrying, Jack remained a drifter of sorts, moving his ever-increasing family up and down California: Glendale, Downey, Midway City, Shafter, Oakland.

Jack was a born loser whose inability to hold a job marked him as more than just antiauthoritarian; his bleak outlook on life, symbolized by a pair of tattoos stretched across his knuckles that read "Hard Luck," bordered on sociopathic. But when he began teaching his sons, Jimmy and Jerry, to box, he saw the possibility of a future materializing. For Jack Quarry, life had been postponed for far too long. Now, the proverbial "good times" were here. With Jerry, a natural pro who wielded both a crippling left hook and a cinderblock chin, Jack found himself, improbably, blessed. Eventually, he had the most popular draw on the West Coast—and in the only division that mattered: heavyweight. Soon the money and the glory began rolling in. By 1967, Jerry was packing the Olympic Auditorium in Los Angeles, drawing celebrities to ringside, and was being touted as a future heavyweight champion of the world. His little brother, Mike, idolized him and soon began hitting the gym to emulate him.

From the beginning, Mike Quarry, six years younger than his famous older brother, was an afterthought. Even his amateur career was cut short when he was disqualified in an Olympic tryout for using the ropes for leverage. After that fiasco, Quarry, encouraged by his father, decided to turn professional. He was still in high school when he made his debut on April 18, 1969, a five-round decision over James Dick on the undercard of Jose Napoles–Curtis Cokes I. Without a second thought, Jack put him on a throwback road not seen regularly since the 1940s. In his rookie year alone, Quarry fought nineteen times, gloving up in prizefight backwaters such as Hawaii, Orlando, Wisconsin, and Minnesota. In a sense, Quarry had re-created the nomadic life of his father, hitting the road every few weeks for a paycheck that would have meant pocket change to someone like Joe Frazier or Muhammad Ali.

By April 1972, only three years after turning pro, Quarry had amassed a record of 35-0. Although he scored a pair of solid wins over ex-title-challengers Andy Kendall and Jimmy Dupree, he was barely above the club fight level. He was talented, but his shortage of power was glaring, and, at twenty-one, he lacked seasoning, even with nearly forty fights under his belt. None of that seemed to bother Quarry, whose cockiness could not be checked. "You might say I have two goals," he said before the fight, "to win the world's light-heavyweight championship and become another Billy Conn, known the world over as not just a boxer but a celebrity."

Quarry took this confidence into the ring with him when he faced Bob Foster, who had been light-heavyweight champion since 1968. Tall and lanky, with a slightly receding hairline, Foster hardly resembled a physical marvel. But he possessed one of the most devastating weapons in boxing: a thunderous hook that left more than one world-class fighter counting atoms on his back as the ring lights fluttered and flashed above him. This included sturdy Dick Tiger, from whom Foster won the light-heavyweight title in 1968. When Foster dropped Tiger for the full count with a cracking hook, the crowd gathered at Madison Square Garden dreaded the possibility of a ring fatality. Tiger, a three-time world champion in two divisions, was unconscious before he hit the canvas.

A deputy sheriff by day, Foster was the most dominant light heavyweight since the 1940s, when Ezzard Charles and Archie Moore were at their peaks. Although Moore reigned as champion for nearly a decade, he was already in his forties halfway through his title run and past his considerable prime.

Success at light heavyweight, however, was a limited blessing. There was little money in the division, which reflected the sagging economy of boxing as a whole. Aside from Muhammad Ali and the heavyweights, a few house fighters at Madison Square Garden, and the Southern California scene, boxing was stuck in a recession it seemed incapable of overcoming. That was why Foster repeatedly challenged heavyweights—and suffered for his temerity. Over the years Foster had been stopped by Doug Jones, Ernie Terrell, Joe Frazier, and Muhammad Ali. At 175 pounds, however, Foster was virtually indestructible. He was already thirty-four years old and making his tenth title defense when he climbed into the ring against Mike Quarry. Foster may have been on the downside, but that fact hardly mattered: Quarry never had a chance.

Despite a record built mostly in the hinterlands, Quarry believed he could outbox the most dangerous light heavyweight in the world. Foster and Quarry met on the undercard of Muhammad Ali–Jerry Quarry II at the Las Vegas Convention Center. In a queasy nod to a far less PC era, this closed-circuit extravaganza was billed "The Quarry Brothers vs. The Soul Brothers."

As if to underscore his modest earning power, Foster entered the ring wearing a ratty terrycloth robe and a pair of trunks that looked like old dishrags stitched together—its beltline was twisted, discolored, gnarled. When the opening bell rang, however, Foster was ready to strike.

It was a sign of just how delusional Quarry was when he broke into a version of the "Ali shuffle" in the first round. A classic boxer who circled the ring on nimble feet and worked behind his jab, Quarry wisely moved to his left—away from the danger zone. To move right meant possibly getting caught by the same hook that nearly annihilated Dick Tiger, Mark Tessman, and many others. For three rounds, Foster stalked, landing occasional rights and a thudding jab, while Quarry tried to avoid incoming artillery. In the fourth round, Quarry began to stand and trade with Foster, a suicidal gaffe. During an exchange, both fighters missed simultaneous rights, and, like images in a funhouse mirror, they prepared to launch hooks synchronously. When Foster landed his left, it was on target—to the jaw—and explosive. No man could sustain such a blow without collapsing. Quarry, whiplashed, suffered a secondary impact when his head crashed against the canvas with an audible thud.

He was unconscious for several minutes while a subdued Foster, worried about what his peculiar talent had done, milled in his corner. Finally, Quarry was revived and helped, gingerly, to his stool, where a television reporter stuck a microphone in his face and asked a few questions. Quarry, who managed to mumble a few distant words, would later confess that he had no recollection of the fight that had left him laid out on his back like a patient etherized on a table. "I don't remember Foster's punch," he would say. "I just remember waking up in the dressing room. Oh, I know I was interviewed in the ring after the fight. So I've been told. But I don't remember any of it. I was unconscious when I was doing that interview. I had to be."

At ringside, Arwanda Quarry fainted when she saw her youngest son poleaxed, and by the end of the night another Quarry rumble had broken out in the crowd. According to Steve Springer and Blake Chavez in their biography of Jerry Quarry, *Hard Luck*, Mike, sufficiently recovered to watch Jerry tangle with Muhammad Ali, encountered hecklers in the crowd. One of them was drunk enough, apparently, to kick him in the crotch, sparking a melee that resulted in arrests.

For his efforts, Quarry earned $40,000. It would prove to be the last title shot of his career. He was twenty-one years old.

Little by little, Quarry slipped into journeyman status, alternating wins and losses with a frequency that eventually forced him out of the light-heavyweight ratings. There was no recovering from what Foster did to him. "I kept fighting," Quarry told *Boxing Illustrated*, "but never really got back to what I was capable of producing."

The travels of a knockaround boxer in the late 1970s were hardly the equivalent of an American Grand Tour. Dreary, seamy, thorny—it was a grinding trade in more ways than one. Television had all but abandoned boxing (the heavyweight division was an exception) and substantial paydays were scarce. To make extra money, Quarry began dabbling in, of all things, karate. In 1975, when Bruce Lee and martial arts were growing fads, roughly eight hundred spectators gathered to watch "Karate Masters versus Boxing Professionals" in Houston, Texas. The main event featured Quarry against "Master" Yong Tae Lee, Korean National Taekwondo Champion and proprietor of a karate school in Los Angeles. "I think full contact karate might become a moneymaking sport in a couple of years," Quarry said, "and if that happens, I want to be prepared. I feel I have an edge with my boxing background. Right now, boxing is my livelihood. But I train in both sports every day." His martial arts debut was a debacle when Lee, being worked over against the ropes, forgot the rules of engagement and headbutted Quarry out of the ring. It was a move that might have made Bobo Brazil proud, but it earned Lee an immediate disqualification.

Quarry went on to become a moderate attraction in Florida and made a fair living headlining nondescript cards at the Orlando Sports Stadium promoted by Pete Ashlock. After all, even in his fighting dotage, at the age of twenty-four or twenty-five, Quarry retained name recognition—even if it was only secondhand.

He was also still capable of scoring the occasional upset. On September 30, 1975, Quarry outpointed streaking light-heavyweight Mike Rossman over ten rounds in Madison Square Garden. But the losses, and the scar tissue, soon began to mount. Two more fights against Rossman ended in defeat for Quarry—including a stoppage due to a gruesome cut above his eye that required multiple stitches.

Until Rossman beat him by TKO, Quarry had failed to go the distance only once, the night Bob Foster demolished him in 1972. Now Quarry began having trouble reaching the final bell. Over the last ten bouts of his career, Quarry went 3-5-2, with four of his losses by knockout.

In 1978, Quarry blew a $20,000 payday against Olympic gold medalist Michael Spinks when he was stopped by Pete McIntyre, a last-minute substitute who entered the ring with a 6-8-1 record.

Like most fighters, who cannot break away from a pursuit ingrained in them from the time they were children, Quarry continued fighting long after he should have retired. He seemed almost out of place at the dawn of the glitzy 1980s, his handsome features now permanently misshapen, and his eyes, beneath the scarred brows, now developing a faraway gaze.

When Quarry retired in 1982, after dropping a decision to a club fighter in Crystal City, Virginia, he did so with resentment at the sport that had promised so much. "If I had to do it all over again," he told *Boxing Scene* in 1986, "I'll tell you one thing, there's no way I'd ever be a fighter. No way. It's a bad business. The professional boxer is abused. He's in the hands of the promoters. Boxing should be outlawed."

Before long, Quarry began behaving erratically. Like his father, who had brawled in labor camps and lumberjack yards during the Depression, Mike Quarry was now a street bruiser. Gerald Early once described the madness of prizefighters who could not resist extracurricular action: "No sane boxer would remotely consider, no matter how severe the provocation short of actual physical endangerment, fighting in a common street brawl: it is felt to be degrading, foolish, and dangerous." Quarry might have disagreed. He lingered outside of bars and strip clubs, under the shimmering moonlight, and goaded unsuspecting drunks into fisticuffs. Although Quarry never won a world title, he was surely the undisputed parking lot champion of the San Joaquin Valley. More than one poor schlub found himself, bridgework loosened, nose newly askew, laid out on some patch of concrete in Bakersfield, courtesy of a left hook that had failed to stop some of the best light heavyweights in the world but was more than enough for paunchy nightcrawlers who trained exclusively on Combos, Alabama Slammers, and Marlboros.

Depressed and struggling to make a living, Quarry was nearing bottom and turned to drugs. "I did cocaine every day for three years," Quarry said in 1986. "It wasn't until I went back East, where I didn't know where to get it, that I finally got off of it."

Abandoning drugs, however, failed to reverse his decline. What followed was that all-too-familiar downward spiral, the fate so common to fighters, from the least talented journeyman to the elite Hall of Famer. He divorced. He squandered his life savings. It was nearly impossible to keep a job. "Boxing separates you from the everyday workweek," Quarry said. "It's tough to come out and find your way." Over the years, Quarry tried his hand at plumbing and hairstyling. He earned a certificate as a physical trainer. He worked as a janitor and an insurance salesman. A gym he ran with his brother, Jerry, failed within weeks of opening.

Almost predictably, he thought about a comeback. He was forty, out of the ring for eight years, inspired by the grotesque return of Jerry, which had ended in a shambles, and the underwhelming talent cashing oversized checks. But as Quarry began to physically deteriorate, he realized that more punches would likely push him over the edge. "One of the elements I had to deal with is short-term memory loss," he told *Boxing Illustrated* in 1992. "It's not that great. Once in a while, I'll forget something. It's humbling to have to write something down to remember it, but that's what I have to do. I have to write things down."

By the mid-1990s, just when his brother Jerry was making headlines battling brain damage, Quarry was struggling with his memory, his motor skills, and his speech. Then came the sad new childhood. In his forties, Mike Quarry was now a man who had to be bathed, fed, and clothed. He would wander off like a preschooler in a supermarket. At times, he woke up screaming in the middle of the night, to punch holes into his bedroom walls, to weep uncontrollably. For Quarry, it was life as a non sequitur. The past, the present, even the future combined and recombined, mixed and matched, randomly, haphazardly, like the cut-up method of William S. Burroughs. And those occasional lucid moments? They let Quarry make cameo appearances in the world, before, finally, not even a flicker of recognition remained. "Life is lived forwards, and learned backwards,"

Quarry would say, perhaps to some of the strangers he stopped in the street for a rambling conversation.

When Quarry began to leave threatening notes around the house for his wife, she had him committed to the dementia unit of Brighton Gardens, in Yorba Linda, California.

Before his career began its tailspin, Quarry was open about his ambitions. He was going to be an actor or an entertainer, with a stand-up routine of some sort. (Incredibly, one of his skits was an impersonation of a punch-drunk fighter, in the vein of "Slapsie" Maxie Rosenbloom and Rocky Graziano.) Instead, he became, at one point or another, a patchwork of the two most important figures in his life: his father, Jack, and his brother, Jerry. Like Jerry, he became a fighter, and as a professional journeyman he replicated the nomadic tendencies of Jack. Then, when he retired, Mike Quarry became a street ruffian, mirroring the days when Jack brawled, bare-knuckled, across the dusty West. A few years later, Mike Quarry was a man unfit for even the most menial job, superficially resembling a young Jack at his most antisocial. Finally, he suffered from the same harrowing disease as Jerry: pugilistic dementia.

No sooner did Jerry Quarry die from complications of what is now known as CTE, in 1999, than genetics was proffered as an explanation for the "Quarry Curse." But Mike and Jerry shared more than just DNA and a hazardous livelihood. They also shared a ring—often. And they often hurt each other, without apparent concern for the acknowledged consequences. (The youngest Fighting Quarry, Bobby, was diagnosed with Parkinson's in the mid-1990s. He, too, sparred countless rounds with Mike and Jerry. Unlike his brothers, however, Bobby had no discernable talent for fighting. He was what is known in the flesh trade as an "opponent," a man whose sole purpose is to provide a body against which better fighters sharpen their damaging skills. This hazardous career choice almost guarantees a diminished future.)

"The hardest punches Mike ever took, except from Bob Foster in their title fight, were from Jerry," publicist Bill Caplan told the *Chicago Tribune*. "It's hard to imagine one brother hitting another like that. I'd ask Jerry, 'How can you do that to your brother?' And he'd say, 'He's in there with me, isn't he? Hey, this is boxing. I've got to get ready for a fight.'"

West Coast promoter Don Chargin also recalled those aberrant sparring sessions. "Their workouts were horrible to watch. I could hardly keep looking. But Mike would go in there day after day." And day after day, he absorbed blows from a world-class heavyweight who viewed their ring time together as a twisted defense of family pride.

Mickey Rourke, who haunted the 5th Street Gym in Miami as a teenager, was shocked, even after the passage of more than thirty years, by the Quarry wars. "They would just beat the livin' piss out of each other . . . you'd actually stop your own work, and watch what was goin' on in the ring with those two, you know?" Rourke told Blake Chavez. "It went on every fuckin' day. They would just tear the shit out of each other . . . and Jerry would get the best out of it."

From his father, Mike had internalized a perverse code of honor (embodied in the unofficial family slogan, "There is no quit in a Quarry") that celebrated toughness and mulishness above all. These qualities, bound up in a reductive notion of pride, were double-edged swords in the ring. When they were applied simultaneously by two Quarrys in a gym, without a referee, they proved disastrous.

Just how dysfunctional was this family? Jerry once emerged from a brawl against Jimmy with a broken arm—courtesy of a baseball bat. Not even a title shot could keep the Quarrys from harming each other. In 2006 Jimmy Quarry recalled the painful whys of how Jerry answered the bell against Jimmy Ellis with a serious back injury. Naturally, the incident took place in a bar. "And you know, you can't get an Irish family together and have their drink and not fight. We thought all you did was fight and drink. Jerry took a swing at me and I ducked, of course. Then I ran into him like a football player would tackle a man. And I ran him across the room, right into the corner of the jukebox." Two months before his championship fight against Ellis, a slick boxer riding a hot streak that included wins over Leotis Martin and Oscar Bonavena, Quarry found himself with a cracked fourth lumbar vertebrae. Quarry dropped a listless decision to Ellis.

Most boxers, through training and fighting, participate in a steady sort of self-immolation: They consume themselves from the inside out after years of slow burning. Mike and Jerry Quarry accelerated that deleterious process. They were—wittingly or unwittingly, who can say?—accomplices to each other's downfall.

No other sport produces so many young has-beens with such regularity. Mike Quarry was twenty-one when Bob Foster demolished him; a few years later, he was considered nothing more than another casualty of boxing. After spending some time in an assisted-living facility, Mike Quarry died on June 11, 2006. He was fifty-five years old.

Jack Quarry, caustic as ever, described the tragic career of a man, his own son, who took up boxing because he idolized his brother. "Michael was too weak, was always sickly as a child, and had a crooked arm from falling off a monkey bar," Quarry said in 1991. "He had a lot of guts and never let you know if you were hurting him. I kept telling him you can't just make guys miss and win fights. Someone once told me he was such a good boxer, he could go through his career without getting hit. Well, that sure turned out to be wrong."

Leftover Life to Kill

WHO WILL REMEMBER CARMELO NEGRON?

n May 10, 2013, explosive 1980s junior featherweight Carmelo Negron died, and hardly anybody seemed to notice. But there was a time when Negron was considered a sure thing, and in a sport where certainty is as scarce as empathy is in a POW camp, that kind of potential, at least back then, was itself noteworthy. Although Negron died of cancer, he also suffered from the most harrowing of boxing fates: dementia.

Over the last decade, one fighter after another has made headlines for sorrowful reasons that make most aficionados flinch. Rocky Lockridge, Matthew Saad Muhammad, Iran Barkley, and Willie Edwards all found themselves homeless. Alexis Argüello committed suicide. Greg Page, who was left paralyzed by injuries suffered during his last fight, died in 2009 when he fell from his bed and, unable to right himself, suffocated. Not long ago, Isidro Pérez, living hand-to-mouth as a neophyte trainer, was hit by a truck and died along a curbside in Mexico City. For months, his body lay unidentified in a morgue. So many fighters have been fatally shot or stabbed on mean streets across the world in recent years that tolling them would take the better part of a day.

Disability, desolation, murder, dementia—these are occupational hazards of a dark art, like the deadly plunge for wire walkers. But what about obscurity? Who will remember the fighters who never headlined HBO, never got their own trading cards, never wore a championship belt around their waists? Who will remember Carmelo Negron? In the end, that bleak combination of vocational blowback and subsequent neglect is almost unbearable. There is very little afterlife for a fighter who has failed to succeed. Not only do most boxers—who remain independent contractors without pensions, unions, or comprehensive health insurance—wind up dispossessed, but, unlike other sports, where minor-league organizations, local television markets, and large coaching staffs offer opportunities for ex-players, boxing offers only a few iffy prospects to its battered alumni in the same grimy environments where fighters first took their steps to glory or failure.

Carmelo Negron, who started boxing in Alphabet City, was one of the hottest fighters in New York in the late 1970s and early 1980s, when the sweet science still meant something. In 1977, for example, Negron fought on a Golden Gloves card at Madison Square Garden that drew more than twenty thousand spectators. Along with Hector Camacho, Mark Breland, Alex Ramos, and Davey Moore, Negron was one of the amateur stand-outs of the *Last Days of Disco* era.

After a few scrapes as a teen in Puerto Rico, Negron moved to New York City and settled in with his mother, who lived in one of several grim housing projects blotting the Lower East Side. In the late 1970s, "Loisaida"—as the neighborhood was colloquially known—was the her-oin capital of the world and a nightmare vision of urban blight made real: Hieronymus Bosch in concrete and asphalt. Luc Sante described what that hell on earth looked like in *Low Life*: "The neighborhood was desolate, so underpopulated that landlords would give you a month's free rent just for signing a lease, many buildings being less than half-full, but it was far from tranquil. . . . In the blocks east of Avenue A the situation was dra-matically worse. In 1978 I got used to seeing large fires in that direction every night, usually set by arsonists hired by landlords of empty buildings who found it an easy choice to make, between paying property taxes and collecting insurance. By 1980 Avenue C was a lunar landscape of vacant blocks and hollow tenement shells."

In those days, New York appeared to be on the verge of anarchy. The chaotic blackout of 1977—which occurred during the terrifying killing spree of David Berkowitz—brought national attention to a city many Americans considered an honest-to-goodness lawless, godless, loveless wasteland. From out of this squalor, poor young men cobbled together flimsy dreams as best they could. For some, pursuing organized violence was, paradoxically, a way out of the disorganized violence that surrounded them around the clock from empty lot to empty lot. Carmelo Negron was one of them. No sooner did Negron arrive on Avenue C than his mother gave him a piece of advice: "The first thing she tell me," Negron told writer William Plummer in 1982, "is go to the gym."

As a young pro, Negron scored seventeen consecutive knockouts to open his career. Joe Colon, who trained Negron in a dilapidated gym above an abandoned methadone clinic, gave Randy Gordon the lowdown on Negron in 1979: "The kid just loves to train and work out. He runs six to eight miles every morning at five o'clock, even when he's not training. He's a runner in the morning, and a pursuer, a killer, in the ring."

At around five-feet-two, Negron charged forward like a mini-siege engine, and initiating that kind of physical contact repeatedly left him open for the kind of punishment he could not, ultimately, endure. Negron was in his early twenties when his aspirations were already distant memories. After suffering his first defeat in late 1981, Negron lost one fight after another, many of them due to cuts. In later years, the scar tissue above his brows was as thick as impasto and splitting those old wounds open was as easy as tearing through balsa wood with a ripsaw. But the blood money was never enough. Negron fought during a time when the extravagant purses of today were mere fantasies. HBO aired only a few bouts a year, Showtime did not yet have a boxing program, and pay-per-view was like a mirage in the desert. There was NBC, ABC, and CBS, however, and Negron could collect a few moderate checks as an opponent.

In 1985 he lost a savage split decision to lethal James Pipps, and the following May he was dismantled by Louie Espinoza in the last major fight of his career. "I was ready to give it all up six months ago," Negron told *Newsday* before the Espinoza fight. "But now, everything seems to be going the way I planned it. I still think I can be a world champion." Negron was on a four-fight losing streak before Espinoza bludgeoned him into retirement, but disillusion is as much a part of boxing as the jab is. Ten years later, Negron was back in the ring, fighting exclusively in his new—and permissive—home state, Illinois, where he scuffled, at risk, until he was forty-one.

Despite being ranked at one point as high as number five in the world at junior featherweight by *The Ring*, only scraps and fragments of his career remain. One of the most interesting is an appearance Negron makes in a photo essay on Alphabet City published in 1992 by Geoffrey Biddle. "Look at the faces," Negron told Biddle, in a Lower East Side gym. "There's a lot of dreams. Like, I'm getting out of this place. They should just do it the smart way. What I did, I trusted my trainer too much. We were big time, and he just bugged out. It takes a lot more than skill. You can't trust anyone when you're in the business of making money in boxing."

Nothing can take away from the terrible symmetry boxing gives its practitioners: a hardscrabble life, followed by a hardscrabble profession, followed by a hardscrabble retirement. Often, boxing is a continuation of privation and not, as many have argued, a reprieve from it. Just two months after undergoing surgery to remove a tumor from his stomach, Carmelo Negron died in Hartford, Connecticut, one of the most dangerous cities on the East Coast.

Who will remember Carmelo Negron?

◆ ◆ ◆

He bled like everybody. He had the same dreams all fighters have. He spent nights soaking in Epsom salt. His jaw was broken once. He saw the black lights now and then. They shouted his name in unison up at the old Felt Forum. The gyms he skipped rope in were begrimed infernos. He rattled heavy bags patched with duct tape and sparred in threadbare rings where hope was mixed with sweat. He watched his weight from day to day. On the streets of Loisaida he passed tatterdemalions huddling over trash can bonfires. Above the FDR Drive, the sun shone through gray fog in the fall and through smog squalls in the summer. When he got the call, he warred for $150, for $5,000, for $650, for whatever he was worth at the time, in Atlantic City neon, or, years later, in the semidarkness of Waukegan, wherever his blood could best be shed. There were cuts, bruises, welts. Did he see barges and scows floating out on the East River during morning runs in 1980? Did he see Greenpoint across the way, with its dark smokestacks racked like blackened cue sticks up against the sky? Did he ever visit the Jardin del Paraiso? So, he was one of the luckless, then; they have an unnerving glaze in their eyes, they wear winding sheets, so to speak, as young men still, with all that leftover life to kill, years before they die.

The Busy World

THE MURDER OF STANLEY KETCHEL

He was only twenty-three years old but already bedraggled. He had been dazzled for years by the bright lights of downtown Boston, San Francisco (Barbary, not Gold Coast), New York City and its Great White Way—all so different from the bonfire nights of his hobo days—and had scrapped hard enough and often enough to find himself disintegrating in his youth. And so, after a detour from Grand Rapids, Michigan, he wound up in Conway, Missouri, for a strange sort of American rest cure. He was sure a few weeks of the simple life would rejuvenate him. What he got instead was a .22 caliber kill shot through his back and a chance for a few last ragged breaths before the end. With his limbs stretched out on a mattress soaked with his own blood, it might have been easy to forget that this was Stanley Ketchel, "The Michigan Assassin," reigning middleweight champion of the world.

◆ ◆ ◆

When Stanley Ketchel retreated from the spotlight in 1910, his best days were already ashes. For years Ketchel had boasted of having had hundreds of undocumented bouts—one of the few claims this dedicated fabulist made that was probably true—and the shambles he represented during his final stretch as a professional fighter seemed to prove it. He was, after all, only a generation or so removed from the era of hardscrabble men who had fought on sandbars, hillocks, barges, and clearings lit only by the moon, and who had boarded mystery trains to their covert battlegrounds, with lawmen sometimes in pursuit. Those fights—the ones Ketchel claimed had never made the ledgers—were of the merciless variety found in roadhouses, saloons, rickety barns, and camping grounds decades before civility became even a half-concept in boxing.

By the time he was twenty-one, Ketchel was the middleweight champion of the world and had earned national recognition with his roughhouse approach in the ring and his freewheeling lifestyle outside of it. In 1909, Ketchel infamously challenged Jack Johnson for the heavyweight championship of the world, in Colma, California, despite the fact that just a few years earlier, he had been a stringy welterweight. But his fame, along with the still-developing Great White Hope angle, forced Ketchel into the ring against Johnson—under circumstances that remain mysterious more than a century later.

It was meant to be just another of the numberless hoaxes so common in the primeval outlaw sport, in those days closer to carnivals or tent-show productions than to organized competition. To capitalize on film footage of the bout, Johnson agreed to carry Ketchel over an unspecified number of rounds. Somewhere along the way, Ketchel—or was it his diabolical manager, Willis Britt?—decided that double-crossing Jack Johnson would pay off. What was intended to be playful suddenly became pitiful when, in the twelfth round, Ketchel unloaded an overhand right that landed like a howitzer shell and, to the shock of the crowd, sent Johnson crashing to the mat. Johnson quickly scrambled to his feet and flattened an onrushing Ketchel with an uppercut whose impact was the sporting equivalent of the great San Francisco earthquake of 1906. Along with losing the fight and temporarily losing his senses, Ketchel also lost assorted teeth and, most likely, more than a smattering of neurons. He was in dreamland until his cornermen dragged him to his stool and revived him.

◆ ◆ ◆

Ketchel was never the same after that. And when his reputation unraveled after a lackluster no-decision bout against Frank Klaus in March 1910 and further stage maneuverings against Sam Langford (another fight openly derided as a fix) in April, Ketchel tried minimizing the stories of his slow ruin. He publicly announced that he had given up both alcohol and auto-mobiles. ("It is hard on the nerves," he said about his reckless driving.) Before his farce with Langford, Ketchel played along with a publicity nar-rative meant to counterbalance his notorious reputation for bed-hopping and bar-crawling: he was reading Oscar Wilde and the Brothers Grimm in hopes of schooling away his rowdiness. Although Ketchel could barely spell, he gamely insisted that self-improvement through letters would be his salvation. To make his image even more wholesome, Ketchel claimed that he had traded tumblers of Gin Fizz for mugs overflowing with nutri-tious buttermilk. (Not even the generally cooperative press took Ketchel seriously. From the *Butte Daily Post*: "Mr. Ketchel should have taken up the buttermilk years ago—the fairy tales come right in line with his business.")

The truth, however, could not be obscured by cornpone: training had become an afterthought to Ketchel, partly because of his harum-scarum outlook and partly because he was no longer capable of pushing himself physically. In fact, Ketchel had been on the verge of collapse for months. *New York Morning Telegraph* columnist (and Wild West legend) Bat Masterson bluntly asked Wilson Mizner, who was managing Ketchel at the time, about rumors of "dissipation." Mizner coolly denied that Ketchel was deteriorating.

◆ ◆ ◆

As if to foreshadow his violent future, the first half of 1910 had been trou-blesome for Ketchel. Against Frank Klaus in a dreary March outing ruled a draw by ringside press, Ketchel suffered a broken hand, forcing him to stall throughout the fight. He performed so poorly that the crowd hissed at him, and the promoter, the Pittsburgh Athletic Club, canceled a future Ketchel engagement.

Then came the frame-up with Sam Langford at the National Athletic Club in Philadelphia on April 27, 1910, a six-round no-decision bout that, according to newspapers, Ketchel lost. In late May, after he swore off driving, Ketchel escaped immolation when his car battery exploded in the Bronx, leaving his automobile in flames. In June, Langford publicly accused Ketchel of double-crossing him after their arranged fight failed to produce a rematch. Similarly, George Little, estranged manager of Jack

Johnson, materialized in the *Chicago Tribune* alleging that the Johnson–Ketchel fight of the previous year had been a hoax from the beginning.

Ketchel tried to drown out the mounting bad press by returning to the ring as soon as possible. After scoring a KO of a rounder named Jim Smith at the National Sporting Club in New York City on June 10, Ketchel had a date against Australian heavyweight Bill Lang set for August. As the fight drew nearer, however, Ketchel asked for a postponement, citing a pair of oversized boils as an excuse to withdraw. Ten days later, shocking headlines assailed the country: Stanley Ketchel had suffered a nervous breakdown and would recuperate on a farm in Grand Rapids, Michigan. "I am in terrible condition right now and I must rest up," Ketchel announced. "My nerves are all gone, but a rest and the simple life will build me up and I will be back in the ring again. For eight weeks or so, few will see me. I'm going into the country and get away from the busy world."

Not since Terry McGovern had such a prominent fighter snapped publicly mid-career. And yet few were surprised that Ketchel had imploded. The hectic life he led after becoming champion was enough to give anybody tired blood. And to the conventional pastimes of every sporting debauchee—women, liquor, fast cars, and dance halls—Ketchel added an unusual twist: opium. Sportswriters sometimes gave this squalid habit the in-between-lines treatment in columns, and sometimes they spelled it out plainly for the typesetters.

Whatever ailed Ketchel, however, it was more than just a fondness for the nightlife. "Several times he started to train," wrote the *Butte Daily Post*, "but never could finish the job, the symptoms indicating that there was something radically wrong with the ordinarily powerful young fellow."

Like his contemporaries, Ad Wolgast and Battling Nelson, two bruisers destined for psychiatric wards and early twilights, Ketchel had a future that seemed tragically settled: a slow decline into a neurological fog.

But Ketchel died before his symptoms could worsen.

◆ ◆ ◆

In Belmont, Michigan, Ketchel relaxed as a gentleman farmer on a plot of land just north of Grand Rapids. He insisted that his convalescence would be a short one. "I am not all in," Ketchel said. "I need a rest, that is all. They say I am broke. Far from it. I have invested most of my ring earnings. And in a month or two you will see the old Stan going down the line doing the same old thing—bringing home the bacon."

By September 15, however, he had accepted an offer to accompany R. P. Dickerson down to Springfield, Missouri. Dickerson was a banker who owned an 868-acre ranch in Webster County and had known Ketchel as a child in Michigan. (Later, whispers across the Midwest would surface, explosively, during the trial: Dickerson was, in fact, more than just a father figure to Ketchel.)

While in Missouri, Ketchel became so enamored with the ranching lifestyle (along with the lushness of the Ozarks) that he decided to leave prizefighting behind. On paper featuring letterhead stamped "Missouri Land and Lumber Co., Stanley Ketchel, President," he wrote to a friend up north about his new direction, albeit with misspellings: "I have quit the Fiting game and I am gowing into the farming bizness. I have bought 32,000 ackers of timber land and 800 ackers of the best farming land in the world."

To give him some practical experience, Dickerson offered him a position as ranch manager on his spread. That was where Ketchel would meet his ruinous fate, in the shifty Walter Dipley and Goldie Smith.

◆ ◆ ◆

They were both young, and they were both running from their pasts.

According to reports, Goldie Smith and Walter Dipley had known each other as schoolchildren in Christian County, Missouri, but had lost touch. Smith wound up in Cherryvale and Coffeyville—with a few taxing stopovers in between—while Dipley joined the navy.

Before she was fifteen years old, Smith had already been married twice. She had given birth to a daughter who had been seized by the county (decades before the concept of child protective services had been established) and had come to epitomize the fallen woman leading a "bad life."

Indeed, long before sharing scandalous headlines with Dipley in 1910 and 1911, Smith had already been a news item in Kansas. In August 1907, Smith had been arrested for streetwalking and was released from jail only after a subscription drive from friends raised enough money to pay off her fine. The *Cherryvale Republican* noted the gloomy circumstances of her life: "Her case is a sad one and she has had a bitter lesson. Twice unhappily married, her home life has not been an agreeable one. Her only home now is with a step-father who is unkind."

A few years later, Smith was arrested for brawling with another woman in Coffeyville, where she had been "conducting a rooming house." After the Ketchel uproar, when reporters began detailing her background, the *Coffeyville Daily Journal* reported that Smith had been "known in police circles" in Kansas and that witnesses acquainted with her there were reluctant to testify at her trial for "fear that they might incriminate themselves by their knowledge."

In the future, these sordid revelations about Smith would leave her at the mercy of both prosecutors and public opinion. More than anything, perhaps, Smith was a by-product of harsh frontier life, the kind that offered few opportunities to an impoverished girl raised in the late nineteenth century.

Walter Dipley had been crisscrossing the Midwest ever since he had deserted the navy a few years earlier. Under various pseudonyms, he went from job to job—zinc miner, copper miner, and barber—never staying anywhere for long. His stint in the navy had also been brief: it had lasted only seventeen months (and included two court-martials, one for assaulting a lieutenant) before he purchased discharge papers from another sailor with a similar name and disappeared into the prairie and the Great Plains. A deserter, Dipley lived in fear of being seized by the navy and thrown into the brig.

On September 11, 1910, Smith and Dipley reconnected by chance in Missouri when they shared a carriage ride from the train station at Chadwick to Blue Creek, where both were bound to visit relatives. During the visits, Dipley and Smith got friendly enough for Dipley to ask her to marry him. Smith declined based on her uncertainty about her current marital status. (She had been married for a third time.) Smith did not know if she was divorced or not and feared incurring a charge of bigamy. Instead, they agreed to live together and pose as a married couple for the sake of a twisted propriety. For over a hundred years, accounts of the Ketchel tragedy would invariably refer to Dipley and Smith as common-law husband and wife, but one month of shacking up as itinerant laborers hardly seems definitive. Their relationship had a pragmatic quality: Both Dipley and Smith were at loose ends, without prospects. Dipley, traveling under various aliases, was essentially a fugitive and feared being tracked by the navy, and Smith was looking for a respite from the hard life she had been living, one that promised her limited future prospects.

Eventually, they wound up in Springfield, Missouri, where an employment agency recommended Dipley and Smith to R. P. Dickerson, who hired them as ranch hand and housekeeper for thirty dollars a month, plus room and board. That was on Monday, October 10. On Wednesday, October 12, Goldie and Dipley arrived at the ranch. On Saturday, October 15, Stanley Ketchel was dead.

◆ ◆ ◆

For two days, Dipley, known to everyone by his alias Walter Hurtz, performed his duties as a ranch hand. He painted a barn, fed the horses, toiled in the field. At one point, he borrowed a rifle from Ketchel—a Marlin .22—for hunting small game. According to his trial testimony, he returned to the main house on Friday evening to find Goldie downcast: "I seen that there was something wrong with Goldie and I asked her what was wrong; she said nothing was the matter. I asked her two or three times, and then she said that Ketchel had made some bad threats. She said, 'I want to leave here.'"

At first, Smith claimed that Ketchel had merely insulted her. "While I was working in the house yesterday, Ketchel insulted me," she told the press only a few hours after the shooting. "I became angry. He was greatly wrought up over the incident and pleaded with me not to say anything to Hurtz about our conversation. He said he would give me the best team of horses on the farm if I would keep quiet. I made him no promise. When Hurtz came home, I told him what Ketchel had said to me. He was very angry. I think that is what caused him to kill Ketchel." By the time Dipley and Smith found themselves indicted for first-degree murder, the story had changed from Ketchel insulting Smith to Ketchel raping her.

The next morning, Dipley, whether out of fury or avarice, was set to act. Before it was even daylight, Ketchel and Dipley crossed paths on the porch. Ketchel went into the dining room and sat down to his last meal: ham, eggs, and a glass of milk.

Later, the prosecuting attorney would describe how Smith had participated in the ambush by rearranging the breakfast table so that Ketchel sat with his back to the door. This new configuration made Ketchel an unsuspecting target.

Dipley claimed that he had decided to quit his new job to avoid trouble, yet he confronted Ketchel. His description of the events leading to the shooting, however, would have been improbable even for a dime novel. Although Ketchel had his back turned, Dipley claimed that they had an acrimonious dialogue, one that ended in tragedy. "He said, 'What in hell are you doing around the house at this time of day; why hain't you out in the field.' I says, 'Why, I am not going out in the field today. I have quit.' He says, 'What in hell is the matter with you this morning?' I says, 'I suppose you are awful damned innocent that you don't know what is the matter.' He said, 'Don't you start nothing here or I will give you some of this,' and he opened his shirt and showed me his gun. I says, 'I guess you would give me some of that, all right.' He said, 'Yes, God Damn you, if you start anything, I will shoot you in two.' I says, 'Will you?' and I jumped to the foot of the bed and grabbed the little rifle that was setting there."

At roughly 6:30 a.m. Dipley, with the .22 caliber rifle in his hands (the same Marlin that Ketchel let him borrow for squirrel hunting), demanded that Ketchel "throw up his hands." Instead of following orders, Ketchel half-rose from his chair, ready, it seemed, to put his lifelong hard-boiled philosophy into effect once again—that rowdy, rebellious, reckless streak that led him from a life in hobo jungles to fame as the middleweight champion of the world.

Before Ketchel could turn, Dipley squeezed the trigger of the rifle, and the country morning shattered with a crack. The bullet struck Ketchel below the right shoulder and tore into his lung, sending him crashing to the floor. Dipley approached the wounded middleweight champion of the world, stripped him of his Colt .45, and bolted from the house. Outside, Dipley crossed paths with C. D. Bailey, the superintendent, who asked Dipley what had happened. The answer: "I shot the son of a bitch!" When Bailey suggested that Dipley wait for Sheriff C. B. Shields to arrive, Dipley decided to flee.

Eventually, Ketchel crawled to his room, leaving a streak of blood behind him, and clambered onto his bed, where Bailey found him muttering on his mattress. "They got me," Ketchel wheezed. Bailey then phoned R. P. Dickerson in Springfield to break the shocking news. In a mad dash,

Dickerson hired a private train and raced to Webster County with two doctors and a reporter in tow. When Dickerson arrived at his Webster County ranch just before noon, he immediately rushed into the bedroom, where a feverish Ketchel was laid out, pale as a waxwork, gasping for water. In anguish, he listened as Ketchel, his lung filling with blood, rasped some of his final words. "I was sitting at the kitchen table," Ketchel whispered, "and I was shot in the back by this man Hurtz. . . . Get the woman too, for she robbed me." (Dipley would be accused of robbing Ketchel as well, a charge he would repeatedly deny.)

When he emerged from the room, Dickerson announced a bounty of $5,000 for the body of Walter (Hurtz) Dipley. Even before the mass media age, that kind of news traveled fast. As a stranger, one that had been in town for less than a week, Dipley had earned none of the clannish loyalty common in the Ozarks. He was running for his life.

The physicians Dickerson brought with him from Springfield examined the fading Ketchel and concluded that his wound was fatal. The bullet lodged in him could not be removed. In a matter of hours, the middleweight champion of the world would be dead. Dickerson ordered that Ketchel be returned to Springfield, where he could die under more comfortable circumstances. They transported Ketchel on the Dickerson Express, as slow as possible, to keep him from suffering, to Springfield, where he succumbed to his wounds at 7 p.m. on October 15. Stanley Ketchel was twenty-four years old.

◆ ◆ ◆

Unfamiliar with the dense terrain of Webster County, Dipley made little progress escaping. For more than a year, he had been a fugitive from the navy; he had tried keeping on the margins, using various aliases, pretending to be married for cover; now he stumbled through the thickets and underbrush of the Osage timber, pursued by bloodhounds led by a posse for whom a $5,000 reward was more than just a windfall. "Dipley apparently wandered about the country aimlessly after the shooting," wrote the *Springfield Leader and Press*. "His course was a wide semicircle, starting southeast and gradually bearing to the south and west after the first few miles." By sundown, Dipley was cold, hungry, and exhausted. He stopped at a farmhouse, requesting food and shelter for the night. It was there, roughly fifteen miles from the Dickerson ranch, that he was ultimately recognized as the assassin who had cut down Ketchel. Crude tattoos from his limited days as a sailor in Hong Kong and the Philippines proved to be the determining factor in identifying him: They were mostly Asian characters inked on his forearms, a language no one in Webster County understood.

Later, when he was already in custody in Marshfield, Dipley would explain why he had fled the scene of what he had insisted had been self-defense instead of waiting for Sheriff C. B. Shields to arrest him. "Well, I was in a little fear," he said. "I didn't know what might happen if I give up there to him." Indeed, even as he sat in jail awaiting trial, Dipley was heavily guarded; Shields feared that vigilantes would target Dipley for some rough justice.

Three months later, on January 17, 1911, Dipley and Smith, charged with first-degree murder, sat in a Webster County circuit court, where their trial scandalized Missouri for years to come. A murdered celebrity, charges of rape, a sketchy drifter, an ex-prostitute dragging a shadow behind her as long as the Beach Road Niangua River Bridge, a prominent citizen, R. P. Dickerson, playing a lead role—all the lurid elements needed for morbid allure.

The Missouri reporters on the scene saw a Dipley conviction as a *fait accompli*; the motive, they agreed, was not self-defense, as his lawyers unconvincingly argued, but robbery, which seemed a likelier incentive for a man on the run. "Dipley on the stand made a poor witness for himself," wrote the *Salina Daily Union*. "It is generally believed Dipley will be convicted."

In addition, the defense spent an excessive amount of time trying to prove that R. P. Dickerson was not just a friend to Ketchel but his biological father as well. It was a curious strategy, one that drove the judge to sustain dozens of objections from the prosecution and might have backfired publicly when Dickerson collapsed from a nervous breakdown a few days after proceedings began.

Because Smith was being tried with Dipley, her survival hinged on the jury believing his tale of justifiable homicide. She certainly had no chance at the trial, where the prosecuting attorneys scythed her character at every opportunity. Her life, suggested Charles Dickey, state prosecutor, "has been so wicked, so vile, and so indecent" that she deserved the same fate as Dipley.

On the stand, Smith faced withering assaults on her character, and her rape charge against Ketchel fared no better. "He threw me on the bed and accomplished the biggest part of what he undertook," Smith testified to the defense. But under cross-examination, she had no response for the fact that she had not only cooked dinner for Ketchel later that night but that she also never told her colleague, a woman named Mrs. Brazeale, about the assault. In fact, all the witnesses at the ranch claimed that Ketchel and Smith had never been in the main house alone together.

In his closing argument for the prosecution, Dickey insisted on death sentences: "Gentlemen of the jury, the evidence in this case shows beyond a doubt that Stanley Ketchel was shot down in cold blood, without a chance to defend himself, and we ask that your verdict be death for both these defendants, who committed one of the foulest murders in the criminal annals of this country."

After deliberating for more than seventeen hours, the jury returned a guilty verdict for both defendants. Dipley and Smith were both given life in prison. It was Smith who had inadvertently saved Dipley. No jury would sentence a woman to the hanging scaffold in 1911 (one of the silver linings of male chauvinism), and because Smith and Dipley were tried together, it meant that leniency for her carried over to him.

A year and a half later, Smith won her freedom on appeal when the Missouri Supreme Court overturned her conviction, citing a lack of evidence against her. Dipley remained in prison until he earned parole in 1934. He died in 1956 and was buried in an unmarked grave in Toquerville, Utah. Smith remained in Springfield for years until she vanished from history sometime in the 1940s.

Stanley Ketchel was buried at Holy Cross Cemetery in Grand Rapids, Michigan, where R. P. Dickerson paid for an ornate marble monument to the man who had died as champion of the world. The inscription reads: "A good son and faithful friend."

Too Far from Home

BATTLING SIKI COMES TO AMERICA

There was nowhere else to go. Only a few months from having lost his light-heavyweight title to an Irishman in Dublin, Battling Siki arrived in America like a refugee or an exile. Just a year earlier, he had been an improbable world champion, the toast of France after having knocked out a national hero, Georges Carpentier, for the light-heavyweight championship of the world in 1922. But for Siki, unpredictable, unruly, and unstable, celebrity status had been as fleeting as his title reign would eventually prove to be, and the esteem he had earned with his fairy-tale exploits would quickly turn into hostility. When Siki arrived in New York City less than a year after upsetting Carpentier, it was in hopes of outstripping the firestorms he had sparked in Europe.

It is almost impossible to separate fact and fiction in the life of Battling Siki, a man who inspired the press on two continents to demonstrate imaginations as vivid and as lurid as those of dime novelists. "He was denounced as a drunk, a thug who enjoyed assaulting strangers, including the police, in the cafes and on the streets, who enjoyed brutalizing his own blue-eyed bride," wrote Peter Benson in his definitive *Battling Siki: A Tale of Ring Fixes, Race, and Murder in the 1920s.* "He was said to have been caught peddling cocaine, to have behaved lewdly in the company of a minor, in short to have been a public disgrace, a permanent blot upon the sport of boxing."

At least these were some of the stories emphasized by sensationalist Parisian newspapers. Until Siki publicly declared that his upset win over Carpentier had been fixed—setting a disastrous chain of events in motion—French *chroniqueurs* viewed Siki with a light touch. To Paris, Siki was not only an exemplar of the offensive "noble savage" conceit and the living embodiment of the primitivism movement that had been in vogue since Gaugin and Picasso, but he was also an odd link to the dandyism of an earlier age when Romantic and Symbolist poets lived outré lives for all to witness. Like Verlaine, he knocked back glass after glass of absinthe; like Rimbaud, he would brawl in public; like De Nerval, he leashed an exotic pet and paraded it down the streets and boulevards (De Nerval walked a lobster; Siki, a lion cub).

But it was one thing to flatten Carpentier in the ring, fair and square; it was another to sully his honor. In humiliating Carpentier, Siki made himself an open target for the corrupt legions of European boxing, whose ranks included sundry newspaper writers on the payroll of managers and promoters.

By first reducing Siki to a caricature and then vilifying him, repeatedly, in the most revolting terms, French sporting society caused Siki enough pain and befuddlement that he began an open letter printed in the newspaper *L'Auto* with a breathtaking declaration: "First of all, I am not a cannibal."

◆ ◆ ◆

Born Amadou M'barick Fall in Saint Louis, Senegal, in September 1897 (the exact date is unknown), the future Battling Siki was raised in a French colonial outpost, a seaport that had often been used as an international trading hub. As a boy, Siki somehow wound up in France, reportedly under the care of a European woman enamored with his happy-go-lucky nature. At some point, Siki found himself on his own, and he scrambled to survive as a street urchin. Years later, to the barbs of race-baiting reporters who speculated on his origins, Siki would reply: "A lot of newspaper people have written that I have a jungle style of fighting—that I am a chimpanzee who has been taught to wear gloves. That kind of thing hurts me. I was never anywhere but in a big city in my life. I have never even seen a jungle."

Various subsistence jobs, from dishwasher to stevedore, kept Siki from starving, but it was a gym—the Premierland Boxing Club in

Marseille—that saved him from poverty. There he chose Battling Siki as his *nom de guerre*.

Only fifteen years old when he became a professional fighter, Siki put his none-too-promising career on hiatus when World War I erupted. When Siki joined the French army in 1914, his documented record as a boxer after nearly two years of milling was 6-7-2, hardly a harbinger of future success in the ring. But on the battlefields of Champagne and the Somme, Siki distinguished himself as part of the Senegalese Tirailleurs (a unit possibly connected to the 8th Colonial Infantry Regiment). For the blood he shed across Europe, Siki earned the Croix de Guerre and the Médaille militaire to go along with enough scars, shrapnel, and stitches to last a pair of wars.

In 1918, Siki resumed his boxing career and became a solid journeyman fighter, eventually building his record to 49-9-3. Along the way, he made barnstorming tours of Northern Europe and posted wins over a slew of local heroes, but his growing reputation in France never merited championship consideration. Not until a manager named Francois Descamps, looking for an easy mark for Georges Carpentier, arrived. Descamps was the kingpin of French boxing, and Carpentier was his meal ticket: a dashing, handsome idol whose fame would not be equaled in France until the arrival of Marcel Cerdan decades later. It had been two and a half years since Carpentier had performed in France, and Descamps decided that Siki would be the perfect foil for a glorious homecoming.

The fight was set for September 24, 1922, but so little did Carpentier think of Siki as an opponent that training became an afterthought. According to the record books (not always an accurate assessment of boxing in pre–World War II Europe), Siki entered his title challenge against Carpentier on a hot streak, having won forty of his previous forty-two fights. His only blemishes over that span were a draw with Harry Reeve in May 1922 and a points loss to Tom Berry in August 1920. What made Carpentier so overconfident that he would barely lift a medicine ball in camp was the fact that Siki had built his exceptional run off the beaten path. In addition to clubbing second-raters in Toulouse and Paris, Siki frequently barnstormed across the boxing backwaters of Belgium and the Netherlands, with an occasional stopover in Spain.

Since being flattened by Jack Dempsey for the heavyweight title a year earlier, however, Carpentier had been less impressive than Siki. Quick knockouts over the undistinguished George Cook and former welterweight champion Ted "Kid" Lewis were not nearly enough preparation for even a raw bruiser like Siki, whose stamina, ruggedness, and power, combined with a hectic schedule, belied his status as a human sacrifice for Carpentier. Yet Carpentier, as haughty as a spoiled dauphin, regarded Siki with nothing but contempt. As his popularity in France reached hero status, Carpentier saw his ego rise proportionately. He would carry his narcissism—along with his disdain for Siki—into the ring, where it would ultimately prove catastrophic.

While Carpentier lollygagged in La Guerche, preferring to hunt or fish instead of spar or run, Descamps began to fret. Descamps not only managed Carpentier, but he was also part-owner of the Stade Buffalo, where the fight would take place, and the co-promoter of the event. Two weeks before the fight, he approached Charlie Hellers, one of a half dozen or so rapscallions who would manage Siki over the last few years of his life, and offered him 200,000 francs for a tank job. Not even a spendthrift like Siki could burn through 200,000 francs in a flash. Grudgingly, Siki accepted the cheerless assignment Hellers relayed from Descamps.

More than 55,000 spectators attended the Stade Buffalo to see Carpentier return. Under an overcast sky, with a slick canvas beneath them, Carpentier and Siki squared off in what was meant to be a choreographed performance. After some desultory two-stepping from both men, Carpentier uncorked a straight right that seemed off-target. No matter—Siki took a knee, anyway. As John Lardner described it in the *New Yorker*, this was a sign of good faith from Siki, the signal to all parties concerned that the script, as written, was now in play.

Referee Henri Bernstein (who had already ominously disqualified two fighters on the undercard) counted to "one" before Siki sprang to his feet to continue the burlesque. Before the first round ended, the crowd in Hauts-de-Seine, long familiar with chicanery in the ring, began to shout, "Fix! Fix!" Embarrassed by this response, Carpentier became increasingly concerned about how an obvious sham might affect his reputation.

If the second round was uneventful, the third was shocking—on the surface, to the spectators, and behind the scenes, to the startled collaborators. A stinging right hand from Carpentier dropped Siki to a knee early in the round. Siki bounced up like a tennis ball, and Carpentier immediately pounced. No longer willing to trade harmless blows for the sake of a shady covenant, Carpentier began letting go, unleashing a legitimate combination that wobbled Siki. Then Carpentier drove a tottering Siki across the ring and into the ropes, where another thumping right sent him to all fours.

It was there, on the grimy canvas, in front of 55,000 spectators, that Siki made the decision that would change his life forever. "Those punches hurt," Siki would say about the shots that put him down. The right that floored Siki—thrown with far more conviction than necessary for a charade—stung physically and emotionally. Losing was one thing, but humiliation was something else altogether: Carpentier had decided to take liberties. And when Carpentier seemed to goad Siki earlier in the bout (in those days, a professional faux pas in both straight and crooked fights), he broke two codes that bound each man as boxers and accomplices.

Either way, Siki had been double-crossed. The harmless exhibition he had expected became a painful battering at the hands of a world-class champion who seemed intent on degrading him. Later, Siki would recall the existential dilemma he faced: "I came to the ring with the intention of going down as they ordered me to. In the first round, in the second, in the third, I went I along . . . but when I was on my knees, in front of fifty thousand people, I thought like this: 'Look at you, Siki, you've never gone down before any man, you've never been on your knees in public the way you find yourself at this moment,' and my blood only circulated once before I was on my feet and punching."

After taking a count of seven, Siki rushed Carpentier and began exchanging whipping shots, toe-to-toe. Then a roundhouse right caught Carpentier square on the jaw, and to the astonishment of all, the Orchid Man collapsed. When the action resumed, Siki landed a series of uppercuts that jarred Carpentier and emphasized a simple, shocking fact: This fight was no longer a humbug. For the next two rounds, Siki battered Carpentier, whose eyes began to swell and who began bleeding from his mouth and nose. Desperate to turn the tide, Carpentier began headbutting at every opportunity, but Siki punished him with arcing shots whenever he got close. Enraged, Carpentier would curse Siki in the clinches. "You bastard," he snarled, "you bastard, go down, go down now."

Finally, in the sixth round, while they swapped blows in a blur, it was Carpentier who went down with a conclusive thud. Referee Henri Bernstein immediately disqualified Siki for tripping, and one of the strangest bouts in history was finally over. But when the outraged crowd protested the decision, French Boxing Federation officials huddled for an emergency meeting. When they eventually emerged, they reversed the decision and named Siki the winner.

The instant Siki earned the title of light-heavyweight champion, his life entered a vortex from which he would never emerge. First, he had cost himself 200,000 francs. And while Siki became an overnight hero to Parisians (who gathered outside his hotel balcony the morning after the fight), he also alienated the charlatans who held his livelihood in their hands.

When Siki was on the margins, fighting biweekly and earning modest sums of guilders, francs, and pesetas, he lived the itinerant life of a journeyman boxer. As a beleaguered champion, he lost control of everything—including his future. Beating Carpentier, in such a violent and treacherous fashion, meant an exponential raise in paydays and a commensurate spike in celebrity status, but it also placed him in multiple crosshairs. Almost instantaneously, Siki became the target of the boxing authorities, the boxing rank-and-file, the boxing enthusiasts. Worse, Siki went on a permanent bender, brawling with waiters, disturbing the peace, and frightening passersby with his pet lion cubs.

Within weeks of scoring his outlandish upset, Siki was stripped of his license and his regional titles by the French Boxing Federation after participating in a post-fight scrum involving a fighter named Ercole de Balzac. Siki, working the corner of de Balzac in a match against Maurice Prunier, shoved a manager during the melee. It was the kind of minor infraction French officials had been hoping for, and it provided the pretext for disciplinary action.

In retaliation, Siki publicly disclosed the Carpentier fix, sparking a scandal that dominated the French sporting world for months. This was equivalent to a magician revealing their secrets or a professional wrestler violating kayfabe. The code of silence in boxing was as sacrosanct as *omertà*, but Siki compounded the transgression of disclosure by admitting that he had also double-crossed Carpentier.

Although France was light-years ahead of the United States when it came to racial prejudice, it lost its national equanimity when it came to Battling Siki. While Paris became a sanctuary of sorts for artistic black Americans—from Josephine Baker, Sidney Bechet, and Ada "Bricktop" Smith in the 1920s to Richard Wright, Chester Himes, and James Baldwin in the 1950s—it also imported black fighters and gave them top billing before World War I erupted, putting an end to sporting frivolity. Sam Langford, Joe Jeanette, and Sam McVea were just a few of the black headliners who milled in France during the teens. Paris even hosted two title defenses by world heavyweight champion Jack Johnson, disappointing waltzes against "Battling" Jim Johnson and Frank Moran. Even that relatively liberal history was not enough to spare Siki from the collective wrath of France. Newspaper reporters turned their backs on Siki, maligning him with every press run. His manager, Hellers, abandoned him, plunging Siki into a financial abyss, and the general public no longer cared for his eccentricities.

Despite being a world champion, Siki, always extravagant, also had to worry about cash. Having betrayed Carpentier, Siki had forfeited his claim to the 200,000 franc bribe he had been offered to perform a sporting Grand Guignol. "I am tired of fighting for glory," Siki announced. "I only got chicken feed for when I beat Carpentier. Why don't they let up on me? I need money for my family." In addition to his household bills, there was also the absinthe, the lion cubs, and the gaudy outfits to factor in as expenses.

Barred from fighting in most of Continental Europe, Siki had few options for remaining solvent. Instead of cashing in on some showcase nontitle fights or a lucrative rematch with Carpentier, Siki found himself performing in exhibitions for small change. That was when Joe Jacobs and Mike McTigue entered the picture. McTigue was an itinerant middleweight with an unusual following in Canada and a fondness for no-decision bouts even during the Walker era, when boxing was legal in New York City, where McTigue lived and where Irish fighters ruled the box office. Jacobs, his scheming manager, who would later gain notoriety by guiding Max Schmeling to the heavyweight title, offered Siki an imperfect escape route from his troubles: a title defense against McTigue in Dublin for a potential purse of 1,500 pounds. The catch? The fight would take place on Saint Patrick's Day. Siki, without much choice, reluctantly agreed to conditions that would reverberate as a punch line for the next century. His first fight since winning the title would take place on March 17, 1923, at the La Scala Theatre in Dublin.

For more than a decade, the upheavals in Ireland had prevented headline matches from taking place in Dublin, and when the Siki–McTigue fight was announced, it stirred an excitement that belied the event itself. After all, the closest McTigue ever got to performing in the Emerald Isle was a KO over Harry Reeve in Liverpool, England, just across the sea. Even so, his status as part of the Irish diaspora (he was born in Kilnamona, County Clare) was enough to cause a stir in a war-torn city weary of bloodshed.

Not only had Siki agreed to fight on unfriendly territory, but he had also agreed to enter another battlefield. It was not the carnage of the Somme or Champagne, but Dublin had been wracked by violence for years. With the Irish Civil War still a few months away from a ceasefire, the threat of sectarian violence on fight night was palpable. By March 1923, the IRA had suffered so many losses (including thousands imprisoned) that it had scaled down its campaign to sabotage and the occasional bombing. On its list of targets was the La Scala Theatre, which received two threats from the IRA in the days leading up to the fight. As a precaution, Siki and McTigue were shadowed by armed guards wherever they went, and on the night of the fight, Criminal Investigation Department (CID) officers set up cordons and frisked everyone who entered the theater. It turned out that the precautions were necessary. "Ten minutes before the fighters entered the ring, La Scala Theatre was silenced by the sound of a mine exploding near O'Connell Street," wrote journalist and author Dave Hannigan. "The Pillar Picture House was damaged, a baby boy was badly injured, and the master of ceremonies, Jim Harris, announced that by order of the military, nobody could leave the venue until after 11:30 p.m."

Despite the explosion, an overflow of thousands lined the streets outside of the theater, waiting to be among the first to know the results of the fight. They gathered hoping that McTigue would become the first Irish-born fighter to win a world title on native soil. A cunning defensive boxer with a lack of firepower, McTigue seemed ill-equipped to fend off the hard-charging Siki for twenty rounds, but he had an advantage (feverish nationalism) that would prove to be insurmountable. After an hour of intermittent action, Siki dropped a dubious decision to McTigue that even the *Irish Times* considered unjust.

Although Siki had enjoyed only a few weeks of the high life as champion before seemingly everyone turned against him, losing the title would only make things worse. In fact, Siki felt the immediate backlash of being just another contender. His standing as a European pariah was underscored the day after the McTigue fight when England refused to allow

Siki to set foot on its shores on his way to France. Forced to scramble for last-minute accommodations and travel a roundabout course, Siki arrived in France more than two weeks later on a tramp steamer. "I am happy to be in Paris," Siki said, "and you can believe that the English have made me realize how cruel they are. I will retain a very bad memory of that adventure."

More bad memories awaited Siki in France, where he lost his first fight as an ex-champion via disqualification to an unexceptional pug named Emile Morelle. A pair of nondescript wins in Montrouge and Bordeaux (along with a falling-out with a short-lived manager named Charles Brouillet, who might have cheated Siki) convinced Siki it was time for self-exile. He sailed for New York City in late August, followed by a past that would pursue him across the Atlantic.

When Siki arrived in New York City on September 1, 1923, he immediately found himself embroiled in controversy. According to the *New York Age*, Siki was detained at Ellis Island, where officials sought to declare him African instead of French and thus ineligible to enter the country. After some confusion, Siki was finally allowed into port and into a new world less hospitable than the one he had just fled.

In America, the press regarded Siki as a low-rent version of ex-heavyweight champion Jack Johnson. If the media had vilified, slandered, and ridiculed Johnson, they still considered him, a Texas-born *bon vivant*, a unique American by-product of sorts. Not so with Siki, who was from Senegal, and, therefore, was ineligible even for the limited homegrown sentiment occasionally extended to Johnson. To newspapermen fond of using the term "darkie" or of invoking animal metaphors or the racist pseudoscientific theories of eugenics, polygenism, and Madison Grant, the arrival of Battling Siki could only be considered a boon. In sports pages across the country, casual racism (such as produced in the purplest of prose by Grantland Rice) vied against the open bigotry of Southern newshawks when it came to black fighters, but Siki sent press row into xenophobic overdrive. "The Singular Senagalese has settled down to his work in Summit, New Jersey," wrote the loathsome Wilbur Wood of the *New York Herald*, only a few weeks after Siki had arrived, "where there are plenty of trees he can swing from when in the mood."

Even Nat Fleischer, founder of *The Ring* and a liberal believer in the egalitarian ethos of boxing, typeset phrases such as "King Kong," "savage," and "wild man" when he wrote about Siki. (In his memoir, *Fifty Years at Ringside*, Fleischer wrote: "Perhaps Siki was only half-human.")

After settling down at a hotel in Yonkers, Siki began to enjoy the night-life in Harlem while he waited for his latest manager, Lucien DeFremont, a timber merchant, to produce a gig. An exhibition tour in Quebec with Jack Johnson proved disastrous for Siki, who clashed with the egoistical ex-heavyweight champion on each stop. Even in his mid-forties Johnson was unwilling to cede the stage to an upstart, and he toyed with Siki whenever they sparred for the public. Eventually, Siki was thrown off a train in Saint-Lambert, Quebec, after attacking some of the exhibition members and wandered the streets for most of a night looking for a hotel that would accept a black man as a guest. Broke, Siki scribbled his signature on a contract from a local promoter in exchange for train fare home. Back in New York, Siki found out that his contract had been sold to a shirtwaist manufacturer named Bob Levy.

Already Siki must have thought that his career in the United States seemed hexed. To make matters worse, the czar of New York boxing, William Muldoon, was a hardcore racist who refused to sanction mixed fights. Even after the tumultuous era of Jack Johnson, black fighters were not barred from boxing, at least not openly. For the black athlete, prohibited from participating in baseball, tennis, football, basketball, and horse racing, boxing was one of the few opportunities open to them. Still, black boxers were often forced to carry opponents, to agree to lose outright, or to settle for being disappointed by crooked scorecards. But Muldoon, chairman of the New York State Athletic Commission, was beyond even such tilts of the playing field. He did everything in his power to eliminate mixed bouts, and no black man would ever be allowed to challenge for the heavyweight title under his oversight.

"I don't like fight colored man," Siki reportedly told a sportswriter, "can't get big money." Siki was well aware that two black fighters squaring off meant a limited payday for all involved. He wanted what was best for the box office, which, in turn, would be best for his wallet: a headline fight against a popular white opponent, preferably reigning heavyweight champion Jack Dempsey. If necessary, he would settle for Harry Greb or even Tommy Gibbons. But he was stymied by Muldoon, who ruled that Siki must abide by a contract previously negotiated by a fly-by-night manager named George Sennett. The opponent would be Kid Norfolk, one of the toughest light heavyweights of his era. In a career that began in 1910, Norfolk had established himself as someone to be avoided. Although Norfolk was forced to ply his trade mostly against other black fighters, he had several quality wins, including a disqualification over Harry Greb and two knockouts of Tiger Flowers.

Out of shape and inactive for more than three months, Siki was now faced with the disconcerting task of swapping blows with Norfolk. His new manager, Bob Levy, proved both inexperienced and incompetent simultaneously. Siki did roadwork and calisthenics but had no training camp and no sparring until less than two weeks before the fight. That was no way to prepare for someone like Kid Norfolk.

◆ ◆ ◆

On November 20, 1923, Siki faced Norfolk in front of 12,180 fans in Madison Square Garden. For a purse of between $15,000 and $18,000, far more than he had received for defeating Carpentier, Siki made his debut in the boxing capital of America. His reputation, it seems, had crossed the Atlantic with him. Compared to the mundane European fighters Siki had faced for much of his career, Norfolk was an *Übermensch*. Yet Siki put up fierce resistance in a thrilling fight that left him bloody and pulped after fifteen rounds.

Although the decision went against him, Siki exited Madison Square Garden with a certain amount of newfound respect from his detractors. That afterglow lasted approximately a month when Siki dropped a decision to Jack Taylor on Christmas Day in Philadelphia. From that point on, Siki rarely participated in a significant bout. His antics in the ring (Siki was a dedicated showboat) and the lurid newspaper clippings he inspired made him an attraction, but only on the club circuit.

From Madison Square Garden, Siki eventually descended to road-show status, fighting palookas and no-hopers in Columbus, Bellaire, Passaic, and Woonsocket. More shocking than his plummet from the marquee of New York City was that Siki lost almost as often as he won. In fact, Siki was through as a contender. His record in America was a dismal 8-13-1, including defeats to several professional losers and run-of-the-mill journeymen. He had less than a year to live when he returned to Madison Square Garden, on short notice and out of shape, as a ritual sacrifice for

Paul Berlenbach on March 13, 1925. For nearly ten rounds, Berlenbach hammered Siki until the mismatch was finally halted in the tenth round.

As if in acknowledgment of the inevitable tragic end, Siki hurtled from one calamity to another in his last remaining months. One bright spot, a vicious KO of Hoboken crowd favorite Jimmy Francis, would possibly backfire against him. In his book on Siki, Peter Benson argues that Siki had agreed to either carry Francis or lose to him outright at the behest of gang forces. Instead, Siki humiliated Francis, obliterating him in less than two rounds. Although Francis was a box-office attraction in New Jersey, his ceiling as a fighter was limited, so there is no telling what the mob had in store for him.

Whether there was a dark agreement in place is unclear, but the fact remains that Siki had gone easy on several fighters in the United States since his arrival on the scene. What happened next, then, after he annihilated Francis, might or might not have been a coincidence. On July 25, 1925, two days after the Francis fight, Siki was hospitalized after a late-night attack left him unconscious, bleeding profusely on the sidewalk. He was admitted to the French Hospital on West 34th Street. According to the *New York Daily News*, Siki was held there for "severed minor arteries under the left ear." Translation: Someone had tried to cut his throat. After a rooftop chase, police collared a man named Joseph Hanrahan for the assault. He was arrested and held on $10,000 bail at Jefferson Market Court.

Before Siki could even get used to the stitches in his neck, he staged a breakout, fleeing his sickroom in a hospital gown, jumping into a taxi, and speeding off into the unknown. A few days later, he refused to press charges against Hanrahan, saying, either brashly or fatalistically, "I don't want to send him to jail; I'll take care of him myself." In a sense, that outlandish comment revealed what few have ever admitted about Siki: that he was, in fact, now part of gangland. By allowing Hanrahan to avoid prosecution, Siki acknowledged the no-snitch policy of the streets. Despite ratting out the biggest power broker in France and sparking a national scandal in 1922, one that ultimately ruined his life, the normally outspoken Siki had no interest in pursuing someone who had just tried to murder him.

Incredibly, Siki was back in the ring two weeks later, losing via disqualification to a stumblebum with a record of 2-6. It would be his last fight in

New York City; the boxing commission, fed up with Siki both in and out of the ring, banned him from competition.

In place of prizefight bureaucrats and wiseguys, it was now the government, specifically immigration, that targeted Siki. A year earlier, Siki had been detained in Havana, Cuba, and barred from entering the United States. When he was finally admitted, Siki, in hopes of establishing citizenship, married a young woman named Lillian Walker. (This act made him a bigamist, at least in America; Siki had a wife and child in Paris.)

This time, however, not even marriage to an American would placate immigration officials. Siki was arrested on August 17, 1925, charged with violating immigration statutes and released on $1,000 bail. For Siki, the downward spiral seemed unending. The day after his immigration arrest, he was battered over ten rounds by Billy Vidabeck in West New York, New Jersey, dropping a clear-cut newspaper decision.

By December 1925, Battling Siki had been barred from several jurisdictions in the United States because of his erratic performances. His drinking had worsened, and so had his temperament. Among the many seamy legends surrounding Battling Siki during his last year in New York City were stories of him challenging cab drivers to fight for fares and knocking strangers off the curb whenever he was in a spiteful mood. Several nights a week, Siki would be spotted reeling home from some gloomy speakeasy in the Kitchen.

The last time Siki was spotted with the staggers was just after midnight on December 16, 1925, when patrolman John J. Meehan came across him emerging from beneath the Ninth Avenue Elevated. Siki, seemingly in a good mood, told Meehan that he was on his way home, only two or three blocks away. When Meehan saw Siki again, a few hours later, the ex-light-heavyweight champion of the world was lying facedown in a gutter, motionless. He had been shot twice in the back with a .32 caliber revolver. Battling Siki, who had survived the carnage of World War I trenches, died in front of 354 West 41st Street after a little more than two years in America. He had three cents in his pocket.

◆ ◆ ◆

His murder led the press, spearheaded by future legends like Paul Gallico and Westbrook Pegler (both syndicated columnists), to turn a tragedy into a purplish clash of civilizations. To them, Siki was a primitive naïf overwhelmed by the temptations of Western luxury and whose death was inevitable.

"Battling Siki, who tried hard to understand civilization but never quite got the idea, will be trundled out over the roads to Long Island today and buried in the civilized way without a single thump of the tom-tom," wrote Pegler, bizarrely.

And Paul Gallico, who became famous after being knocked senseless by Jack Dempsey in a sparring session, echoed the same theme, only without the mystifying tom-tom. "The white man has written an elegant finis to Battling Siki," he wrote. "Possibly, by this time, whatever he and wherever he is Siki may know what the score is. He never quite caught up to it on this earth. Still, the Battler has no kick coming. He owes all of his woes to the white man, but at the same time all of his pleasures."

Like so much written about Siki, this was not just racist malarkey, but it was also a pathetic diversion: Neither man mentioned boxing itself as a possible cause of Siki's death. In Europe, particularly France, boxing was unscrupulous, but only when Siki arrived in America was he thrown into a criminal underworld. In the 1920s, when boxing was made legal in New York at nearly the same time as Prohibition, organized crime began to crystalize into the wildly remunerative force that would thrive until the 1990s. Gangsters and boxers were virtually inseparable during the Roaring Twenties. Among the felonious VIPs involved in boxing at that time were Owney "The Killer" Madden, Dutch Schultz, Jack "Legs" Diamond, Harry "Champ" Segal, George "Big Frenchy" Demange, Pete Reilly, Waxey Gordon, and even the future head of the Luciano family, Frank Costello (childhood pal of future middleweight champion Johnny Wilson). If Siki had remained in Europe, he may have been hounded by officials and skewered by the press (two difficulties he suffered in America as well), but he would have avoided the lawless atmosphere of New York City during the era of the speakeasy and the tommy gun.

Siki was also viciously exploited by several managers, who often disappeared with his purses. And while he had a cordial relationship with Bob Levy, his last manager, it was Levy who threw Siki in with the deadly Paul Berlenbach as a late substitute. By then, Siki was a danger only to himself in the ring. But boxing proved dangerous to him on both sides of the ropes.

In March 1926, police arrested an eighteen-year-old neighborhood thug named Roger Maroney on suspicion of first-degree murder. After a fierce interrogation, Maroney admitted that he had drawn Siki out of a speakeasy with the promise of a few drinks elsewhere. When Maroney and Siki emerged, they were immediately flanked by two other men. One of them shot Siki twice, point-blank. If nothing else, Maroney was acting as a finger man. The question is, for whom? Maroney claimed he was unfamiliar with the men who sidled up to Siki at roughly four in the morning, trigger fingers itchy.

Maroney languished in the Tombs for seven months before officials set him free for lack of evidence. Apparently, confessing to being the decoy that steered Siki to his death was not a crime. No one was ever charged with the murder of Battling Siki.

For fifty years, Amadou M'barick Fall lay in an unmarked grave in Flushing Cemetery in Queens, New York. He finally got a headstone in 1976. Then, in 1993, his body was disinterred, and he was repatriated to Senegal for burial in Saint-Louis. Battling Siki was finally home again.

Sources

BOOKS

Allen, Frederick Lewis. *Only Yesterday: An Informal History of the 1920s.* New York: HarperCollins, 2010.

Anderson, Dave. *In the Corner: Great Boxing Trainers Talk about Their Art.* New York: William Morrow, 1991.

Benson, Peter. *Battling Siki: A Tale of Ring Fixes, Race, and Murder in the 1920s.* Fayetteville: University of Arkansas, 2008.

Berkow, Ira. *Counterpunch: Ali, Tyson, the Brown Bomber, and Other Stories of the Boxing Ring.* Chicago: Triumph Books, 2014.

Biddle, Geoffrey. *Alphabet City.* Berkeley: University of California Press, 1992.

Bodner, Allen. *When Boxing Was a Jewish Sport.* Westport, CT: Praeger Publishers, 1997.

Brock, Pope. *Charlatan: America's Most Dangerous Huckster, the Man Who Pursued Him, and the Age of Flimflam.* New York: Broadway Books, 2009.

Bromberg, Lester. *Boxing's Unforgettable Fights.* New York: The Ronald Press Company, 1962.

Burbank, Jeff. *Las Vegas Babylon.* New York: M. Evans and Company, 2005.

Burke, Carolyn. *Becoming Modern: The Life of Mina Loy.* New York: Farrar Straus & Giroux, 2006.

Callis, Tracy, and Chuck Johnston. *Boxing in the Los Angeles Area: 1880–2005.* Bloomington, IN: Trafford Publishing, 2009.

Cashill, Jack. *Sucker Punch: The Hard Left Hook That Dazed Ali and Killed King's Dream.* Nashville: Thomas Nelson, 2006.

Cavanaugh, Jack. *Tunney: Boxing's Brainiest Champ and His Upset of the Great Jack Dempsey.* New York: Random House, 2006.

Conover, Roger. *4 Dada Suicides: Selected Texts of Arthur Cravan, Jacques Rigaut, Julien Torma & Jacques Vache.* London: Atlas Press, 1995.

Day, Daniel R. *Dapper Dan: Made in Harlem: A Memoir.* New York: Random House, 2019.

Early, Gerald. *The Muhammad Ali Reader.* New York: Ecco Press, 2013.

———. *The Culture of Bruising: Essays on Prizefighting, Literature, and Modern American Culture.* New York: Ecco Press, 1994.

Fleischer, Nat. *Fifty Years at Ringside.* New York: Fleet, 1958.

Florio, John, and Ouisie Shapiro. *One Punch from the Promised Land: Leon Spinks, Michael Spinks, and the Myth of The Heavyweight Title.* Westport, CT: Lyons Press, 2013.

Frazier, Joe, and Phil Berger. *Smokin' Joe: The Autobiography.* New York: Macmillan, 1996.

Freedman, Lew. *Fighting for Life: The Jake LaMotta Story.* Indianapolis: Blue River Press, 2018.

Fried, Ronald K. *Corner Men: Great Boxing Trainers.* Boston: Da Capo Press, 1993.

Giddins, Gary. *Riding on a Blue Note: Jazz and American Pop.* Boston: Da Capo Press, 2000.

Giudice, Christian. *A Fire Burns Within: The Miraculous Journey of Wilfredo 'Bazooka' Gomez.* Sussex, UK: Pitch Publishing, 2016.

———. *Hands of Stone: The Life and Legend of Roberto Duran.* Lancashire, UK: Milo Books, 2006.

Gorn, Elliott J. *The Manly Art: Bare-Knuckle Prize Fighting in America.* Ithaca, NY: Cornell University Press.

Greyvenstein, Chris. *The Fighters.* Cape Town: Don Nelson Publishers, 1981.

———. *This Brutal Glory.* Cape Town: Buren Publishers, 1969.

Grombach, John V. *The Saga of Sock.* New York: A.S. Barnes, 1949.

Hauser, Thomas. *Muhammad Ali: His Life and Times.* New York: Simon and Schuster, 1991.

Hauser, Thomas. *The Black Lights: Inside the World of Professional Boxing.* New York: McGraw-Hill, 1986.

Hauser, Thomas, and Stephen Brunt. *The Italian Stallion: Heroes of Boxing's Glory Days.* Toronto: Sport Media Publishing, 2003.

Haygood, Wil. *Sweet Thunder: The Life and Times of Sugar Ray Robinson.* New York: Knopf, 2009.

Heinz, W. C. *Once They Heard the Cheers.* New York: Doubleday, 1979.

Heller, Peter. *Bad Intentions: The Mike Tyson Story.* Boston: Da Capo, 1995.

———. *In This Corner: Forty-two World Champions Tell Their Stories.* Boston: Da Capo, 1994.

Hoffer, Richard. *A Savage Business: The Comeback and Comedown of Mike Tyson.* New York: Simon and Schuster, 1998.

Holmes, Larry, and Phil Berger. *Against the Odds.* New York: St. Martin's Press, 1998.

Holyfield, Evander: *The Humble Warrior.* Nashville: Thomas Nelson, 2006.

Hotten, Jon. *Years of the Locust.* London: Yellow Jersey Press, 2008.

Johnston, Alexander. *Ten—and Out!* New York: Ives Washburn, 1947.

Kent, Grame. *Great White Hopes: The Quest to Defeat Jack Johnson.* Gloucestershire, UK: Sutton Publishing, 2005.

Kimball, George. *Four Kings: Leonard, Hagler, Hearns, Duran and the Last Great Era of Boxing.* Ithaca, NY: McBooks Press, 2009

Kram, Mark. *Ghosts of Manila: The Fateful Blood Feud Between Muhammad Ali and Joe Frazier*. New York: HarperCollins, 2003.

LaMotta, Jake, and Joseph Carter. *Raging Bull: My Story*. Boston: Da Capo Press, 1997.

LaMotta, Jake, and Chris Anderson. *Raging Bull II: Continuing the Story of Jake LaMotta*. New York: Lyle Stuart Books, 1986.

Lang, Arne K. *The Nelson-Wolgast Fight and the San Francisco Boxing Scene, 1900–1914*. Jefferson, NC: McFarland & Company, Inc., 2012.

Lardner, John. *White Hopes and Other Tigers*. Philadelphia: J. B. Lippincott, 1951.

Liebling, A. J. *Back Where I Came From*. Berkeley, CA: North Point Press, 1990.

Liebling, A. J. *The Sweet Science*. New York: North Point Press, 2004.

Louis, Joe, and Art Rust Jr. *Joe Louis: My Life*. New York: Harcourt Brace Jovanovich, 1978.

Margolick, David. *Beyond Glory: Joe Louis vs. Max Schmeling, and a World on the Brink*. New York: Knopf, 2005.

Marquesse, Mike. *Redemption Song: Muhammad Ali and the Spirit of the Sixties*. London: Verso, 1999.

McNeil, William F. *The Rise of Mike Tyson*. Jefferson, NC: McFarland & Company, Inc., 2014.

Mee, Bob. *Ali and Liston: The Boy Who Would Be King and the Ugly Bear*. New York: Skyhorse, 2011.

Mee, Bob. *The Heavyweights: The Definitive History of the Heavyweight Fighters*. Gloucestershire, UK: Tempus Publishing, 2006.

McCallum, Jack. *The Encyclopedia of World Boxing Champions*. Boston: Chilton, 1975.

McCallum, Jack. *The World Heavyweight Boxing Championship: A History*. Boston: Chilton, 1974.

McIlvanney, Hugh. *McIlvanney on Boxing*. Edinburgh: Mainstream Publishing, 1997.

Monteville, Leigh. *Sting Like a Bee: Muhammad Ali vs. the United States of America, 1966–1971*. New York: Doubleday, 2017.

Moore, Lucy. *Anything Goes: A Biography of the 1920s*. New York: Harry N. Abrams, 2010.

Morgan, Dan, and Jack McCallum. *Dumb Dan*. New York: Tedson Publishing, 1953.

Myler, Thomas. *The Sweet Science Goes Sour*. Vancouver: Greystone Books, 2006.

Nack, William. *My Turf: Horses, Boxers, Blood Money, and the Sporting Life*. Boston: Da Capo Press, 2004.

Nagler, Barney. *James Norris and the Decline of Boxing*. Indianapolis: The Bobbs-Merrill Company, 1964.

Newfield, Jack. *Only in America: The Life and Crimes of Don King*. Sag Harbor, NY: Harbor Electronic Publishing, 2003.

Nicholl, Charles. *Traces Remain: Essays and Explorations*. London: Allen Lane, 2012.

Oates, Joyce Carol. *On Boxing*. New York: Harper Collins, 2006.

O'Connor, Daniel. *Iron Mike: A Mike Tyson Reader*. Boston: Da Capo Press, 2002.

Olsen, Jack. *Black Is Best: The Riddle of Cassius Clay*. New York: Putnam, 1967.

Pryor, Aaron, and Marshall Terrill. *Flight of the Hawk: The Aaron Pryor Story*. Sun Lakes, AZ: Book World, Inc., 1996.

Remnick, David. *King of the World: Muhammad Ali and the Rise of an American Hero*. New York: Random House, 1999.

Riess, Steven. *City Games: The Evolution of American Urban Society and the Rise of Sports*. Champaign: University of Illinois Press, 1991.

Roberts, Randy. *Papa Jack: Jack Johnson and the Era of White Hopes*. New York: Free Press, 1985.

Roberts, Randy, and Johnny Smith. *Blood Brothers: The Fatal Friendship Between Muhammad Ali and Malcolm X*. New York: Basic Books, 2006.

Runstedtler, Theresa. *Jack Johnson: Rebel Sojourner*. Berkeley: University of California Press, 2013.

Sammons, Jeffrey T. *Beyond the Ring: The Role of Boxing in American Society*. Champaign: University of Illinois Press, 1987.

Sanford, Harry. *Stand Up and Fight*. New York: Exposition Press, 1962.

Sante, Luc. *Low Life: Lures and Snares of Old New York*. New York: Farrar, Straus and Giroux, 2003.

Schneider, Eric C. *Smack: Heroin and the American City*. Philadelphia: University of Pennsylvania Press, 2011.

Schulberg, Budd. *Ringside: A Treasury of Boxing Reportage*. Chicago: Ivan R. Dee, 2006.

Schulian, John. *Writers' Fighters and Other Sweet Scientists*. Kansas City: Andrews McMeel Publishing, 1983.

Spivey, Donald. *Sport in America: New Historical Perspectives*. Westport, CT: Praeger Publishers, 1985.

Springer, Steve, and Blake Chavez. *Hard Luck: The Triumph and Tragedy of "Irish" Jerry Quarry*. Westport, CT: Lyons Press, 2011.

Steen, Rob. *Sonny Liston: His Life, Strife and the Phantom Punch*. London: JR Books, 2008.

Streible, Don. *Fight Pictures: A History of Boxing and Early Cinema*. Berkeley: University of California Press, 2008.

Suster, Gerald. *Lightning Strikes: The Lives and Times of Boxing's Lightweight Heroes*. London: Robson Books Ltd., 1996.

Tapia, Johnny. *Mi Vida Loca: The Crazy Life of Johnny Tapia*. Los Angeles: Volt Press, 2006.

Torgoff, Martin. *Bop Apocalypse: Jazz, Race, the Beats, and Drugs*. Boston: Da Capo Press, 2017.

Tosches, Nick. *The Devil and Sonny Liston*. Boston: Little, Brown and Company, 2000.

Tyson, Mike, and Larry Sloman. *Undisputed Truth*. New York: Plume, 2014.

Walsh, Peter. *Men of Steel London: The Lives and Times of Boxing's Middleweight Champions*. London: Robson Books Ltd., 1995.

Ward, Geoffrey C. *Unforgivable Blackness: The Rise and Fall of Jack Johnson*. New York: Knopf, 2004.

Wells, Jeff. *Boxing Day: The Fight That Changed the World*. New York: Harper Collins, 1998.

Wilson, Peter. *Ringside Seat*. London: Rich and Cowan, 1949.

MAGAZINES

Boxing

Boxing Beat

Boxing Illustrated

Boxing Scene

Boxing & Wrestling

Cincinnati Magazine

Fight Beat

Fight Game

Granta

Inside Boxing

International Boxing

Jet

KO

Life

The Literary Review

New York

People

The Ring

The Soil

Sport

Sports Illustrated

Texas Monthly

True Yearbook

The Veteran Boxer

World Boxing

NEWSPAPERS

Akron Beacon Journal

Arizona Daily Star

Boston Globe

Boston Herald

Brooklyn Eagle

Butte Daily Post

Chicago Tribune

Cincinnati Enquirer

Cleveland Plain Dealer

Coffeyville Daily Journal

Desert Sun News

Detroit Free Press

Detroit Metro Times

El Diario

El Mundo

El Nuevo Día

El Paso Times

Hartford Courant

Irish Times

Kenosha Evening News

L'Auto

Las Vegas Sun

Los Angeles Herald

Los Angeles Times

Morning Call

Newsday

New York *Daily News*

New York *Herald Tribune*

New York *Morning Telegraph*

New York *Times*

Oakland Tribune

Orlando Sentinel

Palm Beach Post

Philadelphia Daily News

Philadelphia Inquirer

Pittsburgh Courier-Post

Pittsburgh Press

Sacramento Bee

Salina Daily Union

Salt Lake Tribune

San Francisco Call

San Francisco Chronicle

San Francisco Examiner

Springfield Leader and Press

Star Tribune

St. Louis Post-Dispatch

Tampa Times

Texas Monthly

Toledo Blade

Washington Post

Carlos Acevedo is the author of *The Duke: The Life and Lies of Tommy Morrison*. His work has appeared in *Boxing News*, Hannibal Boxing, *The Ring*, Inside HBO Boxing, and *Boxing Digest*. His stories "A Darkness Made to Order," "A Ghost Orbiting Forever," and "The Duke of the West Side" all won first place awards from the Boxing Writers Association of America. He lives in Brooklyn, New York.

Sporting Blood is set in 10-point Sabon, which was designed by the German-born typographer and designer Jan Tschichold (1902–1974) in the period 1964–1967. It was released jointly by the Linotype, Monotype, and Stempel type foundries in 1967. Copyeditor for this project was Shannon LeMay-Finn. The book was designed by Brad Norr Design, Minneapolis, Minnesota, and typeset by New Best-set Typesetters Ltd.

CPSIA information can be obtained
at www.ICGtesting.com
Printed in the USA
JSHW050441100822
29066JS00001B/2